English Corpus Linguistics

(18794)

This book is affectionately dedicated to
Jan Svartvik
by its editors, contributors and publishers.

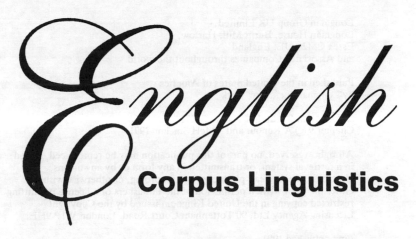

English
Corpus Linguistics

Studies in Honour of
Jan Svartvik

Edited by Karin Aijmer & Bengt Altenberg

LONGMAN
London and New York

Longman Group UK Limited,
Longman House, Burnt Mill, Harlow,
Essex CM20 2JE, England
and Associated Companies throughout the world.

Published in the United States of America
by Longman Inc., New York

First published 1991

British Library Cataloguing in Publication Data
English corpus linguistics : studies in honour of Jan Svartvik.
1. English language. Linguistics
I. Aijmer, Karin   II. Altenberg, Bengt   III. Svartvik, Jan
420
ISBN 0-582-05931-3 csd
ISBN 0-582-05930-5 pbk

Library of Congress Cataloging-in-Publication Data
English corpus linguistics : studies in honour of Jan Svartvik /
   edited by Karin Aijmer and Bengt Altenberg.
      p.   cm.
   Includes bibliographical references and index.
   ISBN 0-582-05931-3 (cased). — ISBN 0-582-05930-5 (paper)
   1. English language — Research — Data processing.   2. English
language — Discourse analysis — Data processing.   3. Linguistics
research — Data processing.   I. Aijmer, Karin.   II. Altenberg,
Bengt.   III. Svartvik, Jan.
PE 1074.5.E5   1991
410'.285—dc20   90-24334
                                                                         CIP

Set in Linotron Times 10/12pt
Produced by Longman Singapore Publishers (Pte) Ltd.
Printed in Singapore

Contents

Contributors

JAN AARTS, Department of Language and Speech, University of Nijmegen

KARIN AIJMER, Department of English, University of Lund

BENGT ALTENBERG, Department of English, University of Lund

DOUGLAS BIBER, Department of English, Northern Arizona University

WALLACE CHAFE, Department of Linguistics, University of California, Santa Barbara

PETER COLLINS, School of English, University of New South Wales

DAVID CRYSTAL, Department of Linguistics, University College of North Wales, Bangor

JOHN DU BOIS, Department of Linguistics, University of California, Santa Barbara

EDWARD FINEGAN, Department of Linguistics, University of Southern California

SIDNEY GREENBAUM, Department of English, University College London

M. A. K. HALLIDAY, Department of Linguistics, University of Sydney

OSSI IHALAINEN, Department of English, University of Helsinki

STIG JOHANSSON, Department of English, University of Oslo

GRAEME KENNEDY, English Language Institute, Victoria University of Wellington

GÖRAN KJELLMER, Department of English, University of Gothenburg

GEOFFREY LEECH, Department of Linguistics and Modern English Language, University of Lancaster

CHARLES F. MEYER, Department of English, University of Massachusetts at Boston

DIETER MINDT, Didaktik der englischen Sprache und Literatur, Freie Universität Berlin

RANDOLPH QUIRK, Department of English, University College London

ANTOINETTE RENOUF, School of English, University of Birmingham

MATTI RISSANEN, Department of English, University of Helsinki

JOHN MCH. SINCLAIR, School of English, University of Birmingham

GABRIELE STEIN, Anglistisches Seminar, University of Heidelberg

ANNA-BRITA STENSTRÖM, Department of English, University of Stockholm

SANDRA THOMPSON, Department of Linguistics, University of California, Santa Barbara

GUNNEL TOTTIE, Department of English, University of Uppsala

Jan Svartvik

This book is a tribute to Jan Svartvik and his pioneering work in English corpus linguistics. Although Jan Svartvik has many linguistic interests, it is corpus linguistics that has been closest to his heart and the field where he has made his most important contributions ever since he began his career as Randolph Quirk's student over thirty years ago. It is therefore natural that we have chosen corpus linguistics as the theme of this volume.

Jan Svartvik's contributions to corpus linguistics are well known and need no special presentation. They are amply illustrated in this book and in the many references to his work. We hope that the thematic arrangement of the volume and the selection and content of the articles will capture something of his own wide-ranging interests in corpus linguistics and the study of English.

As editors, we thank the contributors for their generous participation in the volume. We also want to thank Ami Gayle for her invaluable help in preparing the manuscript and Jean Hudson and Muriel Larsson for helpful comments on various parts of the text.

KARIN AIJMER   BENGT ALTENBERG

Books by Jan Svartvik published by Longman

(with R Quirk, S Greenbaum and G Leech. 1972) *A Grammar of Contemporary English.*

(with G Leech. 1975) *A Communicative Grammar of English.*

(with S Greenbaum and G Leech. 1980) *Studies in English Linguistics: For Randolph Quirk.*

(with R Quirk, S Greenbaum and G Leech. 1985) *A Comprehensive Grammar of the English Language.*

Acknowledgements

We are indebted to Cambridge University Press for permission to reproduce an extract and Tables from *Apposition in Contemporary English* by Charles Meyer (to be published 1992).

1   Introduction

KARIN AIJMER AND BENGT ALTENBERG

The orientation of much linguistic research is undergoing change... I think this is a good development for humanistic subjects: it calls for more academic cross-fertilization and fresh approaches to old problems which, hopefully, will lead to a better understanding of the complexities of natural language and the marvel of human language processing. There is, in this field, a real need for people who have experience from working with 'real' language data...
(Svartvik 1990: 85–6)

Corpus linguistics can be described as the study of language on the basis of text corpora. Although the use of authentic examples from selected texts has a long tradition in English studies, there has been a rapid expansion of corpus linguistics in the last three decades. This development stems from two important events which took place around 1960. One was Randolph Quirk's launching of the Survey of English Usage (SEU) with the aim of collecting a large and stylistically varied corpus as the basis for a systematic description of spoken and written English. The other was the advent of computers which made it possible to store, scan and classify large masses of material. The first machine-readable corpus was compiled by Nelson Francis and Henry Kučera at Brown University in the early 1960s. It was soon followed by others, notably the Lancaster-Oslo/Bergen (LOB) Corpus, which utilized the same format as the Brown Corpus and made it possible to compare different varieties of English.

In 1975 Jan Svartvik and his colleagues at Lund University undertook the task of making the spoken part of the SEU Corpus available in machine-readable form. The resulting London-Lund Corpus of Spoken English has greatly stimulated studies of spoken

1

English and inspired a number of research projects (see e.g. Svartvik *et al*. 1982, Tottie and Bäcklund 1986, Svartvik 1990, Altenberg and Eeg-Olofsson 1990).

There now exists a large number of computerized corpora varying in size, design and research purpose, and others are under development (see the Appendix at the end of this volume). The great research potential offered by these corpora has given rise to a dramatic expansion of corpus-based research that few could have foreseen thirty years ago.

Computerized corpora have proved to be excellent resources for a wide range of research tasks. In the first place, they have provided a more realistic foundation for the study of language than earlier types of material, a fact which has given new impetus to descriptive studies of English lexis, syntax, discourse and prosody. Secondly, they have become a particularly fruitful basis for comparing different varieties of English, and for exploring the quantitative and probabilistic aspects of the language.

In all these respects, the availability and use of computerized corpora have expanded the domain of linguistic inquiry in significant ways. At the same time, this expansion has led to the development of more sophisticated research methodologies and new linguistic models. Many tasks which previously had to be done by hand can now be achieved automatically or semi-automatically by means of computer programs and other kinds of software. The most fruitful efforts in corpus linguistics have concerned automatic grammatical analysis of texts (tagging and parsing), but recently there have also been attempts to develop automatic programs for the analysis and generation of speech, and for interpreting the meaning and coherence of texts. Such programs require precise rules which simulate the knowledge that is part of the native speaker's linguistic competence. In the development of such programs computerized corpora have served both as a source for the creation of probabilistic models of language and as a testbed for theoretically motivated language models.

The benefits of using machine-readable text corpora, especially grammatically 'annotated' ones, are now so widely recognized that it is probably true to say that most text-based research makes use of a computerized corpus in one way or another. This growing dependence on machine-readable material and on the computer as a research tool has forced 'traditional' linguists to cooperate with computational linguists and computer scientists to an increasing extent. In this sense, corpus linguistics has more and more become an interdisciplinary field, where team-work has prospered and different approaches have met and fertilized each other. But the central goal has remained the same: to reach a better understanding of the workings of human language. Even when corpus-based research has had a predominantly practical aim, such as providing data for language teaching, lexicography or man–machine communication, the linguistic goals have been in the forefront. Thus corpus linguistics has developed into an important framework where description, model-building and practical application prosper side by side.

Only some of these aspects can be reflected in this volume. The computational side of corpus linguistics has had to be left out almost completely. Instead, the focus has been placed on theoretical and methodological questions and the description of particular linguistic phenomena in different varieties of English.

The book is arranged in four main sections focusing on different aspects of corpus linguistics. Part 1 describes the place of corpus studies in linguistic research and discusses the goals and methods of corpus work. From its humble beginnings in the late 1950s corpus linguistics has now emerged as a recognized research paradigm with its own particular methodologies and specific goals. The landmarks in this development and the present state of corpus linguistics are outlined by Geoffrey Leech (Chapter 2), who shows how the creation of new text corpora has led to an upsurge of research on many different fronts.

Like Leech, M. A. K. Halliday emphasizes the importance of corpus studies as a source of insight into the nature of language (Chapter 3). Viewing language as inherently probabilistic, he stresses the need to investigate frequencies in texts to establish probabilities in the grammatical system – not for the purpose of tagging and parsing, but for discovering the interaction between different subsystems and for a better understanding of historical and developmental change and the variation of language across registers.

An important problem in corpus linguistics concerns the status of corpus data. Any corpus is likely to contain constructions which, although they belong to language use, should not be part of a theoretical grammar describing the speaker's competence. Jan Aarts' article (Chapter 4) deals with the problem of deciding which types of phenomena should be included in the grammar and which should be excluded.

The articles in Part 2 deal with the design and development of new computer corpora. These are problematic tasks which require careful consideration of such matters as corpus and sample size, stylistic composition and coverage, systems of transcription, encoding principles, etc.

The lack of a corpus of spoken American English has long been felt among researchers interested in comparing speech and writing in different regional varieties. In Chapter 5, Wallace Chafe, John Du Bois and Sandra Thompson describe their projected new corpus of spoken American English at Santa Barbara. Another important corpus in the making is the Corpus of International English. This is going to consist of both spoken and written material and will include countries where English is spoken as a second or foreign language. The organization and design of the corpus are described by Sidney Greenbaum, coordinator of the project (Chapter 6).

Methodological and descriptive problems are the subject of Part 3, which deals with the exploration of corpora.

Collocations and 'prepatterned' language represent the intersection of lexicon and grammar, an area which can be fruitfully studied in corpora. Graeme Kennedy (Chapter 7) uses the LOB Corpus to show that the prepositions *between* and *through*, although they are partly similar and are often confused by learners, differ considerably in their major functions and linguistic 'ecology'. Göran Kjellmer (Chapter 8) uses an inventory of collocations in the Brown Corpus to demonstrate the prepatterned nature of a text taken from Jan Svartvik's *The Evans Statements*. He also discusses the role collocations play in the native speaker's mental lexicon and their importance for language learning and teaching. On the basis of the large Birmingham Corpus, Antoinette Renouf and John Sinclair demonstrate that grammatical 'frameworks' (like *a . . . of*) are statistically important and form an interesting basis for studying collocation (Chapter 9).

Corpora are particularly useful for comparing regional and stylistic varieties of English. This may cause methodological problems if the corpora are not assembled and designed in the same way. How such problems can be solved is shown in Peter Collins' article (Chapter 10) in which a comparison is made of the modals of necessity and obligation in three corpora representing British, American and

Australian English. Variation is also the subject of Charles Meyer's article (Chapter 11) comparing the use of appositions in the Brown, LOB and London-Lund corpora. The questions raised are how and why appositions vary between speech and writing and between different textual categories. Dieter Mindt (Chapter 12) is concerned with the relationship between syntax and semantics. Using three English corpora, he reveals systematic correspondences between semantic distinctions and their syntactic correlates in three areas: the expression of futurity, intentionality and the functions of *any*.

The material needed for a particular purpose can be quite small and need not be computerized. Gabriele Stein and Randolph Quirk demonstrate in their article (Chapter 13) that even a small corpus of fictional works can provide new insights into verbal–nominal phrases such as *have a drink*.

One area where computerized corpora have proved particularly useful is the study of linguistic variation and the stylistic properties of texts and genres. Drawing on their own large-scale explorations of computerized corpora, Douglas Biber and Edward Finegan (Chapter 14) discuss the methodological questions connected with corpus-based studies in general and multi-feature/multi-dimensional approaches in particular, such as the design of text corpora, the representativeness of text samples, the nature of text types and genres, and the form–function correspondences of linguistic features. The stylistic distinctiveness of texts is also the concern of David Crystal (Chapter 15), who considers the possibilities of extending to stylistics an analytical approach used in clinical linguistics. The procedure he explores – 'stylistic profiling' – is reminiscent of Biber and Finegan's approach, but while theirs depends on multivariate statistical analysis of tagged texts, Crystal's does not. Hence, the two approaches supplement each other in interesting ways.

While the use of 'genuine' examples from written sources has a long tradition in the study of English, research on natural speech data is a fairly recent development. Spoken corpora can be used for many different purposes, such as the investigation of prosodic phenomena or the functions of particular discourse items. Anna-Brita Stenström (Chapter 16) uses the London-Lund Corpus to study the repertoire and function of expletives employed by adult educated English speakers. She demonstrates that the women in the material resort to expletives more often than the men, but that they use different items in functionally different ways. Gunnel Tottie

(Chapter 17) compares the use of 'backchannels' in British and American English conversation, showing that such a comparison is possible and can yield interesting results, although the British and American spoken corpora she uses are designed and transcribed in somewhat different ways.

Two other areas where computerized corpora have only recently begun to demonstrate their usefulness are historical linguistics and dialectology. Matti Rissanen's diachronic study of *that* and zero as English noun clause links (Chapter 18) traces the gradual spread of zero, at the same time as it illustrates the methodological problem of how one can search for grammatical phenomena that have no overt lexical realization in the corpus. Ossi Ihalainen (Chapter 19) shows how machine-readable transcriptions of dialect material can provide evidence about syntactic variation across a dialect continuum in cases where questionnaires are of little use.

In the final chapter, Stig Johansson takes on the difficult task of looking into the future of corpus linguistics. Stressing the many problems that the explosive expansion of corpus studies has left unsolved, he nevertheless predicts a bright future for corpus linguistics, characterized by continued technical advances, new types of material, and exciting research possibilities.

Part 1

Goals and methods

2   The state of the art in corpus linguistics

GEOFFREY LEECH

2.1   Historical background

When did modern corpus linguistics begin? Should we trace it back
to the era of post-Bloomfieldian structural linguistics in the USA?
This was when linguists (such as Harris and Hill in the 1950s) were
under the influence of a positivist and behaviourist view of the
science, and regarded the 'corpus' as the primary explicandum of
linguistics.[1] For such linguists, the corpus – a sufficiently large body
of naturally occurring data of the language to be investigated – was
both necessary and sufficient for the task in hand, and intuitive
evidence was a poor second, sometimes rejected altogether. But
there is virtually a discontinuity between the corpus linguists of that
era and the later variety of corpus linguists with whose work this
book is concerned.

The discontinuity can be located fairly precisely in the later 1950s.
Chomsky had, effectively, put to flight the corpus linguistics of the
earlier generation. His view on the inadequacy of corpora, and the
adequacy of intuition, became the orthodoxy of a succeeding generation of theoretical linguists:

Any natural corpus will be skewed. Some sentences won't occur because
they are obvious, others because they are false, still others because they are
impolite. The corpus, if natural, will be so wildly skewed that the description
would be no more than a mere list.
(Chomsky, University of Texas, 1962, p. 159)

In the following year or two, the founders (as is now clear in
hindsight) of a new school of corpus linguistics began their work,
little noticed by the mainstream. In 1959 Randolph Quirk announced

8

his plan for a corpus of both spoken and written British English – the Survey of English Usage (SEU) Corpus, as it came to be known. Very shortly afterwards, Nelson Francis and Henry Kučera assembled a group of 'corpus-wise' linguists at Brown University, and out of their deliberations eventually came the Brown Corpus – a 'standard sample' of printed American English 'for use with digital computers' (Francis and Kučera 1979/1982). We can regard the second era of corpus linguistics as that which began with the collection of the SEU and Brown corpora in 1961 and has been dominated by the power of the computer; and yet the SEU Corpus was not conceived of as a computer corpus.[2] The drawback of computer corpora – their tendency to disfavour spoken data (because of problems of transcription and input) – did not therefore apply to the SEU, which was to be (approximately) 50 per cent spoken and 50 per cent written. Its particular strength was to be in the 'non-computable' data of speech.

It was left to the vision and perseverance of Jan Svartvik, with the team he assembled at Lund, to capitalize on the combined strengths of the Brown and SEU corpora.[3] His Survey of Spoken English began, in 1975, the arduous task of rendering machine-readable the unscripted spoken texts of the SEU corpus. The arduousness was especially due to the detailed prosodic coding in which the texts had been transcribed. The resulting London-Lund Corpus (LLC) remains to this day an unmatched resource for the study of spoken English.[4]

In the thirty years since 1961, corpus linguistics (of the newer computational variety) has gradually extended its scope and influence, so that, as far as natural language processing by computer is concerned, it has almost become a mainstream in itself.[5] It has not revived the American structural linguist's claim of the all-sufficient corpus, but the value of the corpus as a source of systematically retrievable data, and as a testbed for linguistic hypotheses, has become widely recognized and exploited.[6] More important, perhaps, has been the discovery that the computer corpus offers a new methodology for building robust natural language processing systems (see 3 below).

2.2   The corpus data explosion: bigger means better?

At a basic level, the resurgence of corpus linguistics can be measured in terms of the increasing power of computers and of the exponentially increasing size of corpora, viewed simplistically as large bodies of computer-readable text. The Brown Corpus (like its British counterpart, the LOB Corpus – see Johansson *et al*. 1978) can be thought of as a 'first-generation' corpus; its million-word bulk seemed vast by the standards of the earlier generation of corpus linguistics.[7] But this size was massively surpassed by a 'second generation' of the 1980s represented by John Sinclair's Birmingham Collection of English Text (Renouf 1984, Sinclair 1987) and the Longman/ Lancaster English Language Corpus, which benefited from the newer technology of the KDEM optical character-recognition device, freeing corpus compilation from the logjam of manual input. And perhaps the title 'third generation' may be given to those corpora, measured in hundreds of millions of words, almost all in commercial hands, exploiting the technologies of computer text processing (in publishing and in word-processing, for example) whereby huge amounts of machine-readable text become available as a by-product of modern electronic communication systems. Machine-readable text collections have grown from one million to almost a thousand million words in thirty years, so it would not be impossible to imagine a commensurate thousand-fold increase to one million million word corpora before 2021.

2.2.1   *Why size is not all-important*

To focus merely on size, however, is naive – for four reasons. Firstly, a collection of machine-readable text does not make a corpus. The Brown and SEU corpora were carefully designed as systematic collections of samples, so as to have face-validity as representative of 'standard' varieties of English. The third-generation corpora have been more in the nature of computerized archives (of which the best-known example is the Oxford Text Archive: cf. Oxford University Computing Service 1983): that is, they have been collected more or less opportunistically, according to what sources of data can be made available and what chances for collection arise. The Birmingham Collection is an interesting intermediate case: data have been collected beyond the bounds of what is required for the lexicographic purpose in hand, so that an ongoing archive – what Sinclair and his associates call a 'monitor corpus' (Renouf 1987: 21) – exists alongside the lexicographic 'main corpus'. New initiatives, notably the ACL/DCI (Association of Computational Linguistics

Data Coding Initiative) in the USA, aspire to make the concept of an archive almost comparable in scope to that of a national copyright library.[8] But there still remains the task of 'quarrying' from such a vast data resource the corpus needed for a particular purpose – for ultimately, the difference between an archive and a corpus must be that the latter is designed or required for a particular 'representative' function.[9] In terms of 'representativeness' we may distinguish relatively general-purpose corpora, such as the Brown and SEU corpora, from corpora designed for a more specialized function – a domain-specific corpus representing the language of the oil industry, for example.[10]

Secondly, the vast growth in resources of machine-readable text has taken place exclusively in the medium of written language. Until speech-recognition devices have developed the automatic input of spoken language to the level of present OCR (optical character-recognition) devices for written language, the collection of spoken discourse on the same scale as written text will remain a dream of the future. The transcription of spoken discourse into written form, as a necessary step in the collection of spoken corpora, is a time-consuming process fraught with problems.[11] In this context, the abiding importance of the London-Lund Corpus must again be emphasized.

Thirdly, while technology advances quickly, human institutions evolve slowly. This platitude has particular relevance to the collection and distribution of computer corpora, where that most slowly evolving of human institutions – the legal system – retards the full availability of the resources which technology makes possible. The law relating to copyright – not to mention other legally enforceable rights such as that relating to confidentiality – forbids the copying of text (including the inputting of texts to a computer) without the express permission of the copyright holder, typically the originator, author or publisher of the text. Since the granting of copyright permission can be held to have a commercial value, it is not likely to be granted on a *carte blanche* basis, and substantial fees are liable to be charged. Although certain corpora (such as the Brown, LOB and LLC) are distributable for non-commercial research applications, others are not publicly available at all, and the concept of a corpus which is in the public domain – available unconditionally for all users – does not so far exist, except for texts too old to be in copyright.

Fourthly, another platitude – current within the computer world – is that, while hardware technology advances by leaps and bounds, software technology lags like a crawling snail behind it. In the present context, software may be taken to include not the 'raw' or 'pure' corpus, which can be collected more or less automatically in its original machine-readable form, but the annotations which linguists and others may add to it, and the computer programs designed to process corpora linguistically. Clearly, a corpus, however large, when stored orthographically in machine-readable form, is of no use unless the information it contains can become available to the user. Therefore, as a first step it is necessary for the corpus-derived information to be accessed through a search and retrieval facility, a simple example of which is a KWIC concordance program. Such programs are the most familiar and basic pieces of software to use with a corpus; more sophisticated search and retrieval packages such as the Oxford Concordance Program (OCP), WordCruncher and KAYE are known to many users.[12] But to make more linguistically interesting use of a corpus, it is necessary to analyse the corpus itself, and therefore to develop tools for linguistic analysis. Such tools are at present relatively primitive, with a consequent limit on the extent to which large corpora can be linguistically exploited.

2.2.2   The need for annotated corpora

Concordance programs essentially sort and count the objects they find in a corpus – which, in the 'raw' corpus, are words, punctuation, and the characters of which words are composed. Unless appropriate additional information is somehow built into the corpus, the concordancer cannot tell the difference between *I* (personal pronoun) and *I* (roman numeral); between *minute* (noun) and *minute* (adjective); or between *lying* (telling untruths) and *lying* (in a recumbent posture). How is this information to be provided? Can the analysis, as in the post-Bloomfieldian paradigm, be induced from the corpus by discovery procedures, or does the researcher need to impose distinction on the text by means of human 'intuition' or analysis?

2.2.3   Arguments in favour of large corpora

Shortly, I will answer the above question by pointing to the variable division of labour between human analyst, corpus and software; but before leaving the issue of size, I wish to balance my above deprecation of large corpus size by arguments in its favour.

The corpus linguist of the 1950s could entertain without too much difficulty the idea of a corpus providing the data for an exhaustive description of a language.[13] This was probably because the linguists of that day focused on phonemics and morphophonemics – levels where the inventory of linguistic items is small by comparison (for example) with syntax or the lexicon. When Chomsky shifted the centre of attention from phonology to syntax, he was able effectively to debunk the notion that the corpus could provide a sufficiency of data. He argued that the syntax of a language is a generative system, producing an infinite number of sentences from a finite number of rules. This illustrates how the notion of what is an adequate corpus shifts significantly as one moves from one linguistic level to another. However, Chomsky in his turn could not have conceived, in the 1950s, of a corpus of 500 million words capable of being searched in a matter of minutes or hours. While it is unlikely that foreknowledge of such a phenomenon would have changed Chomsky's view of corpora at that time (see Section 2.1 above), we can see, in historical retrospect, how the availability of vastly increasing computer corpus resources has enabled syntactic and lexical phenomena of a language to be open to empirical investigation on a scale previously unimagined.

Ironically, this development has caused investigators to become aware, with a degree of realism not previously possible, of the open-ended magnitude of languages not only in their lexis (where the openness of the linguistic system has long been acknowledged) but also in their syntax, where recent research has indicated that syntac-tic rule systems are themselves open-ended, rather than a closed set such as Chomsky envisaged.[14] However, this sobering awareness should not dishearten the corpus linguist. Whereas the view of a corpus as an exhaustive reservoir of data is scarcely tenable today, our new 'megacorpora' can provide the means for *training* and *testing* models of language so as to assess their quality. The statistical measure known as *perplexity* (see Jelinek 1985b) provides an evalu-ation of how good a grammar (or language model) is in accounting for the data observed in a corpus. Here is a precise measurement comparable to the 'simplicity measures' which Chomsky, in his earlier writings, regarded as a basis for the evaluation of linguistic descriptions (see Chomsky 1965: 37–47). Corpus linguistics need no longer feel timid about its theoretical credentials, nor does the earlier Chomskyan rejection of corpus data carry such force.[15] At the same time, the development and testing of probabilistic models of language require the availability of very large corpora.

2.3   The processing of corpora: how humans and machines interact

The linguistic annotation or analysis of corpora demonstrates a need for a partnership between man and machine, or (drawing the lines in a slightly different way) between human processing, computer processing and corpus data. Neither the corpus linguist of the 1950s, who rejected intuition, nor the generative linguist of the 1960s, who rejected corpus data, was able to achieve the interaction of data coverage and insight that characterizes the many successful corpus analyses of recent years.[16]

There are a number of ways in which human, software and corpus resources can interact, according to how far the human analyst delegates to the computer the responsibility for analysis. At one end of the scale, the computer program (e.g. a concordance program) is used simply as a tool for sorting and counting data, while all the serious data analysis is performed by the human investigator. (Most of the studies mentioned in Note 16 belong to this category.) At the other extreme, the human analyst provides no linguistic insight, just programming ability; the machine discovers its own categories of analysis, in effect implementing a 'discovery procedure'. Such experiments as have been carried out in this field have been mostly limited to simple tasks, such as the discovery of English word classes by clustering words on the basis of their distribution.[17] Their results are fascinating in showing, on the one hand, some striking resemblances between the classes discovered by the machine and those recognized by grammatical tradition (prepositions and modals, for example, emerge as clearly distinguishable classes), and on the other, that the classes found often correspond only partially to established English word classes (*her*, for example, falls uneasily between possessives and objective pronouns, since the program cannot account for word class ambiguity). Such experiments appear to show that the machine can discover some, but not all, of the truth; they provide reassurance to those, like myself, who believe that successful analysis depends on a division of labour between the corpus and the human mind.

Somewhere between the two poles of unequal collaboration mentioned above there is a third type of human–machine partnership, where the human linguist's role can be characterized as that of an 'expert' whose specialized knowledge is programmed into a computer system. Consider the example of a grammatical word-tagging system.[18] The human expert here – say, a grammarian or a lexicographer – proposes a set of grammatical tags to represent the set of English word categories; a lexicon and other databases are built, making use of these categories; and programs are written to assign an appropriate word tag to each of the word tokens in the corpus. The program achieves its task at a success rate of x per cent (x being typically in the region of 96–7 per cent); the errors that it makes – judged to be errors on independent linguistic grounds – are fed back to the expert, who then proposes modifications to the original set of categories, or the program, or both. The program and analytic system can now be tested on fresh corpus material, and it can be observed how far the modifications have brought about a better success rate (see Figure 2.1).

In this model, then, there is a truly interactive relation between analyst, software and corpus, whereby two different analyses can be

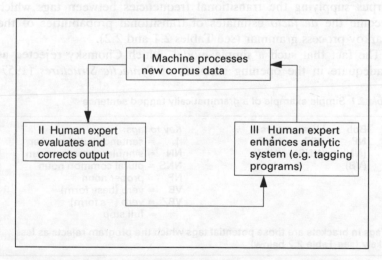

Figure 2.1   A 'symbiotic' relation between human and machine in corpus processing

compared and evaluated by an independent criterion of success. After the human post-editor has completed the task of annotating the corpus, the results are twofold: (a) an analytic device (in this case an improved grammatical tagger), and (b) an analysed, or annotated, corpus. The symbiosis is evident in the relation between the analytic device, which brings about an analysis of the corpus, and the analysed corpus, which (through feedback) brings about an improvement in the analytic device (cf. Aarts, this volume).

This symbiosis is all the more necessary when we add a probabilistic dimension. Probabilities, like corpora,[19] were given no place in the Chomskyan paradigm, but in areas such as speech recognition, probabilistic models have been found to be more capable than non-probabilistic models,[20] even though the latter may claim greater verisimilitude as imitations of human language processing. While it is evident that detailed probabilities are not 'intuitively' available to the native speaker or the linguist, realistic estimates of probability can be made on the basis of observed corpus frequencies. The most successful grammatical tagging systems appear to be those based on a simple finite-state grammar with probabilities (derived from corpus frequency data) assigned to the transitions between states – i.e. a Markov process model.[21] An essential source of data for such a system is a grammatically tagged corpus supplying the transitional frequencies between tags which become the *de facto* estimates of transitional probabilities of the Markov process grammar (see Tables 2.1 and 2.2).

The fact that such a simple model, which Chomsky rejected as inadequate in the opening chapters of *Syntactic Structures* (1957:

Table 2.1 Simple example of a grammatically tagged sentence

↑	Bob	likes	toys	.	Key to tags:
↑	NP	VBZ	NNS	.	↑ = sentence initial marker
	(NN)	(NNS)	(VBZ)		NN = singular common noun
	(VB)				NNS = plural common noun
					NP = proper noun
					VB = verb (base form)
					VBZ = verb (−s form)
					. = full stop

Tags in brackets are those potential tags which the program rejects as less likely (see Table 2.2 below).

Note: Punctuation marks and the sentence initial marker ↑ are treated as word tags for this purpose.

Table 2.2 Transitional probability estimates for pairs of tags

↑ — NP 533	NN — VBZ 116	NP — NNS 151	NNS — NNS 30	VBZ — VBZ	0
↑ — NN 312	NN — NNS 301	VB — VBZ 0	NNS — VBZ 24	NNS —.	1301
↑ — VB 108	NP — VBZ 152	VB — NNS 204	VBZ — NNS 136	VBZ —.	310

Note: The figures represent relative frequencies of tag transitions in the Lancaster-Oslo/
Bergen Corpus as numbers of occurrences per 10,000 words. Multiplying together the
figures for each possible sequence of tags in the table shows that the correct sequence of
tags, on the basis of these observed frequencies, is the one which is most likely to occur.

21), proves unexpectedly adequate to the task of automatic grammatical tagging and throws an interesting light on the contrast
between the non-probabilistic and cognitive orientation of
Chomskyan linguistics, and the probabilistic non-cognitive orientation of much corpus-based research. The 'cognitivists' will say that
a machine for manipulating probabilities cannot represent a realistic
model of language, i.e. a model of human linguistic knowledge.
From their point of view, the probabilities at best provide a means
whereby the machine, lacking human knowledge and cognitive
abilities, can achieve a limited resemblance to human ability, like
that of an ingenious mechanical doll full of springs and machinery.
The 'probabilists' will say that the model is a model of human
linguistic behaviour – precisely that, and no more; but it may even
so provide insights into the psychology of language, on the grounds
that probabilities enter into human language processing and understanding to an extent that has been overlooked (see Sampson
1987b). One thing in favour of probabilistic language processing
systems is that they are eminently *robust*. They are fallible, but they
work; they produce a more or less accurate result, even on un-
restricted input data, in a way that outperforms most rule-driven
language modelling systems.

2.3.1   Self-organizing methodology

Here, brief mention should be made of a more advanced model of
the partnership between human and machine in the development of
probabilistic language models, one which gives a larger role to the
machine. The major disadvantage of the symbiotic model described
above is that it requires massive human intervention at two points:
(a) at an initial stage, where an extensive manual corpus analysis is

needed in order to arrive at preliminary probabilistic estimates for the language model; and (b) at the crucial stage of diagnosis of errors in the corpus analysis, and the feedback of those errors into the corpus analysis. I call the human role here 'massive' because the analysis of a million words by hand (which may be what is needed to give the minimum satisfactory result in terms of probabilistic grammar) requires the dedication of many thousands of human hours to the work.

A self-organizing methodology (see Bahl, Jelinek and Mercer 1983) is one which avoids the human feedback stage intervening between one iteration of model enhancement and another. The basic idea is that the machine 'learns' to improve its language model on the basis of the data it encounters and analyses. To start the iterative process, it is sufficient to have some rough initial estimates of probability. The iterative process constitutes the training of the language model so as to adjust its probabilities in order to maximize the likelihood, according to the model, of the occurrence of the observed corpus data (see Jelinek 1985a, Sharman 1989a: 33–6). At present, the training of language models by self-organization is extremely demanding on computer resources, and only the largest computers are adequate to the task. In the future, as computers increase in storage and processing power, we may hope that self-organizing methodology will take over much of the human effort at present invested in corpus analysis. This becomes all the more necessary as we develop more complex probabilistic models and the opportunity arises for these to be trained and tested on larger and larger corpora.

In Section 2.3 I have presented four different paradigms of research balance between the role of the human analyst and the computer. These can now be listed in the form of a scale, from most human intervention to least human intervention:

(1) 'Data retrieval model'
    Machine provides the data in a convenient form.
    Human analyses the data.

(2) 'Symbiotic model'
    Machine presents the data in (partially) analysed form.
    Human iteratively improves the analytic system.

(3) 'Self-organizing model'

Machine analyses the data and iteratively improves its analytic system.
Human provides the parameters of the analytic system and the software.

(4) 'Discovery procedure model'
Machine analyses the data using its own categories of analysis, derived by clustering techniques based on data.
Human provides the software.

2.4   Annotated corpora

One example of corpus annotation that I have mentioned is grammatical tagging – the assignment of grammatical word-class labels to every word token in a corpus. A consequence of the corpus analysing methodology outlined in Section 2.3 above is an annotated corpus – no longer the 'raw' (or 'pure') corpus which was originally input to the computer but a version in which linguistic information, of particular kinds, is exhaustively provided.

Once a computer corpus has been annotated with some kind of linguistic analysis, it becomes a springboard for further research; it enables a concordance program, for example, to search for grammatical abstractions (such as instances of the passive voice, of the progressive aspect, of noun–noun sequences, etc.) rather than for words. Probably the most important spin-off is the use of an annotated corpus to provide initial statistics for probabilistic language processing (see Section 2.3 above).

At present, a number of different corpora have been grammatically tagged and are available in tagged versions, for example the Brown Corpus, the LOB Corpus and the Spoken English Corpus (SEC).[22] There are, however, many other levels at which annotation must eventually take place if the corpus is to incorporate full information about its linguistic form. With speech corpora, phonetic and phonemic labelling has a high priority (see Moore 1989). The prosodic annotation of the LLC is itself a complex form of annotation – although in this case the annotation is also a part of the transcription of the text itself.

Beyond word tagging, higher levels of grammatical tagging can be undertaken, as in the grammatically annotated part of the London-Lund Corpus (see Svartvik et al. 1982, Svartvik 1990). Various syntactically analysed sub-corpora, known as *treebanks*, have come into existence. They are 'sub-corpora' because, as already noted in Section 2.3 above, the syntactic analysis, or parsing, of corpus sentences is a laborious activity, and even the analysis of a million words (e.g. of the Brown or LOB Corpus) is a vast enterprise, so that in practice we have had to be content to build our treebanks from subsections of such corpora.[23] Recent research at Lancaster, however, has resulted in a simplified syntactic analysis technique known as 'skeleton parsing', which can be performed very quickly by human operators using a rapid input program (see Leech and Garside 1991).

The annotation of corpora does not stop with parsing. Semantic analysis and discoursal analysis of corpora are likely to be the next stage in this development of corpus annotation. The annotation of the LLC for discourse markers (Stenström 1984b, 1990) is one example of higher-level analysis. Another example is an 'anaphoric treebank' which is now being undertaken (with IBM funding) at Lancaster and which includes not only skeleton parsing but also markers of anaphor–antecedent relationships.

2.5   Where are we now, and where are we going?

I conclude this survey of the 'state of the art' in corpus-based research by considering the present situation and future prospects under three headings which identify priority areas both for immediate and for longer-term development (see also Johansson, this volume):

(1) basic corpus development
(2) corpus tools development
(3) development of corpus annotations.

We are now in a position where corpus-based research has truly taken off, not only as an acknowledged paradigm for linguistic investigation but as a key contribution to the development of natural language processing software. Hence research on the three fronts mentioned is likely to attract not only academic attention but also the governmental and industrial funding that will be necessary if the progress wished for is to take place.

2.5.1 Basic corpus development

The basic acquisition, archiving, encoding and making available of text corpora has recently taken a big step forward in many countries. A recent unpublished survey of European language corpora, by A. Zampolli,[24] showed corpus development, either completed or in progress, for sixteen European languages. France (with its enormous historical corpus of the *Trésor de la langue française*) was a pioneer in this field, but many other countries have recently followed, perhaps seeing the value of national corpus resources from two contrasting points of view: that of commercial investment (e.g. for dictionaries) and that of the patriotic investment in a national language. Zampolli's data for languages excluding English showed, in all, 365 million words already collected (the largest quantities being 190 million words of French and 60 million words of Dutch), and a further 63 million words planned. However, the gulf between the quantities of written material (348 million) and of spoken material (17 million) was all too obvious. English was excluded from Zampolli's survey, but he noted that even in non-English-speaking European countries, English corpora, and projects involving them, were pre-eminent over those of other languages.

In the English-speaking world, where up to now the largest collections of data have been those acquired (e.g. by IBM) for industrial or commercial research (see Section 2.2 above), a number of public corpus collection initiatives have recently begun or are about to begin. The Association for Computational Linguistics has launched a Data Collection Initiative (ACL/DCI) aiming initially at a corpus of 100 million words, largely of American English. The corpus will be encoded in a systematic way, using the Standard Generalized Markup Language (SGML), in coordination with a further initiative, the TEI (or Text Encoding Initiative).

Alongside these American-based (but not exclusively American) initiatives, the compilation of a British-based (but not exclusively British) 30-million word corpus, the Longman/Lancaster corpus, is now available to academic researchers. Two other ambitious British-led corpus-building initiatives are expected to begin shortly. One is a national corpus initiative led by Oxford University Press, with a number of collaborators including Oxford and Lancaster Universities, Longman Group UK Ltd and the British Library. The aim of this consortium, like that of the ACL/DCI, is 100 million words – a quantity which seems to have become the 'going rate' for corpora in the 1990s, just as one million was the rate set by the Brown Corpus and the SEU Corpus for the 1960s and 1970s. A second initiative is that of the International Corpus of English (ICE), coordinated by Sidney Greenbaum at the Survey of English Usage and involving the compilation of parallel corpora of English from a wide range of countries in which English is the primary first or second language (see Greenbaum, this volume).

The three British-based corpora mentioned above will all contain a combination of written and spoken material. It is generally acknowledged now that the overall neglect of machine-readable spoken transcriptions in the past is something which must now be corrected as a matter of the highest priority. A problem yet to be thoroughly confronted, however, is that of how to provide a set of standards or encoding guidelines for the transcription of spoken discourse, so that the needs of various users can be met (see Chafe *et al.*, this volume). These range from, at one end of the scale, the need of speech scientists to have meticulous spoken recordings linked to detailed labellings of phonetic features, to the need for lexicographers, for example, to have access to many millions of words of speech – which, of necessity, could be only crudely transcribed.

2.5.2   *Corpus tools development*

It is widely acknowledged today that a corpus needs the support of a sophisticated computational environment, providing software tools both to retrieve data from the corpus and to process linguistically the corpus itself. In spite of the relatively wide availability of some tools, such as concordance packages (see Section 2.2.1 above) and – increasingly – grammatical tagging systems, most tools exist only in prototype forms and in home-grown settings, without adequate documentation or public availability.

Some of the tools for which a fairly general need is felt are as follows.

(a) General-purpose corpus data retrieval tools which go beyond the existing concordance facilities, in being able to handle corpora in complex formats – including the non-linear formats of treebanks – in being able to sort and search in varied ways, and in being able to derive from an (annotated) corpus various kinds of derived data structures (such as corpus-based frequency lists, lexicons or grammars).

(b) Tools to facilitate corpus annotations at various levels. These might be used for automatic processing (like current tagging systems), for semi-automatic interactive use (like the LDB parser at Nijmegen – see van den Heuvel 1987) or for accelerated manual analysis and input (like Garside's skeleton parsing program – see Leech and Garside 1991). Interactive windowing facilities have much unrealized potential in this field. One tool for which there is a strong demand is a robust corpus parser: something that will be able to provide a reliable though 'shallow' parse for large quantities of text.[25]

(c) Tools to provide interchange of information between corpora and lexical and grammatical databases. At the most simplistic level, a program which derives lexical frequency lists from raw corpora is a device for deriving lexical information from a corpus – in fact, for creating or updating a lexicon. From a tagged corpus, a lemmatized frequency list may be derived; and from a treebank, a probabilistic grammar may be derived (using observed frequencies of rules as first-approximation probabilities). These are examples of how corpora can create or augment linguistic databases. From the opposite direction, a testing algorithm can use observed corpus data as a means of evaluating the coverage of a grammar or the performance of a parser. From these and similar instances we can see that between corpora and linguistic databases or linguistic models is an important and rather complex channel of information transfer, for which special tools are required.

2.5.3   Development of corpus annotations

As more and more analysis or annotation is carried out on corpora, it is natural that annotated corpora themselves provide a platform of linguistic analysis on which further research can build – by no means limited to research undertaken by the original annotators.[26] In this connection various requirements are beginning to arise with some urgency.

(a) There is an increasing need for detailed documentation of the linguistic schemes of analysis embodied in annotations, e.g. tagging schemes (cf. Johansson *et al.* 1986) and parsing schemes (cf. Sampson 1987b).

(b) The devisers of such schemes of analysis generally seek to incorporate 'consensually approved' features such as (in the simplest case) traditional parts of speech. But ultimately, there is no such thing as a consensus analysis: all schemes are likely to be biased in some way or another – however minor – towards a particular theoretical or descriptive position. For future annotation schemes, some kind of consultation process, or even a 'popularity poll', should be carried out among interested members of the academic community, to ensure that the annotations are as far as possible the most useful for the greatest number of potential users. In some cases, alternative annotations for different communities of users may be advisable.

(c) At the same time, there is much to be said for a harmonization of different annotation schemes. As things are, tagging schemes and parsing schemes have arisen piecemeal, and if any standardization has taken place it has been no more than the *de facto* standardization accorded to a widely used scheme (such as the Brown Corpus tagset). It is widely felt that standardization of annotation schemes – in spite of its attractions in the abstract – is too high a goal to aim at; instead, our goal should be of annotation 'harmonization' – using commonly agreed labels where possible, and providing readily available information on the mappings, or partial mappings, between one scheme and another. Such a goal should be easier to attain in a flexible annotation system allowing for both hierarchies of annotation levels and degrees of delicacy in the specification of categories. (Spoken corpora may need special tags for speech-specific items.)

(d) Up to the present, the attention given to different levels of annotation has been very patchy, as the following rough list attempts to indicate.

Linguistic level	*Annotations carried out so far*
phonetic/phonemic	widespread in speech technology corpora or databases
syllabic	none known
morphological	none known

prosodic	little (the LLC and SEC are notable exceptions – see Note 4)
word class (i.e. grammatical tagging)	widespread
syntactic (i.e. parsing)	rapidly becoming more widespread
semantic	none known
pragmatic/discourse	little – but developing

It is likely that in the relatively near future certain levels of annotation – especially the semantic and pragmatic/discourse levels – will begin to receive greater priority.

(e) Finally, an annotated corpus should never totally replace the corpus as it existed prior to annotation. The original 'raw' corpus (including the original sound recordings) should always be available, so that those who find the annotations useless or worse can recover the text in its virgin purity.

2.6   Conclusion

Those who work with computer corpora are suddenly finding themselves in an expanding universe. For years, corpus linguistics was the obsession of a small group which received little or no recognition from either linguistics or computer science. Now much is happening, and there is a demand for much more to happen in the future. This is exhilarating and gratifying for those who, like Jan Svartvik, have been on the corpus bandwagon since it was a little donkey cart – when corpus work was, indeed, little else but donkey work. But gratification is also mixed with irony and nostalgia. After all, driving the donkey cart was much more fun!

Notes

[1] See especially Harris (1951: 12–14). I am grateful for the background to corpus linguistics provided by Mark Sebba, in his unpublished MSc dissertation (Sebba 1989). As Sebba points out, some American structuralists reasonably took the view that the corpus was not the *sole* explicandum of linguistic description. For example, Hockett (1948: 269) made it clear that 'the purpose [of the structural linguist] is not simply to

account for all utterances which comprise his corpus' but to 'account for utterances which are not in his corpus at a given time'.

2 See Quirk (1960) on the planning of the SEU Corpus, and Francis (1979) on the planning of the Brown Corpus.

3 See Svartvik *et al.* (1982) and Svartvik (1990) on the computerization of spoken English data, with particular reference to the London-Lund Corpus.

4 Mention should be made, however, of various more recent projects for the development of spoken English corpora. The Spoken English Corpus (SEC) compiled by IBM and Lancaster University (see Knowles and Lawrence 1987) is a particularly relevant example. The corpus is small (consisting of *c*. 50,000 words), but is available in coexisting machine-readable versions (prosodically transcribed, tagged, parsed, orthographic, etc.), as well as in the original sound recordings. On the plan for a corpus of spoken American English, see Chafe *et al.*, this volume.

5 Corpora have now become widely regarded as essential 'infrastructure' for software development in natural language processing. In the United Kingdom, for instance, the following quotation is from a strategy document issued by the Department of Trade and Industry after extensive consultation and discussion among those researching into speech and natural language technology:

> Availability of large amounts of annotated data is critical in both speech and natural language processing, regardless of the approach taken . . . but corpora of the right scope, size, quality, and accessibility do not yet exist in the UK. (Thompson 1989: 17)

Later, the same document states that 'corpora for speech and language work are an essential component of every speech and natural language project' (*ibid.*: 21). A few months after this document was produced, in January 1990, the Department of Trade and Industry sponsored a workshop on a national initiative to develop 'corpus resources' (see Note 25 below). This rather sudden popularization of computer corpora in the UK has parallels in other countries, such as the USA, Japan and the EC countries.

6 A glance at the relevant bibliographies (Altenberg 1986, 1991) shows how extensive has been the use of computer corpora such as the Brown, LOB and LLC for varied spheres of linguistic research on modern English. However, the recent sudden upsurge of interest in corpus-based methodology has arisen mainly through its application in such commercially exploitable areas as lexicography, speech recognition (cf. Jelinek 1985b), speech synthesis (cf. Knowles and Lawrence 1987) and machine translation (Brown *et al.* 1988).

7 The American Brown Corpus and the British LOB Corpus are matching

corpora of written English, both containing data from publications in the year 1961. Each corpus contains 500 text extracts classified in terms of fifteen text categories. Other corpora built to the same general design are the Kolhapur Corpus of Indian English (Shastri 1988) and the Macquarie Corpus of Australian English (Collins and Peters 1988, Collins 1988b).

[8] ACL/DCI is currently aiming at a collection of 100 million words of text, with the objective of making this material available for academic research at cost and without royalties – see Liberman (1989). An important component of the plan is the coding of the text in a standardized format, to be specified by a parallel initiative known as the TEI (Text Encoding Initiative).

[9] In practical terms, a corpus is 'representative' to the extent that findings based on its contents can be generalized to a larger hypothetical corpus. For instance, the Brown Corpus is often assumed to be representative of American English, of written English, or of English in general. At present, as assumption of representativeness must be regarded largely as an act of faith. In the future we may hope that statistical or other models of what makes a corpus representative of a large population of texts will be developed and will be applied on existing corpora. (On representativeness, see Rieger 1979.)

[10] Examples of domain-specific corpora are the JDEST Corpus of English in science and technology (see Yang 1985a), the Guangzhou Petroleum English Corpus (Qi-bo 1989). Other types of specialized English corpora include, for example, corpora of learners' language or of children's language – the latter illustrated by the CHILDES child language database (MacWhinney and Snow 1990).

[11] The SEU and SEC corpora both involved careful and detailed prosodic transcription, necessarily the work of more than one skilled phonetician, whose transcriptions required cross-checking for the sake of intersubjectivity and consistency. Even so, there are problems regarding the reliability of such transcriptions (see Knowles and Alderson, forthcoming). The transcription of very large quantities of spoken data, such as is envisaged for current projects, requires a radically simplified notion of transcription, but here again, the nature and extent of such simplification require careful consideration (cf. Chafe et al., this volume).

[12] On the OCP, see Hockey and Martin (1988); on WordCruncher, Jones (1987); on KAYE, Kaye (1989, 1990). Another widely used concordancing package is CLAN (see MacWhinney and Snow 1990: 17–20).

[13] However, Harris (1951: 13) did acknowledge that different linguistic levels might require corpora of different sizes:

> How large or variegated a corpus must be in order to qualify as a sample of the language, is a statistical problem.... For example, in phonological investi-

gations a smaller corpus may be adequate than in morphological investigations. (Quoted in Sebba 1989)

[14] Sampson's (1987a) argument, based on corpus evidence, is that the set of grammatical rules is open-ended, and that the grammatical/ungrammatical distinction exists only in terms of a statistical scale of likelihood. This argument is opposed by Taylor *et al.* (1989) and Briscoe (1990) on the grounds that Sampson's phrase structure grammar model provides an inadequate test, but is supported by Sharman's (1989b) finding that grammatical rules, like words, conform to Zipf's statistical law of type-token distribution.

[15] Arguments against the rejection of corpus evidence are presented, *inter alia*, by Aarts and van den Heuvel (1985).

[16] From the point of view of linguistics, perhaps the best argument in favour of corpus-based research is the wealth of serendipitous descriptive studies based on corpus data which can be scanned in the bibliographies of Altenberg (1986, 1991). As a particularly notable example of the range of such studies, we may refer to the Swedish studies of extempore spoken English reported, in many publications, by Aijmer, Stenström and Tottie (among others) based on the LLC data.

[17] One such experiment is reported in Atwell and Elliott (1987: 132–4). More extensive experiments on the discovery of word classes have been undertaken, using the more powerful computing facilities required, by Robert Mercer (personal communication) at IBM Yorktown Heights, New York.

[18] Examples of grammatical tagging systems are CLAWS (developed at Lancaster by Roger Garside and others – see Garside *et al.* 1987: 30–56), Volsunga, developed by DeRose (1988), and the systems developed for the London-Lund Corpus by Eeg-Olofsson (1985, 1990). These systems, being probabilistic, make use not only of 'humanly devised' analytic categories but of corpus-derived frequency data. Thus CLAWS, used for the grammatical tagging of the LOB Corpus, depended for its initial statistics on frequency information from the tagged Brown Corpus, generously made available by Francis and Kučera.

[19] Chomsky (1957: 16) takes the view that 'one's ability to produce and recognize grammatical utterances is not based on notions of statistical approximation and the like'.

[20] See the conclusions of the ARPA empirical test of speech-recognition devices undertaken in the USA in 1971–6, as reported in Sampson (1987b: 29).

[21] On the advantages of a Markov process model in grammatical tagging as compared with non-probabilistic methods, see Marshall (1987: 42–7).

[22] On the tagged Brown Corpus, and issues of grammatical tagging, see

Francis (1980). On the tagged LOB Corpus, see Johansson *et al.* (1986) and Garside *et al.* (1987: 30–56, 99–119).

23 On treebanks and the methods employed in their compilation, see Leech and Garside (1991).

24 Presented in January 1990 to the UK Speech and Language Technology (SALT) Club's Workshop on Corpus Resources, Wadham College, Oxford.

25 On experiments in corpus parsing, see Garside *et al.* (1987: 66–96); also Aarts and van den Heuvel (1985).

26 The best testimony of this is the number of copies of tagged corpora (particularly the Brown and LOB tagged corpora) which have been acquired for research purposes around the world. For example, 89 institutions acquired copies of the tagged LOB Corpus in the five years 1986–90. It is only fair to mention, on the other hand, that some researchers are suspicious of this imposition of humanly derived linguistic analyses on the data: for them, the 'raw' corpus is the 'pure' corpus, whose authenticity is uncontaminated by the intervention of the analyst. John Sinclair put this point of view forcefully at the Wadham College Workshop, mentioned in Note 24 above.

3   Corpus studies and probabilistic grammar

M. A. K. HALLIDAY

In the Preface to his book *On Voice in the English Verb*, which was published a quarter of a century ago, Jan Svartvik wrote that 'corpus-studies will help to promote descriptively more adequate grammars' (Svartvik 1966: vii). This modest claim ran against the ideology prevailing at that time, according to which corpus studies had nothing to contribute towards an understanding of language. Chomsky's theory of competence and performance had driven a massive wedge between the system and the instance, making it impossible by definition that analysis of actual texts could play any part in explaining the grammar of a language – let alone in formulating a general linguistic theory.

Explicitly rejected was the relevance of any kind of quantitative data. Chomsky's sarcastic observation that '*I live in New York* is more frequent than *I live in Dayton Ohio*' was designed to demolish the conception that relative frequency in text might have any theoretical significance.[1] Svartvik recognized, however, that the significance of linguistic frequency measures was not something that could be trivialized out of court in this way. As well as using data from the corpus to establish a taxonomy of classes of the passive in English, and to set up the 'passive scale' in the form of a serial relationship (implicational scaling), he also calculated the ratio of passive to active clauses and compared the frequency of passives across a range of different registers. Such patterns could not be reduced to accidental effects like the population of American cities, or people's preferences in the personal names they bestowed on their children.

There is no longer any need to argue for the importance of corpus studies as a source of information about the grammar of a language, and indeed as a source of insight into the nature of grammar in general. Svartvik's own subsequent work, and that of the Survey of English Usage quartet of which he has been a permanent member, has shown beyond doubt how much can be learnt from what the corpus contains. But the theoretical status of corpus frequencies is still an open issue, and it is to this topic that I would like to return here.

It had always seemed to me that the linguistic *system* was inherently probabilistic, and that frequency in text was the instantiation of probability in the grammar. In working on Chinese grammar, in the 1950s, I used such text frequencies as I had available and assigned crude probabilities to the terms in the grammatical systems.[2] Firth's concept of 'system' provided the necessary paradigmatic base. It seemed to me self-evident that, given a system 'polarity' whose terms were 'positive/negative', the fact that positive was more frequent than negative was an essential property of the system – as essential as the terms of the opposition itself. Analytically, of course, it was necessary to separate the statement of the terms of the system from the statement of their relative probabilities; but what was involved was a single phenomenon, not two.

It turned out that some people felt threatened by this suggestion, regarding it as an attack on their freedom as individuals to choose what they wanted to say. It was rather as if by stating people's probable sleeping behaviour one would be denying them the freedom to lead a nocturnal existence if they chose. But there was an interesting contrast here. Occurrences in vocabulary had been being counted for some time, and the results had been used, by Zipf (1935), to establish general principles such as the relationship between the relative frequency of a lexical item and its place in the rank order; and while it could be questioned what significance such generalizations might have, the fact that word frequency patterns could be systematized in this way was accepted as a property of language.[3] It was a systematic feature of English that *go* was more frequent than *walk* and *walk* was more frequent than *stroll*, and nobody was particularly upset by it. Why, then, the resistance to quantitative patterns in the grammar?

This might be explained if there were some fundamental difference between lexis and grammar; but this seemed to me unlikely. I have always seen lexicogrammar as a unified phenomenon, a single level of 'wording', of which lexis is the 'most delicate' resolution.[4] In a paradigmatic interpretation, the 'two' form a continuum: at one end are the very general choices, multiply intersecting, which can readily be closed to form a paradigm, such as 'polarity: positive/ negative', 'mood: indicative (declarative/interrogative)/imperative', 'transitivity: material/mental/relational', and these are best illuminated by being treated as grammar; while at the other end are choices which are highly specific but open-ended, with each term potentially entering into many term sets, e.g. *run* contrasting (i) with *walk*, (ii) with *hop*, *skip*, (iii) with *jog*, etc. and these are best illuminated by being treated as lexis. Midway along the continuum are things like prepositions and modals which do not yield a strong preference to either form of treatment. But both lexicographer and grammarian can occupy the whole terrain; 'lexis' and 'grammar' are names of complementary perspectives, like the synoptic and dynamic perspectives on a semiotic process, or wave and particle as complementary theories of light, each explaining different aspects of a single complex phenomenon.

Given this concept of lexicogrammar, it does not make sense to condone relative frequency in lexis but deny its validity in grammar. Admittedly, grammar is the 'deeper' end of the continuum, less accessible to conscious attention, and this may be why the treatment of grammar (in any form) always engenders more resistance. But the concept of the relative frequency of positive: negative, or of active: passive is no more suspect than the concept of the relative frequency of a set of lexical items. It is, on the other hand, considerably more powerful, because the relative frequencies of the terms in a grammatical system, where the system is closed and the number of choices is very small (typically just two or three), can be interpreted directly as probabilities having a significance for the system of language as a whole.

It is clear that the significance of such probabilities is not that they predict single instances. What is predicted is the general pattern. We might establish that, for any clause in English, the probability of its being negative is (say) one in ten; but that will not enable us to specify in advance the polarity of any one particular clause. However, this is not to say that probability has no significance with regard to the single instance. It has; but its relevance lies not in predicting but in interpreting. Part of the meaning of choosing any term is the probability with which that term is chosen; thus the meaning of negative is not simply 'not positive' but 'not positive, against odds of nine to one'. This is one of the reasons why grammatical choices may mean different things in different registers, where the odds may be found to vary.

For register variation, in fact, probability is the central concern. As Svartvik found in his study of voice in English, corpus studies suggest that grammatical frequencies will vary across the diatypic varieties, or registers, of a language but that they will vary within certain limits. Thus for his main corpus of novels and science texts the overall proportion among finite clauses was 88 per cent active to 12 per cent passive. When the frequency of passive was expressed as the number of passive clauses per thousand words, the figure, obtained from a larger corpus, came out at 11.3; this corpus consisted of eight text sets in different registers, within which the number of passives per thousand words varied from 23 in the science texts to 3 in the advertising ones. Four out of the eight clustered between 12.7 and 8.2, with the one sample of speech showing 9.2.[5] Svartvik did not give the active: passive ratio for the different text sets; but assuming that the average figure of 11.3 passives per thousand words corresponds to the 12 per cent of passive clauses in the smaller corpus, this would suggest that, while the overall probability of active: passive is 0.88: 0.12, it would vary between 0.76: 0.24 and 0.96: 0.04 in a range of different registers, with all but science and advertising falling between 0.84: 0.16 and 0.94: 0.06. This is the sort of picture that is borne out by subsequent investigations – with the stipulation, of course, that passive is not always identified in the same way.[6] But the critical observation that Svartvik made was that 'the frequencies for most of the texts of a text group are remarkably similar'. Register variation can in fact be defined as systematic variation in probabilities; 'a register' is a tendency to select certain combinations of meanings with certain frequencies, and this can be formulated as the probabilities attached to grammatical systems, provided such systems are integrated into an overall system network in a paradigmatic interpretation of the grammar.

Diachronically, frequency patterns as revealed in corpus studies provide explanations for historical change, in that when interpreted as probabilities they show how each instance both maintains and perturbs the system. 'System' and 'instance' are of course not different things; they form yet another complementarity. There is only one phenomenon here, not two; what we call language (the system) and what we call text (the instance) are two observers of that phenomenon, observing it from different distances. (I have used the analogy of 'climate' and 'weather'.) To the 'instance' observer, the *system* is the potential, with its set of probabilities attached; each instance is by itself unpredictable, but the system appears constant through time. To the 'system' observer, each *instance* redefines the system, however infinitesimally, maintaining its present state or shifting its probabilities in one direction or the other (as each moment's weather at every point on the globe redefines the global climate). It is the system which has a history – that is, it is the system-observer who perceives depth in time; but the transformation of instance into system can be observed only through the technology of the corpus, which allows us to accumulate instances and monitor the diachronic variation in their patterns of frequency.

Now that it is possible to store and process massive quantities of text, and programs of great elegance are available for quantitative studies, the main limitation on the use of corpuses for probabilistic grammar is the familiar catch that what is easy to recognize is usually too trivial to be worth recognizing. It is not that the categories we have to retrieve are necessarily very delicate ones – that would merely increase the size of the corpus needed in order to retrieve them, which is hardly a problem these days. On the contrary; at this stage we still need statistics for very general categories of the grammar. But they have to be categories with real semantic power, not distorted so as to suit the capabilities of a typically simplistic parser.[7] For example, the clause *it occasionally happens* would be positive, *it rarely happens* negative; the clause *a replay would be your only hope* active, *your only hope would be a replay* passive. With systems such as voice and polarity it is fairly easy to parse mechanically so as to identify perhaps 70–75 per cent of instances; but it then becomes exponentially more costly as one approximates 100 per cent. A human parser, of course, does not attain 100 per cent, because some instances are inherently indeterminate and humans also make mistakes; but there is still a critical gap between what the machine can achieve and what the human can achieve. So in deriving grammatical probabilities from a corpus we still depend on human participants for carrying out the text analysis.

Given, then, a paradigmatic grammar, based on the concept of the 'system' in Firth's sense of the term, frequency information from the corpus can be used to establish the probability profile of any grammatical system. From this profile – the probabilities of each of the terms – we can derive a measure of the information that is generated by that system, using Shannon and Weaver's formula (1949: 8–16)

$$H = - \Sigma \, p_i \log_2 p_i$$

where p_i is the probability of each term in the system taken separately. The value of H (information) will vary from 1, where all terms are equiprobable, to a vanishingly small number as they become more and more skew, but reaching 0.08 when the ratio of two terms is 99 : 1. (The formula can be applied to systems with any number of terms.) $1 - H$ (1 minus the information value) gives the value R (redundancy).

It has been shown that those who know a language can make an informed guess about the relative frequency of its words – to return to the example above, they will recognize that *go* > *walk* > *stroll*. This is just an aspect of 'knowing the language'. Provided they have some understanding of grammatical concepts and categories (and do not feel threatened by being asked to reflect on them), they can do the same for the grammar. Speakers of English can recognize that active is more frequent than passive, positive than negative, declarative than interrogative, *the* than *this* or *that*, simple tenses than compound tenses. They will be uncertain, on the other hand, of the relative frequency of singular and plural, *this* and *that*, *a* and *the*, past and present. This suggests that some systems tend towards being equiprobable and hence have a higher information value, while others are notably skew and thus display a greater degree of redundancy (in the technical sense of that term in information theory).

I had found some such pattern emerging when I counted instances in Chinese, where it seemed that very general grammatical systems fell into two such broad types. This seemed to account for our sense that some systems have an 'unmarked term', whereas others have not. An unmarked term is a default condition: that which is selected unless there is good reason for selecting some other term. It is not *defined* by frequency, but it is likely to correspond to the more probable term in a system whose probabilities are skew.

When I started counting occurrences of comparable features in texts in English, a similar pattern appeared. For example, simple past and simple present, while they might be very unequal in any given register, appeared roughly equal in their frequency overall. Likewise the three major process types of material, mental and relational; these form a transitivity system of three terms whose occurrence in any particular text type is liable to be quite skew, but the three terms show up as fairly evenly distributed when the figures for the different types are combined. Some systems, on the other hand, remained skew over a wide register range: positive was more frequent than negative, active than passive, declarative than interrogative, simple tenses than compound tenses. My figures were not large; I counted simply until the least frequent term had reached 200 occurrences. But as far as they went they suggested that grammatical systems vary in their probability profiles.

But the variation was not random, and the more interesting feature was the particular bimodal pattern that seemed to emerge. In principle, any set of systems might distribute themselves evenly over the whole scale of probability values, from 0.5 : 0.5 to 0.9 : 0.01 (from equiprobable to maximally skew). But we are considering semiotic systems, which are systems of a particular kind. We know they are unlikely all to be equiprobable; such a grammar would have no redundancy at all, and no human semiotic could work with such restraint.[8] On the other hand, it seems equally unlikely that they could be spread over all possible values; a semiotic system of this kind would be virtually impossible to learn. The figures suggested, rather, that grammatical systems fell into two main types: (i) the equiprobable, those tending towards 0.5 : 0.5, and (ii) the skew – and that these latter tended towards a ratio of one order of magnitude, which we could represent ideally as 0.9 : 0.1. Svartvik's frequency figures for active and passive defined a system of this second type (probabilities 0.88 : 0.12).

It is interesting to note that this skew profile of 0.9 : 0.1 is just at the point where, in Shannon and Weaver's theory of information, the redundancy measure works out at 50 per cent. (To be exact, $H = R = 0.5$ where the probabilities are 0.89 : 0.11.)[9] This, as it happens, was the value they had calculated for what they rather quaintly referred to as 'the redundancy of English', meaning by this the redundancy of English orthography interpreted as a system of twenty-seven symbols (twenty-six letters and a space) and calculated up to strings of 'about eight' letters. As a property of English orthographic sequences this made only a very limited appeal to linguists, since it was not clear what implications it had for other languages or for other linguistic levels – and in any case it rested on a not very adequate characterization of the orthography of English. But it would be a matter of some significance if it turns out that grammatical systems tend towards a bimodal probability distribution where one mode is that of almost no redundancy and the other is that where redundancy is around 50 per cent. The actual values showing up in my own informal frequency counts would be defined by the following limits:

(i) equiprobable
p　　0.5 : 0.5 ～ 0.65 : 0.35
H　　1　　　　～ 0.93

(ii) skew
p　　0.8 : 0.2 ～ 0.89 : 0.11 ～ 0.95 : 0.05
　　　　0.72　　～ 0.5　　　　～ 0.28

In other words, the redundancy was either (i) less than 10 per cent or (ii) somewhere in the region of 30–70 per cent, and often towards the middle of that range, close to 50 per cent. If this is in fact a general pattern, it would suggest that the grammar of a natural language is organized around the interaction between two modes of quantizing information: one where each act of choice – each instance – is maximally informative (it might equally well have been the opposite), and one where it is largely uninformative (since you could pretty well have guessed it already). Furthermore, it might be the case that these two kinds of system occur in roughly equal proportion.

A semiotic of this kind would have enough 'play' in it to allow for functional variation in register, but enough constraint to ensure that such variation was systematic – without which it could not, of course, be functional. Svartvik's figures showed both effects: the global probabilities, those of the grammar of English, and the locally conditioned probabilities, those of this or that particular register. To refer again to the analogy of the climate, it is entirely meaningful (as we all know today) to establish probabilities for the global climate as well as the local probabilities conditioned by season, latitude, height above sea level, time of day and so on. It is equally valid to talk of global probabilities in a language while still recognizing that every text is located somewhere or other in diatypic space. And just as we define regions of the globe by reference to their weather patterns, so (as suggested above) we can define registers by reference to their grammatical probabilities: register variation is the resetting of the probabilities in the grammar. But it seems likely that these probabilities will typically remain within the values defined by the system type; and that only in rather specialized registers (Firth's 'restricted languages') should we expect a categoric shift such as a reversal of marking – for example in predictive texts like weather forecasting, where future leaps over past and present and becomes the most frequent tense. Generally, this external conditioning of the probabilities, realizing variation in the context of situation, is probably not such as to perturb the overall profile of the system.

A corpus which is organized by register, as all the great first-generation ones have been, makes it possible to study such external conditioning of probabilities, and to show how the grammar of doing science differs quantitatively from that of telling stories, advertising and so on. But the corpus also enables us to study the conditioning effects from within the grammar itself: to ask what happens if we intersect the frequency patterns of two simultaneous systems (that is, systems that have the same point of origin but such that neither is dependent on the other), like voice and polarity as systems of the clause. Are they truly independent? Are the probabilities for active: passive the same whether the clause is positive or negative, and are the probabilities for positive: negative the same no matter whether the clause is active or passive?

Table 3.1 shows some possible effects, with typical values attached, using two imaginary systems: system I with terms m, n, and system II with terms p, q (see Halliday forthcoming). In (a) – (c) the two systems are unassociated; in (d) – (g) there is some association between them. Where two systems are associated in this way, there may be one-way favouritism, such that m favours p but p does not favour m, as in (e), or vice versa, as in (f); or two-way favouritism, such that m favours p and p favours m, as in (d). There may also be a reversal of marking, as in (g), where the two favoured combinations are m with p and n with q. A real situation of type (g) is described by Nesbitt and Plum (1988), working with a corpus of spoken English texts. Overall, the system of interdependency, or 'taxis' (parataxis: hypotaxis), is within the equiprobable range (0.6 : 0.4), as is that of projection (locution: idea). But there is an

Table 3.1 Intersection of probabilities of two simultaneous systems.

II \ I	m	n	T
p	100	100	200
q	100	100	200
T	200	200	400

(a) Both systems have no unmarked term

II \ I	m	n	T
p	324	36	360
q	36	4	40
T	360	40	400

(b) Both systems have one term unmarked

II \ I	m	n	T
p	180	180	360
q	20	20	40
T	200	200	400

(c) System I has no unmarked term, system II has one term unmarked

II \ I	m	n	T
p	140	60	200
q	60	140	200
T	200	200	400

(d) Both have no unmarked term, but *m* favours *p*, *n* favours *q*

II \ I	m	n	T
p	140	100	240
q	60	100	160
T	200	200	400

(e) Both have no unmarked term, but *m* favours *p*

II \ I	m	n	T
p	140	60	200
q	100	100	200
T	240	160	400

(f) Both have no unmarked term, but *p* favours *m*

II \ I	m	n	T
p	180	20	200
q	20	180	200
T	200	200	400

(g) Both have one term unmarked, but marking is reversed

association on the one hand (a) between parataxis and locution, such that:

    (a) within parataxis, locution: idea   = 0.87 : 0.13
        within locution, parataxis: hypotaxis = 0.86 : 0.14

and on the other hand (b) between hypotaxis and idea, such that:

    (b) within hypotaxis, idea: locution = 0.80 : 0.20
        within idea, hypotaxis: parataxis = 0.81 : 0.19

In other words, the favoured combinations are those of 'direct speech' and 'indirect thought', and the reverse combinations appear as marked terms.

We can also use the corpus to establish transitional probabilities within the text. Given a system of the clause, how are its probabilities affected by choices in the preceding clause – both within the same system and in other systems? Sinclair has shown that the probabilities of lexical items are affected transitionally by collocation within a span (lexical distance) of up to about four (Sinclair *et al.* 1970, Sinclair 1985); and we may find similar effects obtaining in the grammar. It seems likely that the kinds of predictions we make as listeners and readers would depend on Markov properties of the lexicogrammar as a whole.

There are good reasons for thinking that an important semogenic process, whereby new meanings are created in the evolution of the system through time, is that of the dissociation of associated variables, whereby one system of two terms with complex realizations evolves into two simultaneous systems:

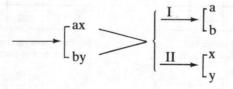

Where this happens, it is highly likely that systems I and II would, initially at least, be partially associated; the pattern of parataxis: hypotaxis and locution: idea described by Nesbitt and Plum is suggestive of just such a change in progress, as they point out. In other words, one may postulate an earlier stage consisting of a single system, 'direct speech/indirect thought' (paratactic locution/ hypotactic idea), from which the present pattern has evolved. The pattern might stabilize in its present form, or it might evolve further to one in which the two systems become fully independent, with neither conditioning the choice within the other. One can think of many other systems which might have had this kind of a history; for example, tag questions, where in present-day English the tag may select either 'polarity reversed' or 'polarity constant', the latter being the marked term, may have evolved through a stage where the only possible form was that with polarity reversed. This same process, whereby associated variables gradually become dissociated from one another, is also a characteristic feature of children's language development. The most favoured combinations are construed first, forming a system on their own; these are then deconstrued, and the remaining, less favoured combinations introduced as additional choices.[10]

Corpus studies have a central place in theoretical investigations of language. There are many ways in which a corpus can be exploited, of which the one considered here – by no means the only one – is that of providing evidence of relative frequencies in the grammar, from which can be established the probability profiles of grammatical systems. These in turn have implications for at least five areas of theoretical enquiry: developmental, diatypic, systemic, historical and metatheoretic. Children construe the lexicogrammar, on the evidence of text frequency, as a probabilistic system; a probabilistic model can help to explain the growth of their meaning potential. Diatypic variation, or register, is variation in the probabilities of the grammar; this is the major resource for systematically construing variation in the environment (the 'situation'). Systematically, the grammar of a language can be represented paradigmatically as a network of choices, each choice consisting of a small number of alternatives related by probability; these probabilities appear to form a pattern related to the construing of 'information'. Historically, both semogenesis, the creation and maintenance of meaning, and its opposite, the destruction of meaning, can be explained in terms of probabilities, in the way grammatical systems evolve towards more, or less, informative states. Metatheoretically, the key concepts for interpreting a semiotic system, as a stratified dynamic open system, are those of realization and instantiation; the corpus shows how a system of this kind persists through being constantly perturbed, with each instance reconstructing the potential of the whole. The immense scope of a modern corpus, and the range of computing resources that are available for exploiting it, make up a powerful force for deepening our awareness and understanding of language. The issues raised in this paper relate to a small fraction of this whole domain.

Notes

[1] Made in the course of a denunciation of corpus studies in a lecture at the Linguistic Society of America Summer Institute, Bloomington, July 1964.

[2] See Halliday (1959), especially Chapter 6 and Appendix C; also Halliday (1956).

[3] Cf. however Gross's (1972 : 154) comment that Zipf's law 'has been found to be of such generality that no precise use of it can be made in linguistics'.

[4] See Halliday (1961). The concept of lexis as most delicate grammar is developed by Hasan (1987) and exemplified in detail in Hasan (forthcoming).

[5] Svartvik gives the following figures (Table 7: 4, p. 155)

Text set	No. of words	No. of passives	Passives per 1000 words
Science	50,000	1,154	23.1
News	45,000	709	15.8
Arts	20,000	254	12.7
Speech	40,000	366	9.2
Sports	30,000	269	9.0
Novels	80,000	652	8.2
Plays	30,000	158	5.3
Advertising	28,000	83	3.0

[6] Quirk *et al.* comment (1985: 166): 'There is a notable difference in the frequency with which the active and passive voices are used. The active is generally by far the more common, but there is considerable variation among individual *text types*' (my italics).

[7] There are, obviously, many forms of human–machine collaboration in retrieving grammatical frequencies from a corpus. An example would be Peter Collins' (1987) use of the London-Lund Corpus for his work on clefts and pseudo-clefts.

[8] The most obvious reason for this is that there is too much noise. But there are other, more fundamental reasons to do with the nature of a dynamic open system: no system which persists through constant perturbation from its environment could remain in a statement of almost zero redundancy.

[9] It may be helpful to give values of H (information) and R (redundancy) for some probability profiles of a binary system, to two places of decimals:

Probabilities	H	R
0.5 : 0.5	1	0
0.6 : 0.4	0.97	0.03
0.67 : 0.33	0.91	0.09
0.8 : 0.2	0.72	0.28
0.9 : 0.1	0.47	0.53
0.99 : 0.01	0.08	0.92

The 'hinge' probability profile, where H and R become equal at 0.5, is 0.89 : 0.11 (H = 0.499916).

[10] This appears clearly from Painter's (1984) systemic interpretation of child language development.

4 Intuition-based and observation-based grammars

JAN AARTS

4.1 Introduction

For the past seven or eight years, a research team of linguists and computer scientists at the University of Nijmegen has been engaged in the computational analysis of corpora and in writing formal grammars for that purpose. The corpora we have been analysing contain almost exclusively written material and the type of analysis made of them is predominantly syntactic. For each utterance in a corpus the analysis yields a tree with a function and a category label at every node, together with additional information which may be morphological and/or semantic in character.

In the course of the years, we have been confronted with various kinds of problems: problems raised by the grammatical formalism and its implementation, by the need for making our descriptive syntactic framework fully explicit, and problems raised by the nature of the corpus data. Many of the issues that cropped up proved to have wider implications for both the theory and the methodology of linguistic research in general. In this article I will concentrate on one of these issues: the interaction between the syntactic description contained in the formal grammar used for the analysis on the one hand, and the nature of corpus data on the other. I will occasionally simplify or idealize aspects of the analysis process that do not form the topic of this article, without wanting to imply that in reality they may not be much more complex than is suggested here. Before going on to discuss our experiences, however, I will first outline briefly the methodological premises and the most important research tools that form the basis of the corpus linguistic research carried out at the University of Nijmegen. I shall henceforth refer to these as 'the Nijmegen approach'.

In the Nijmegen approach, a corpus is understood to be a collection of samples of *running text*. The texts may be in spoken, written or intermediate forms, and the samples may be of any length. Since the corpus provides the data, corpus linguistics by definition deals with *language use*. The data contained in corpora are subjected to analysis, which is largely *syntactic* in nature although it incorporates some semantic elements. The choice for a syntactic analysis is not theoretically motivated but made for practical reasons – so far, we are unable to give sufficiently formal expression to the semantic notions we would like to include in our analyses. However, insofar as we are able to make this judgement now, the grammatical formalism that we employ seems to be suitable enough to accommodate a semantic component. The grammatical formalism that is used belongs to the class of attribute grammars or two-level grammars; the level of the attributes is appropriate to introduce semantic notions. In linguistic terms, the formalism has *context-sensitive* power.[1]

The formal grammar is not seen merely as a tool serving to produce an analysed corpus. For corpus linguists the grammar is also the vehicle in which they express their hypotheses about the (syntactic) structure of the language, which can be tested on the basis of the corpus data. As a corollary of this, the corpus, too, has a double function: on the one hand a corpus, especially in an enriched form, serves as a linguistic database for linguists studying the structure of the corpus language, and on the other the corpus in its raw form is for the corpus linguist the testbed for his hypotheses about the language, which he has expressed in a formal grammar. The two roles of the grammar – the 'practical' and the 'theoretical' – are sometimes in conflict; but the problems raised by this do not constitute the topic of this article.

About the way in which such a formal grammar comes into being, I have said elsewhere (Aarts 1988):

The (corpus) linguist first writes a formal grammar for some well-delimited part of the corpus language, for example the noun phrase. This grammar is written on the basis of the linguist's intuitive knowledge of the language and whatever is helpful in the literature. The first version of the grammar is then tested on a set of sentences made up by the linguist himself. On the basis of the analysis results the grammar is revised, tested again, and this process is repeated until the linguist has the conviction – or perhaps better, the illusion – that his grammar is tolerably reliable and complete. At that moment the grammar is tested on the sentences of a corpus – which is always a dismaying experience. Only linguists who use corpus data themselves will know that a corpus always yields a much greater variety of constructions than one can either find in the literature or think up oneself. ... The process of writing partial grammars, of testing and revising them is continued until a complete grammar of the corpus language is arrived at – or rather a grammar that is as complete as the linguist wants it to be. Certain low-frequency constructions may be left unaccounted for if they would 'mess up' the grammar to an unacceptable extent; but that is another story.

The last part of this quotation ties up directly with the topic of this article. It is said that the linguist makes a decision about the 'completeness' of the grammar. On what grounds he makes this decision about completeness, and with respect to what kind of phenomena the grammar is (in)complete, are questions that remain unanswered. The present paper is the tentative beginning of the 'other story' mentioned in the quotation.

4.2   From intuition-based to observation-based grammar

After these preliminaries, I can now give a clearer characterization of the nature of the problems we have been confronted with in applying formal grammars to corpus material. Such grammars are 'complete' if they give a description of all the data for which they are written. Hence the question about the (in)completeness of a grammar shifts from the grammar to the data it is supposed to account for. Basically, then, our question is the old one of what sort of data a linguist should describe when he wants to describe language or a language.

Let us see, therefore, what linguistic phenomena a grammar intended for the analysis of a corpus will describe *in any case* and what phenomena it *might* describe. For that purpose, let me return to the first stage of writing the grammar. As I said, the first version of the grammar is written on the basis of the linguist's intuitive and explicit knowledge of the language and whatever is helpful in the literature. Basically, this is an *intuition-based* grammar and as such it can be looked upon as an explicitation of the facts of competence rather than an account of 'language use'. I shall call the products of competence 'grammatical sentences' and the products of language use 'acceptable sentences'. Although it is hard to delimit the notion of competence and therefore the class of grammatical sentences, most linguists will agree that the set of grammatical sentences is not identical with that of acceptable sentences and that the latter class will include sentences that are not members of the class of grammatical sentences (for an example, see sentence (2) below). For the time being, I use the term 'language use' to indicate products of linguistic activity based on competence rules but not necessarily restricted by them. The term should not be understood as entirely synonymous with 'performance'. I return to this question below.

Ideally, the intuition-based grammar, through its confrontation with corpus data, becomes an *observation-based* grammar, i.e. one that also accounts for the facts of language use – a procedure of which Itkonen (1980: 344) said: 'Clear cases, i.e. well-established rules, can and must be investigated by means of intuition. Unclear cases, i.e. less than well-established rules, as well as actual linguistic behavior in general, must be investigated by means of observation.'

The original version of the grammar, then, is turned, in a few testing and revision cycles, into a final version which is used for the analysis of the corpus. The confrontation with the test corpus will show up straightforward lacunae and mistakes in the grammar, but the consistent observation of the corpus data will also bring to light phenomena that might be called 'unclear cases', which have received little attention so far and which are typically within the realm of language use. In order to achieve a good coverage of the various aspects of language use, it is advisable to change the test corpus in every cycle, so that the grammar is tested on a large number of different language varieties.

Although the above is a rather simplified account of the process of writing a grammar for automatic analysis, we can say very roughly that the revision cycle starts from a grammar that mainly accounts for competence and the related set of grammatical sentences, and results in an observation-based grammar that accounts for language use, that is, the set of acceptable sentences. An intuition-based grammar will therefore always be at the basis of an observation-based grammar; they are not two different things. If in the rest of this article I talk about them as if the two were distinct, I do so for the sake of the clarity of the argument.

4.3   The question of language use

It will be clear that the process leading from the initial to the final stage of the grammar consists of a series of decisions by the linguist which should, ideally, be prompted by a clear idea of the nature of a grammar of language use. I do not want to pretend that we have such a clear idea yet, but we have been forced to think about it; this article therefore describes the problems encountered in confronting a formal grammar with corpus data, but does not provide ready-made answers to them.[2]

First of all, let's take a look at the relation between an intuition-based and an observation-based grammar. In Figure 4.1, the intersection of the two circles contains sentences that are both grammatical and acceptable – 'normal sentences' or clear cases, therefore, whose number will be larger in the reality of language use than is suggested by the figure. An example of a grammatical (i.e. grammar-generated) but unacceptable sentence is given in (1); it comes from an article by Paul Ziff entitled 'The number of English sentences' (Ziff 1974: 528).

(1)   My grandfather's grandfather's father's grandfather's grand-
       father's father's grandfather's father's grandfather's grand-
       father's father's father was an Indian.

Ziff called such sentences 'Mathlogicenglish'; it is a phenomenon we do not need to dwell upon, for they are an inevitable product of any formal grammar which, also inevitably, must contain recursive rules.

Sentence (2) is an example of an acceptable, but by all accounts of English grammar ungrammatical, sentence and is from the spoken part of the Nijmegen corpus.

(2)   And what a performance by the man *who* some of us thought
       that may be the pressure of being the favourite of Wimbledon
       might not let *him* win.

In this sentence of course *him* should not be there because it is raised in the form of *who* to the beginning of the relative clause. The interesting thing about the example is that native and non-native speakers alike reject the grammatical version of the sentence and prefer the ungrammatical one.

What can we expect to find if we confront this picture with a corpus of English sentences? This situation is represented in Figure

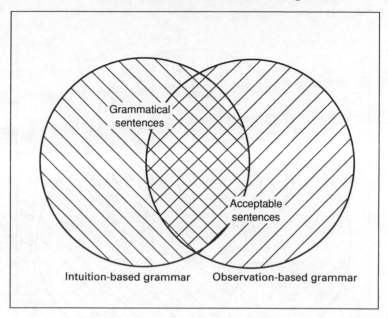

Figure 4.1   Relation between an intuition-based and an observation-based grammar

4.2. In the first place, we will find sentences that will be accounted for by both types of grammars; in the average corpus, sentences that are both grammatical and acceptable will constitute the majority of the total number. The intersection of corpus sentences and sentences that are generated *only* by an intuition-based grammar will be empty; it would be inherently contradictory if *in language use* we should come across a sentence that is grammatical but at the same time not accounted for by an observation-based grammar. After all, a grammatical sentence is a product of an intuition-based grammar and this, in its turn, forms the basis and is the first version of an observation-based grammar. It is the intersection of corpus sentences with the sentences accounted for by an observation-based grammar in the making that constitutes the greatest problem for a corpus grammarian; or, to put this in terms of Figure 4.2: the crucial question for corpus grammarians is to decide where the broken line

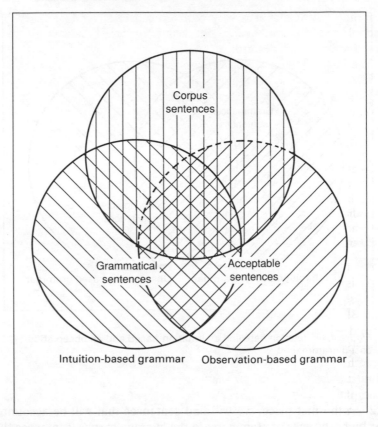

Figure 4.2 Testing a grammar on a corpus

should be positioned that separates the acceptable sentences in the corpus from the utterances that, although they do occur, are not, and should not, be accounted for by any grammar. They cannot, of course, let the grammar decide which corpus sentences belong here and which do not, for their grammar is still in the making, and they are using their corpus precisely for the purpose of turning an intuition-based grammar into an observation-based grammar. For every corpus sentence, therefore, that is not accounted for by their intuition-based grammar, they have to decide whether or not they want to give it the stamp of acceptability by inserting rules into their grammar that account for the structure that is represented by the sentence.[3] And that is a very hard thing to do, because, strangely enough, they do not know exactly what they want their observation-based grammar to describe.

The last sentence may at first sight seem to contradict what I said in the introductory paragraphs of this article, namely that 'corpus linguistics by definition deals with *language use*'. Unfortunately, however, it is not really clear at all what we mean when we talk about language use. Let me illustrate this with a short passage from an article by Morton Bloomfield (1985: 269):

> The determination of the facts of usage is by no means a simple matter. To rely completely on usage can lead into a morass of confusion. There are signs that some linguists are beginning to recognize this, and to acknowledge that it is necessary to study prescription in order to understand actual use and even more to understand attitudes towards a language by its speakers and writers.

If we take this passage literally, it seems to say that in trying to establish the facts of usage we should not rely on the facts of usage, because this will only result in confusion. The truth is, of course, that Bloomfield's term 'usage' covers two different notions. In his second sentence, presumably, 'usage' is intended to refer to everything people say and write, whereas in the first it seems to indicate something like 'acceptable language use' in which prescription and linguistic attitudes are in some way involved. Apparently, therefore, Bloomfield makes a distinction between usage in a non-normative and in a normative sense. We recall the passage from Itkonen (1980: 344, see above), who seems to make a similar distinction between two notions of language use when he makes his tripartite division into: 'well-established rules' (i.e. the rules of competence), 'less than well-established rules' and 'actual linguistic behavior'. Unfortunately, he does not enlarge upon the status of the set of 'less than well-established rules', but it is clear, in any case, that they account for an area that must be investigated by means of observation, while at the same time it is not the realm of performance, for that is covered, presumably, by 'actual linguistic behavior'.

Saying, then, that the grammar should account for language use does not automatically provide an answer to the question of what phenomena it should describe; 'language use' proves to be too elusive a concept, so far. One way of evading the issue of what exactly constitutes language use or what utterances should be called acceptable constructs would be to maintain that an utterance, if it occurs in a corpus, is by definition acceptable and should therefore be incorporated into a grammar of language use. This position seems to be taken by Crystal in an article entitled 'Neglected grammatical factors in conversational English', when he says: '[in informal conversation] the discrepancy between standard descriptive statement and observed reality is most noticeable . . . neglected features of this variety . . . will have to be incorporated into standard descriptions' (Crystal 1979: 153). It is not entirely clear what Crystal means by a 'standard description', but if we can read this as 'a grammar accounting for language use', I think that this position is untenable, for two reasons. In the first place it ignores the fact that every corpus will contain sentences that the writer *wanted* to be ungrammatical (in the widest sense of the word) by deliberately violating the rules of the grammar, or *knows* to be ungrammatical, as when he breaks off sentences, repeats (parts of) constituents, uses elements from a substandard variety of the language, and so on. Another reason why it is undesirable to equate the occurrence of sentences in a corpus with their (linguistic) acceptability is the fact that, if we write a grammar that accounts for every single sentence in a corpus, that grammar loses its (potential) generalizability and we are doing exactly what corpus linguistics in the 1960s and early 1970s was denounced for: we are making linguistic statements about the sentences in the corpus only, and we have no idea about the generalizability of these statements to the whole of the language.

4.4   Some examples

To remove the discussion from the rather abstract level on which we have conducted it so far, and give it some more substance on the level of the actual data, an appendix has been added to this article. It contains a number of utterances, taken from both our corpora, which in one way or another have raised the question: should an utterance of this nature be accounted for in our grammar of contemporary British English usage? For the sake of presentation, the examples in the appendix have been classified roughly according to the type of problem they exemplify. Here I give a short selection from the examples, not because I want to single them out for special comment but in order to illustrate briefly that it is impossible to draw a clear line between utterances that a grammar of language use should, and those it should not, describe. The examples have been ordered so as to show a (subjective and impressionistic) scale, ranging from utterances that typically belong to performance and therefore should not be described by a general grammar of usage, to utterances which, although they are of marginal status in all existing accounts of English grammar, would seem to be candidates for inclusion in a grammar of language use.

(3)   Man who build big library should not forget small words.
(4)   'I – I put out my arms to come to me.'
(5)   'Do,' he hesitated, 'do you remember anything?'
(6)   'Share . . .' He stopped, as though words escaped him, '. . . your secrets.'
(7)   The things, oh Jesus in Heaven, the things he had done.
(8)   Suddenly – out of the dark – a dog.
(9)   'It's so long . . .' was all he could say: a limping banality.
(10) What if it hadn't drifted in by accident?
(11) One glimpse of his twelve-bore, and Lawrence whizzed off . . .
(12) It is better to train lightly then add to the training set as a text is being scanned.

Sentence (3) is perhaps the clearest case of an utterance that should not be accounted for by a grammar, because it is an example of intended ungrammaticality: in the context in which it occurs the main point of the sentence is precisely that it is ungrammatical. The writers of sentences (4)–(6) will also have been aware that their sentences were ungrammatical and, in a way, the ungrammaticality is also intended here; such sentences are typical of dialogue in fiction, where the writer wants to imitate the sort of performance disfluency that is characteristic of spontaneous speech. Very often a writer achieves this effect by repetition of elements or by breaking off sentences before they have reached their grammatical conclusion. Repetition of elements may occur at all linguistic levels: at the phonological and morphological levels (stuttering), at the lexical level as well as at the syntactic level, when constituents or parts of them are repeated. It will be clear that any (formal) grammar that would allow repetition of elements or allow any constituent to be incomplete – and thus create innumerable new and hardly predictable constituents – would not only lack any practical value, since it could never be used for analysis, but would not even be a 'grammar' in the proper sense of the word because it would fail to make any sort of meaningful generalization. Sentence (7) resembles instances of repetition in performance disfluency and for that reason poses the same sort of problem. It is typical of a 'vivid' style, which is not necessarily restricted to narrative prose. Example (8) illustrates a kind of telegraphic style that is not uncommon in descriptive narrative. It is typified by utterances in which the arguments are specified but in which, due to the absence of a verb, no explicit syntactic clue is provided as to their semantic roles. Sentence (9) belongs to a rather large group of sentences containing what we have called 'floating noun phrases' (see appendix). Usually these are noun phrases that are predicated of a concept referred to or associated with a constituent in the same sentence without any overt syntactic marker to indicate this. Examples (10)–(12) are the most likely candidates for inclusion in the set of acceptable sentences that a grammar of language use would have to account for, in spite of the fact that they are of marginal status and have received little or no attention in descriptions of English so far. Sentence (10) exemplifies a sentence pattern which is 'formulaic' in character in that it shows a syntactically and partly lexically fixed form. In (11) we find an instance of 'irregular' coordination (noun phrase + sentence), which is not at all uncommon but difficult to incorporate in a formal grammar without creating undesirable side effects. Finally, in example (12) we find a surprisingly frequent and widely distributed use of *then*; it occurs between two coordinated sentences and is not preceded by a comma, so that such occurrences cannot be looked upon as instances of zero coordination. The best way to deal with them would be to regard *then* as a coordinator that is semantically marked for chronological sequence.

Note that, in a way, utterances like the ones illustrated in (3)–(6) might also be called 'acceptable' in the sense that in most cases they are not inappropriate – given the particular type of discourse and the communicative setting of the particular piece of discourse in which they occur. In other words, a deliberately ungrammatical or unacceptable sentence may well be – for stylistic or other reasons – appropriate at the particular place where it occurs in a running text; such stylistically appropriate utterances might be called *metagrammatical*, for their stylistic appropriateness in itself does not make the utterance acceptable in a linguistic sense. We therefore agree with

Bloomfield when he implies that everything that is used by speakers/ writers does not necessarily belong to 'language use' in the sense of 'belonging to the set of linguistically acceptable sentences yielded by a grammar'. In other words, language use, like linguistic competence, is a normative idea, although the norms holding for the two are probably not of the same nature.

4.5   Drawing the line between 'language use' and 'performance'

Decisions about whether or not to account for the structures of sentences in a corpus that are not represented in an intuition-based, competence-like grammar are, as we have seen, inevitable. The question is, on what grounds such decisions can be based. In the practice of writing our English grammar such decisions have been almost entirely prompted by intuitions. These intuitions are, of course, of a different nature from the primary judgements on the basis of which the first, competence-like version of the grammar was written. Basically, such primary judgements are of a dichotomous nature; they are about the question whether or not a sentence in isolation belongs to the set of English sentences. Nor are such intuitions similar to those that are called upon to determine the 'acceptability' (as distinct from the 'grammaticality') of sentences; for such intuitions usually take the form of the question: can this sentence be contextualized? Whereas intuitions about grammaticality or contextualizability are firmly rooted in *productive* skills, intuitions about the inclusion of structures in a grammar for language use seem to derive primarily from *recognition*. Or, to put this differently, they seem first and foremost to be based on knowledge of language use by others, rather than on knowledge about (what one thinks is) one's own language use. However vague this may be as a first approximation of the question of how an observation-based grammar should come into being, let us now give a name to such intuitions and call them intuitions about the *currency* of certain structures.

Before looking more closely at the notion of currency, let me discuss a concrete example of the sort of decisions that actually had to be made in the process of writing the grammar. In two consecutive samples of our corpus we came across utterances such as:

- Pity we can't include Tom
- Better we look silly than . . .

Such structures were not incorporated in the grammar, so that, in view of the fact that we were dealing with a recurrent structure, we had to ask ourselves whether or not the grammar should account for them. Do we, then, have any idea how 'normal' or 'current' such constructions are? The first thing we can say about them is that, although they may not be straightforwardly grammatical, they are certainly not intuitively rejected as highly deviant or unacceptable. The next thing to establish is whether the construction is flexible enough to allow a reasonable range of lexical variation. This appears to be the case; it is not difficult to find utterances which show a similar structure, for by the side of the above examples we have examples like:

– Very nice that you could come
– Unthinkable that such a thing should happen
– Not that I want to go

It would seem, then, that the construction is sufficiently 'current' to warrant inclusion in the grammar. (It may well be, of course, that the set of rules accounting for it will turn out to be variety-specific; it is not at all unlikely that the construction is limited to spoken English. This is supported by the fact that the corpus examples all occur in dialogue.)

A secondary, but essential consideration in making the decision as to whether or not a given structure should be incorporated in the grammar is whether it is possible to assign a good structural description to the construction in question – that is, one that is in line with the modular structure of the grammar and the basic notions on which it is based, implicitly or explicitly. These notions include constituenthood and rankscale as well as the assumption that there is an essential difference between phrases on the one hand and sentences/clauses on the other. If we look at our examples from that angle, we find that they all clearly have the same structure: they start with a predicating word (usually an adjective or adjective phrase, but *not* and a limited set of nouns are also possible) and are followed by a clause of which the initial word or phrase is predicated. The clause in question can be finite (see the examples) as well as non-finite ('very nice of you to come'). From this short description it is already clear that our descriptive apparatus is such that it enables us to impose a reasonable structure on such constructions.

If, as in these examples, a particular construction is intuitively judged to be a current one, and if it appears to be possible to account for it in the terms and notions of our descriptive framework, we may, in principle, decide to incorporate a description of the construction in our grammar.

As I said earlier, the condition of currency is the primary one and may overrule the second, in which case major revisions of our descriptive apparatus would be needed. So far, we have not found such major revisions to be necessary. All the additions that we made could be fitted in without changing either the design or the nature of our grammar.

It should be mentioned in passing that whenever we decide not to incorporate in the grammar a particular construction found in one or more utterances, the utterance(s) in question do(es) not, of course, receive an analysis in the database. This makes it necessary to mark them in the database not only for their unanalysability but also, where possible, for the type of construction that has remained unanalysed. This marking has a double purpose: it makes it easier to identify such constructions if at a later date we should decide to incorporate their description in the grammar after all, and it also gives easy and immediate access to interesting linguistic material.

But let me return to the question on what grounds we can make decisions about what should and what should not be included in a grammar describing language use. As already mentioned, in our opinion the notion of currency of constructions is crucial in this respect. Let us look at this concept a little more closely by noting, first of all, how the term is defined in two English dictionaries whose editors use the term themselves when talking about dictionary making: the COBUILD dictionary and the *Longman Dictionary of Contemporary English* (*LDOCE*). The COBUILD dictionary says in the entry for *currency*: 'expressions . . . have currency if they are used and accepted by many people at a particular time', while the *LDOCE* defines one of the meanings of *currency* as: 'the state of being in common use or general acceptance'. Keywords in these definitions are *many, common* and *general acceptance*. It is clear that, our knowledge of language use being what it is at the moment, we have no objective measure for such notions as 'common use' or 'general acceptance' when we are dealing with syntax.

One important aspect of any conception of currency is inevitably the fact that it has to do with frequency of occurrence (cf. *many* and *common*). Can we assume that the currency of a syntactic construction can be entirely defined in terms of its frequency in a corpus? The answer to that question is largely dependent on the answer to another, namely whether or not 'common use' and 'general acceptance' are identical notions. I think that they are not. For it is certainly not unthinkable that certain constructions are 'generally accepted' in the sense that they are 'felt' to be 'normal'. Personally, I have the feeling of 'normalcy' about most of the utterances in the appendix under I–V. The examples under VI–VIII would seem to be metagrammatical in character, while the examples under IX form a mixed category. I think that this judgement is separate from any intuitions about the frequency of the constructions concerned. It may well be, for example, that in certain texts anacolutha and broken-off sentences are much more frequent than instances of the construction discussed above ('Pity we can't include Tom'), so that frequency of occurrence cannot be the only yardstick for deciding whether or not a construction is current. Now, if the currency of a construction is determined both by its observed frequency and, independently of this, by its 'normalcy', it is quite clear that the first criterion for currency is within easy reach – it will not be long before reliable data become available about the frequency of constructions, even of grammatically marginal ones. The notion of normalcy, however, is much harder to capture and to translate into operational terms. Quite possibly, as Bloomfield pointed out, it has to do with linguistic attitudes, determined among other things by prescription. In that respect, a grammar of language use might well be a *normative* grammar, if we understand 'normative' as 'based on the norms set by a not insignificant part of the language community' – that is, a grammar of structures used (frequency) as well as accepted (normalcy) by a large number of language users.

4.6   Conclusion

Summing up, we can say that if we want a formal grammar to be more than just a tool to produce an analysed corpus and want it also to contain a description of language use, we start from an intuition-based grammar consisting of a set of well-established rules, and confront this grammar with the material contained in a corpus. This confrontation will lead to an expansion and revision of the original, intuition-based grammar, which in the course of this process becomes an observation-based grammar that can be used for analysis.

What expansions and revisions are made cannot be entirely dictated by the corpus material. In other words, a grammar describing language use cannot be written by trying to account for each and every fact of performance; language use and performance are two distinct notions. Whether or not a particular construction found in the corpus should be accounted for in the grammar is determined by the currency of that construction. The currency of a construction is compounded of its frequency of occurrence and its 'normalcy'. The first of these criteria is easy enough to make operational; the second is not, but the criterion of 'normalcy' will exclude, in any case, those utterances that we have called metagrammatical. So far, however, we have no other alternative than to rely on our intuitions with respect to the currency of a particular construction, until we can give the notion an empirical grounding.

Notes

[1] The same formalism is being used at the moment for the analysis of written corpora in four languages: English, Spanish, Modern Arabic and Classical Hebrew. From the description given here it will be clear that at this stage we do not use a probabilistic grammar. There is a variety of reasons for this, the most compelling of which is the purely practical consideration that in the present state of the art there is simply not sufficient analysed material from which to derive probabilities, at least on the level of syntax (as distinct from morphology).

A fuller account of the Nijmegen approach is given in Aarts and van den Heuvel (1985).

[2] As far as English is concerned, the data in question are the texts contained in two corpora: the Nijmegen corpus and the TOSCA corpus. The Nijmegen corpus is a comparatively small one, consisting of some 130,000 words. Of these, 120,000 are printed English, while the rest consists of spoken English (TV commentary). The printed samples each comprise 20,000 words of running text. All the texts were published between 1962 and 1966. The Nijmegen corpus has been fully analysed, and in its analysed form is made available to academic institutions in the Linguistic Database (LDB), which was specially designed for the purpose of making syntactically analysed corpus material available to linguists who have little or no experience with computers. Keulen (1986) gives more details about the texts included in the corpus as well as an account of the way in which it was analysed. The TOSCA corpus numbers 1.5 million words of post-1985 printed English. Like the Nijmegen corpus, its samples have a length of 20,000 words. A full

account of its compilation and the principles underlying it is given in
Oostdijk (1988a and b). In a current project, one million words of the
TOSCA corpus are being analysed. This analysis yields basically the
same results as those of the Nijmegen corpus (i.e. analysis trees with
function and category information), except that the nodes of the TOSCA
analysis trees are also provided with feature information. The analysed
corpus will be made available in the same way as the Nijmegen corpus,
i.e. in LDB format and to academic institutions only. Most of the
examples in the appendix come frome the TOSCA corpus. A detailed
description and evaluation of the analysis of the TOSCA corpus is to be
found in Oostdijk (1991, forthcoming).

[3] This sort of problem has of course long been familiar to the lexicographer who has constantly to decide whether or not a particular word
should be included in the dictionary. Sinclair, in his Introduction to the
COBUILD dictionary, puts it as follows: 'However much . . . the editors
[of a dictionary] may say that they are only recording and following
usage, there is no doubt whatsoever that they take thousands and
thousands of decisions which contain an element of subjective judgement' (1987b: xxi). For example, the decision not to include a word may
be prompted by the judgement that it 'should not be given a place in the
language that implies permanence' (xx).

Appendix to Chapter 4

I   *Truncation*

(1)   Make life a lot easier, he did something like that, huh?
(2)   Always have. | Always strawberries.
(3)   Pity we can't include Tom.
(4)   And then yesterday.
(5)   Better we look silly than end up with a knife in our throat.
(6)   Told you so, it shouted. Told you so!

II   *Floating noun phrases*

(1)   Well, he'd hear it, ghosts or no ghosts.
(2)   Whitehead had never imagined it would be like this: a hushed
       debate in a white tiled room, two old men exchanging hurts
       against him.
(3)   'It's so long . . .' was all he could say: a limping banality.
(4)   Holman felt himself almost mesmerized by her words and

began to relax, a combination of his own tiredness, the soft
chair he was sitting in and the easy manner in which she was
talking to him.

(5)   They kept the illegal gun hidden behind the transmit unit, a
secret agreement among themselves and many other aeroplane
crews, as a protection against the increasingly frequent hijack-
ings.

(6)   It was blossom she was looking at, brilliant white heads of
it caught in sun or starlight.

(7)   He couldn't make sense of it at first: the uncertain whiteness,
the fluttering, as of snowflakes.

III   *Floating adjective phrases*

(1)   The European was a trespasser here: unarmed, unaided.

(2)   Hypothetical constructs themselves are of three different
kinds, physiological, mentalistic and mechanistic.

(3)   'A tiny thing: so vulnerable.'

IV   *Coordination*

(1)   One glimpse of his twelve-bore, and Lawrence whizzed off
back into the bushes and left Mrs Simpson to her own devices.

(2)   The whole of Salisbury Plain and you have to pick the bloody
spot where you planted a deadly disease fifteen years before.

(3)   During the war, our airfields had what was called the F100
system, another expensive process and little used since.

(4)   It was too absurd: like a fairground side-show, but played
without razzmatazz.

(5)   ...and so on I ...or whatever I ...but the reverse
...and vice versa I (you deaf, stupid) or both

V   *Juxtaposition*

(1)   It is better to train lightly then add to the training set as a text
is being scanned.

(2)   For a moment the eyes looked at the policeman then swivelled
back towards Holman.

(3)   He held her tightly to him, knowing the hurt was seeping
through, his words had spurred it to.

(4)   The old man had been here recently, that much was apparent.

VI   *Intended ungrammaticality*

(1)   Man who build big library should not forget small words.
(2)   Besides, I been talking to Rossi, and I ain't so sure James even
        made the doll.

VII   *Repetition*

(1)   Y–you did this to her. You m–made her do this.
(2)   'I–I put out my arms for her to come to me.'
(3)   The things, oh Jesus in Heaven, the things he had done.
(4)   'Do,' he hesitated, 'do you remember anything?'
(5)   Could it have – Holman had hesitated to say it – could it have
        intelligence?

VIII   *Inserts*

(1)   ...far up the Parana (had it been?) where they kept the
        calculating horse and the disassociated girl.
(2)   'We have a meeting in', he looked at his watch, 'ten minutes.'
(3)   ...so that we can combine our various skills to combat this
        growing – and I mean that literally – threat.
(4)   'Share...' He stopped, as though the words escaped him,
        '...your secrets.'
(5)   'Gentlemen,' he began, 'and lady,' he smiled briefly at Janet
        Halstead, 'you all know the facts...'

IX   *Miscellaneous*

(1)   Strauss, probably: the man had become restless recently.
(2)   Suddenly – out of the dark – a dog.
(3)   What if it hadn't drifted in by accident?
(4)   Look, what about calling a truce?
(5)   'Y–e–s'
(6)   'What are you saying, that the aristocratic ones taste better?'
(7)   What's the danger mark, that fat-looking line?
(8)   'The dogs –'
        '– are dead.'
(9)   You might check if Altman's ever hired carpenters, maybe
        for...

Part 2

Corpus design and development

5 Towards a new corpus of spoken American English

WALLACE L. CHAFE, JOHN W. DU BOIS and
SANDRA A. THOMPSON

5.1 Background

At the University of California, Santa Barbara, we are proposing to create a moderately large (200,000-word) computerized database of spoken American English, which we will publish both in book form and in an interactive computer format that will allow simultaneous access to transcription and sound.[1] This research tool will make possible a wide range of types of research, including both traditional language corpus research and research of a kind that has not previously been possible.

During the last few decades several extensive computerized corpora of the English language have been created. The primary differences between these have to do with the distinction between regional varieties and the difference between written and spoken English. So far as British English is concerned, there is the Lancaster-Oslo/Bergen (LOB) Corpus, consisting of material published in the year 1961 (Johansson et al. 1978), and the London-Lund Corpus of Spoken English, collected in Britain mainly in the 1960s and early 1970s (Svartvik and Quirk 1980, Svartvik et al. 1982, Greenbaum and Svartvik 1990). For written American English there is the Brown Corpus, consisting of written material published in the United States in the year 1961 (Kučera and Francis 1967, Francis and Kučera 1982). These corpora were originally made available to researchers in the form of mainframe computer tapes, and more recently have also been distributed on diskettes for use with micro-computers. In addition to these three corpora of English as used by adults, a project is currently being sponsored in the United States by the MacArthur Foundation to create a major archive of English child language. In recent years, the set of written corpora has been increased through the addition of new corpora for British, Indian and Australian English (Taylor and Leech 1991).

It is obvious to all concerned that there is a conspicuous gap in these materials: a comparably large computerized corpus of spoken American English as used by adults. Such a corpus would provide a rich source of data for all those interested in the nature of spoken American English and, more generally, of spoken language, whether their interests are descriptive, theoretical or pedagogical. For example, it has been suggested that the grammar of spoken language is still little understood (Halliday 1987); the Corpus of Spoken American English (CSAE) will provide materials for extensive studies of all aspects of spoken English grammar and lexicon. It will at the same time have an obvious value for studies of differences between speech and writing, and thus can contribute to an understanding of how the educational system can facilitate the child's transition from accomplished speaker to accomplished writer. It will be of obvious value to sociologists and linguists studying the structure of conversational interaction. It will constitute a basic source of information for those engaged in teaching English as a second language, who will be able to draw on it in either a research or a classroom setting for examples of linguistic and interactional patterns that are characteristic of conversation. And, because the transcription into standard English orthography will be linked with sound, linguists and speech researchers will gain a useful tool for studying the relation of auditory phenomena to linguistic elements, which will ultimately contribute to the goal of enabling computers to recognize speech. In a larger time frame, this corpus will provide an invaluable source of information on the English language as it was spoken colloquially in America towards the end of the twentieth century.

In addition to these considerations, there is a strong theoretical thrust to this project. We are convinced that current understandings of language suffer in a fundamental way from reliance on inadequate data. Many discussions of theoretical issues depend on concocted English sentences or the literal translations of such sentences into other languages. Those of us who have sought theoretical insights in the data of actual language in use have been continually impressed with the rich and systematic insights such data provide into the nature of language and the motivations for linguistic form, as well as the relations between language, thought and social interaction. We anticipate that making this corpus available to the linguistic community will help to stimulate some badly needed changes in the relation between linguistic theory and the data linguistics should explain but at present fails even to notice. There have been hundreds of publications based on the London-Lund Corpus. Because of the unique additional features we will include and the widespread interest in American English, we have every reason to expect the CSAE to follow in the great tradition of that corpus as a stimulus for new research.

While a corpus of spoken American English following in the traditional pattern of existing corpora would no doubt be of great value in its own right, recent developments in microcomputer and mass storage technology have opened exciting new possibilities for increasing the accessibility and usefulness of such a corpus. Interactive mass storage devices such as CD–ROM optical disks now allow the simultaneous presentation of both visual and auditory information. We intend to make use of this emerging potential by publishing our corpus in an interactive computer format so that researchers will be able to see a transcription on their microcomputer screen and to hear it at the same time. Moreover, users will be able to search the written transcripts for relevant key words using standard English orthography and then hear the corresponding passages, thus gaining access to what is in effect an auditory concordance. This capability will open up a wide variety of new kinds of research such as, for example, studies of the statistical correlation of particular pitch patterns with particular discourse functions.

5.2   Comparability

One question that immediately arises is the feasibility of comparing this new corpus with existing corpora. How should the goal of comparison affect corpus design considerations? The design of any corpus is subject to demands which may to some degree conflict with the demands on other corpora. On the one hand, one would like the design of a new corpus to follow the pattern set by earlier corpora to which it might be compared, making comparisons as straightforward as possible. The obvious point of comparison in this case is the London-Lund Corpus. This consideration would argue for building the CSAE along the lines originally set for that corpus. On the other hand, one would also like to allow a new corpus to take advantage of all that has been learnt, and all that has come within our technological grasp, in the interval since the structure of the earlier corpus was set. One would like the design of the CSAE to take account of new technological and theoretical developments during the quarter-century since decisions were made which fundamentally determined the character of the London-Lund Corpus.

We have sought to balance these two considerations as far as possible, attempting to retain as much comparability with the London-Lund Corpus as is feasible while not shying away from new insights and technologies. For example, we will take advantage of the capability of CD–ROM to allow simultaneous access to transcription and sound. But this provision of full access to audio information raises both practical and ethical issues.

A CD–ROM disk can hold a maximum of nineteen hours of speech (in the 'Level C' format), but with allowance for the text, concordance and indexing data that also have to be placed on the disk, the practical limit will be approximately fifteen hours. The result is that only about 200,000 words of conversation can be included on a disk. While it would be possible in principle to put the data on two or more disks, this expedient would complicate systematic access to the information, and would increase the expense both for publication and for the user. Another consideration that argues for a corpus of about 200,000 words is the time and expense of transcribing. We estimate that transcribing and checking this amount of material at the level of precision and accuracy we seek will occupy the greater part of a three-year period. While one would like to match the London-Lund Corpus's 500,000 words, this goal would exceed the scope of what is presently feasible.

The London-Lund practice of cutting off transcriptions at an arbitrary point so that all speech samples will contain the same number of words no longer seems necessary. In the light of current discourse research, with its interest in examining the sequence of events in extended interactions, it seems preferable to include whole conversational interactions as far as possible. Conversations will thus differ from each other in their natural length, allowing discourse researchers access to the amount of context that they need.

A new corpus must also adapt to some changing practical realities regarding privacy. It would not be desirable (or, for that matter, legally feasible) to publish the words of speakers who had not consented to being recorded. In this respect, the CSAE unavoidably differs from the London-Lund Corpus. However, our experience has been that this constraint makes little difference in the naturalness of speech, so that the comparison of surreptitious with non-surreptitious recordings will not be a serious problem.

Transcription is also an important issue. While the London-Lund transcription system is rich and capable of great precision, especially with respect to intonation, non-specialists tend to be overwhelmed by the density of information and symbols. We have sought to develop a discourse transcription system (Du Bois *et al.*, forthcoming a, b; see examples below) which, while it does not contain as much detailed intonational information, will be easier to implement in the transcription stage and more accessible to the non-specialist, while still incorporating the most important advances of the last two decades in the understanding of discourse and its transcription.

Recognizing the need for differences, we have found that there are ways to enhance comparability with the London-Lund Corpus. For example, if one considers only the category of face-to-face conversation, the London-Lund Corpus contains 250,000 words, a figure close to the projected size of the CSAE. Since many discourse researchers would take face-to-face conversation to be the most important genre of spoken discourse, and since users of the London-Lund Corpus often choose to use only this category for their studies, we believe that 200,000 words of face-to-face conversation will allow adequate comparisons with the relevant portion of the London-Lund Corpus. In general, we believe that the similarities between the CSAE and the London-Lund Corpus will be more significant than the differences, and that any differences will be justified by the need to adapt to changing conditions and to take advantage of new developments in technology and discourse research.

5.3   Sampling

In discussing our plans with others, we have found that scholars quickly think of all that is desirable in such a corpus, and all that could be done under ideal conditions. We ourselves have been able to envision many features which are beyond the reasonable grasp of even a major three-year effort. For example, to speak of a corpus of 'American English' suggests to many a body of data that would document the full sweep of the language, encompassing dialectal diversity across regions, social classes, ethnic groups and age groups in ways that would make possible massive correlations of social attributes with linguistic features. Some also envision data that would encompass the genre diversity of American English in ways that would allow comparison across service encounters, sermons, doctor–patient interactions, legal proceedings, planned and un-planned class lectures, hallway conversations, and so on. While we appreciate the attractions of such visions, we also find it significant that existing corpora, especially those of spoken language, have not generally aimed at this kind of breadth.

The CSAE, as proposed, will consist of about thirty half-hour conversations in 'Standard American English'. Given this fact, it is useful to clarify (1) what we mean by Standard American English, (2) the relationship of this linguistic variety to social variables such as class and ethnicity, and (3) why this linguistic variety was chosen. It will also be useful to clarify the distinction between corpus linguistics and another type of research that uses spoken material, variational sociolinguistics.

While Standard American English (SAE) is often characterized as the variety of English used in spoken and written journalism, linguists would usually apply the term to a broader range of uses. Spoken SAE encompasses formal and informal styles, preaching, cursing, bureaucratese, slang, Southern accents, New York accents, and a host of regional, class, gender and ethnic accents. What unifies it is a shared set of grammatical rules and structures, which among spoken varieties of American English come closer than any other to the written variety as used in journalism, government publications, textbooks, and so on, while of course still differing from the written variety in the many ways that speaking may differ from writing. Because SAE encompasses a variety of accents, regis-ters and styles, it is not the sole property of any particular group in American society. For every ethnic group of any size in the United States, there are members who speak SAE and members who do not. Why, then, should SAE be selected for this corpus? The alternatives would be to use several different varieties, of which SAE might be one, or to use some other single variety.

In considering the multiple-varieties option, it is important to take into account the size of the proposed corpus. Given that modern standards of discourse research require fairly extended samples of discourse for access to the necessary context, the corpus will provide an extract of approximately half an hour from each conversation. It will also include some smaller conversations of the kind that last between thirty seconds and a few minutes, but these brief conversations, though possibly numerous, will represent no more than about 5 per cent of the total number of words in the corpus. Assuming that an average of about three speakers participate in each half-hour conversation, the corpus will have a total of about ninety speakers, each represented on average by only ten minutes of speech (along with a number of other speakers represented by very small amounts of speech). Moreover, since the conversations will be naturally occurring and not experimentally induced, the ninety speakers cannot be selected independently of each other. In effect there will be only thirty selections available – one for each of the conversations that will make up the bulk of the data. The corpus simply will not be large enough to sustain statistically viable differentiations based on social variables such as regional dialect, ethnic group or socio-economic status.

Projects in variational sociolinguistics typically gather data by interviewing a large sample of speakers within a single speech community. To handle the hundreds of hours of interview speech that may result, researchers typically do not transcribe the material fully but search for instances of a linguistic variable that has been selected for study. This variable will then be examined for correlation with the social variable of interest. The partial analysis of large volumes of interview data from a single community is uniquely suited to the discovery of facts about the role of social variables in language use.

Projects in corpus linguistics, on the other hand, generally involve a rather different approach to spoken material. The most important difference is that *all* the data in the corpus must be subjected to an intensive transcription process in order to obtain the level of detail, precision and accuracy that must accompany publication of the data in their entirety. We estimate that a trained team of researchers will require approximately six person-hours to transcribe and check each minute of conversation. As a result, published corpora of speech can hope to represent only a single variety – which to date has been virtually without exception the standard variety. What emerges is a different kind of tool, used to answer different questions, from that generated by a sociolinguistic project. Both tools are useful to students of language, and in many cases the same scholar will turn to each of them, asking different questions.

There are several reasons why the standard variety of American English is preferred for this corpus over other varieties. The CSAE will enable comparisons with existing corpora of written English (both American and British) and of spoken British English. All of the major corpora in these categories are corpora of the standard variety. Another major function which the CSAE is expected to serve is that of a resource for teaching English as s second language. Again, the first need for non-native speakers is for materials that will allow them to learn the standard variety.

While neither the selection of a non-standard variety nor the subdivision of this small corpus into several varieties is a viable alternative, this in no way means that the social diversity of the American population will be excluded from the picture. For example, speakers from ethnic minorities will be included as representative speakers of SAE. We seek a body of speakers who are diverse in ethnicity, sex, occupation and geographic origin as far as is possible within the rather severe limitations on corpus size.

In sum, we have carefully considered the question of the kind of sample our corpus will' contain. We have decided to construct a corpus that is relatively homogeneous with respect to Standard American English but varied with respect to such features as age, sex, region, educational level and occupation, but we will not attempt to have the corpus reflect a rigorous sampling procedure. We will aim for a reasonable balance in our choice of speakers, trying to find a wide representation of adult speakers of Standard American English. We will also try to vary the recording situation to ensure a variety of contexts, including face-to-face conversations at family gatherings, among close friends, and among those who know each other less well, such as co-workers. Conversations will be allowed to flow naturally, and will not be directed in any way by the person doing the recording. We feel that defining the scope of the CSAE in this way will produce a solid foundation for the kinds of discourse research that will interest most potential users.

5.4   Organization

The goal of creating a computerized corpus of approximately 200,000 words of carefully transcribed language and making it accessible to a wide range of researchers will call for organization of a sort that we will outline here very briefly, giving most of our attention to the most innovative aspect of the project, the development of the CD–ROM format.

The development of the corpus will be managed jointly by the three authors of this chapter, in periodic consultation with an advisory board, outside consultants and research assistants. The research assistants will undergo an intensive training programme, including both course work and on-the-job training. The conversational data will be recorded in the most natural circumstances possible, with the use of small portable tape recorders and microphones that will yield the highest audio quality feasible in realistic field conditions. At the time of recording, basic ethnographic information about the speakers and circumstances of the speech event will be documented, using forms developed by Du Bois (Du Bois *et al.*, forthcoming a). Each original tape will be copied to ensure data security, but ultimately the digitized computer-readable version will constitute the safest and most permanent form of archival preservation. From the tapes that we record we will make selections for further processing, the final selection defining a corpus of about 200,000 words, or fifteen hours, of conversation.

Each selection will be transcribed, with special attention to such phenomena as pauses, intonation unit boundaries, intonation contours, segment lengthening, primary and secondary accent, vocal noises such as inhalation (a significant cue for turn-taking behaviour), truncation of words and of intonation units, rate of speech, laughter, speaker turn-taking and speaker overlap. For a full discussion of the features included, the reasons for notating them, the conventions for representing them and the criteria employed, see Du Bois *et al.* (forthcoming a, b). The transcribing methods and conventions we will use are those which we feel most effectively balance the trade-off between the time and effort expended by the transcribers and the needs of a broad range of potential users. While for any transcription it will always be possible to add new detail, we have sought to provide a system that is both viable for general research and cost effective to implement. Because we will distribute the audio recordings along with the transcriptions, any researchers who wish more detail in areas of specialized interest will have access to it. In order to ensure accuracy, we have devised a system of checking by both research assistants and project directors that will ensure maximum review of transcriptions before final versions are accepted.

The tape-recorded sound signal will be digitized for storage on computer-readable media. In this digitization process, a tape will be played into an IBM–PC microcomputer equipped with a Sony audio encoding board which is designed for converting data to the CD–ROM format. The digitized audio segment can then be edited on the microcomputer in order to remove extraneous noise. Each segment will then be stored on an optical disk.

Indexing software will then be used to create a cross-referenced relative index of the conversational transcript and its associated audio segments. The transcripts will be structured according to the following hierarchy of discourse units, from largest to smallest: conversation, intonation unit, word. Each of these units will receive a unique (compound) index. Each intonation unit will be cross-referenced to the identifier for the corresponding digitized audio segment. The resulting index allows interactive Boolean keyword searches (including searches for intonation contour patterns, speaker labels, etc., which in our system are effectively treated as keywords), in which all intonation units containing the specified keywords can be both seen and heard, along with the desired amount of context. Software that will allow the corpus user to retrieve information in the ways described above will be purchased and customized to meet the specific needs of the CSAE project.

5.5   Dissemination

The final product will be published in two major forms: a CD–ROM optical disk and a printed book. Each is expected to serve somewhat different functions and to complement the other. In addition, the corpus will be made available in two minor formats to researchers with specialized interests.

The CD–ROM format has already been described. We feel that this format will present the corpus as a research tool in its most powerful form. Corpus users will be able to carry out a rich variety of searches through the conversational transcript data, and to hear the corresponding audio, with the desired amount of surrounding discourse context. The research potential provided by this unique new tool is considerable.

We expect to sell the CD–ROM version of the corpus for about $80.00, which is comparable in price to some academic books. In addition, users will need a microcomputer (an IBM–PC or IBM-compatible personal computer with 512K to 640K of memory) and a CD–ROM XA drive. The relatively low cost of the corpus on CD–ROM will mean that both the corpus and the drive to use it can be purchased for about the current cost (in 1990) of a high-quality dot matrix printer. We believe that microcomputer owners with research and/or educational interests that would benefit from using the corpus will feel that the research potential of this microcomputer accessory justifies its cost. The availability of other language-oriented CD–ROM research tools, such as the *Oxford English Dictionary* on CD–ROM drive, will of course enhance its attractiveness.

We also plan to publish the corpus transcriptions in the form of a printed book, which will contain about 60,000 lines of transcript (200,000 words) in as many as 1200 pages. This book will contain the full text of all the conversations, each as a separate chapter, and appropriate explanatory material. The book will serve several important functions. Many researchers who wish to make extended analyses of whole transcribed conversations (rather than of, say, uses of a particular class of adjectives) may find it easier to work through the conversations in the pages of a large-format book than to work with a computer screen. There will be some users who will not have access to a CD–ROM drive. Many users may wish to use the corpus in both printed and electronic forms.

We believe that the CD–ROM version and the printed book version of the CSAE will serve complementary functions and reach partly distinct audiences. We also expect that each version will promote awareness and use of the other. These two forms of the CSAE will be of the greatest value and widest interest, but two other versions will be made available to limited numbers of researchers who need them. We will present the corpus transcriptions on microcomputer diskettes, for those who wish to have computational access to the data and are willing to forgo the benefits of the specially designed retrieval software and the audio sound, available only on CD–ROM. There will be approximately two megabytes of transcribed data on about six diskettes.

We also hope to be able to make copies of the audio tapes available to qualified researchers on demand. These tapes may be useful to some researchers who want access to the sound but do not have access to a CD–ROM drive, and who are willing to accept the inconvenience of dealing with multiple cassettes. This version will consist of approximately fourteen ninety-minute cassette tapes.

5.6   Examples

We close with examples of transcriptions and concordances in the styles that are contemplated for presentation of the CSAE. To make

Table 5.1 Glossary of symbols for discourse transcription (Du Bois *et al.*, forthcoming a, b)

{carriage return}	Intonation unit boundary
--	Truncated intonation unit
{space}	Word boundary
- {hyphen}	Truncated word
.	Final contour class
,	Continuing contour class
?	Yes–no question contour class
!	Exclamatory contour class
\	Falling terminal pitch
/	Rising terminal pitch
\/	Falling–rising terminal pitch
/\	Rising–falling terminal pitch
_ {underscore}	Level terminal pitch
:	Speaker attribution and turn beginning
[words]	Speech overlap
...(.,n)	Long (timed) pause
...	Medium pause
..	Very short pause; tempo lag
(0)	Latching
^	Primary accent
`	Secondary accent
=	Lengthening
(TEXT)	Non-verbal vocal sound
%	Glottal stop
(H)	Inhalation
(Hx)	Exhalation
@	Laugh syllable
<Y words Y>	Marked quality
<@ words @>	Laughing while speaking
<Q words Q>	Quotation quality
((COMMENT))	Researcher's comment
<X words X>	Uncertain hearing
X	Indecipherable syllable

it more accessible, the book version will consist primarily of conversational transcriptions in a relatively broad transcription, without
a great deal of fine prosodic detail. The CD–ROM version will
contain both broad and narrow transcriptions in electronic form, as
well as full concordances with varying amounts of context, all of
which will be linked to the corresponding audio.

Example (1) illustrates the type of broad discourse transcription
that will be used in the book version and in one of the two
alternative transcriptions in the CD–ROM version. The transcription
segment is taken from a small body of conversations recorded and
transcribed by the authors and their research assistants.[2] A glossary
of the discourse transcription symbols used appears in Table 5.1. In
general terms, the following conventions apply: carriage return
indicates the beginning of a new intonation unit; multiple dots
indicate pauses of various durations (with the duration of long
pauses in parentheses); punctuation symbols indicate various intonation contours; square brackets mark the overlap of one speaker's
talk with another's; one or two hyphens indicate truncation of words
and intonation units, respectively; and the '@' sign represents a
syllable of laughter. (Full explanations and illustrations of usage are
given for each of these symbols in Du Bois *et al.*, forthcoming a, b.)

(1)
G: For most people it's celebration,
    for me,
    it's it's a time,
    to --
    to get in bed,
    to- to put the mustard plaster on,
    a time to take . . . fifteen grams of vitamin C a day,
    . . . (2.2) and,
    of course,
    a lot of herb tea,
    when I'd rather be drinking whisky.
K: . . . (1.3) You don't drink whisky.
    . . . (1.5) @
G: I would if I wasn't sick.
K: @
    . . . No you wouldn't.

G: Yes I would.
   I used to drink bourbon every Christmas.

A broad transcription is naturally the easiest to read, and the most accessible to the widest audience. But many researchers will be eager to have access to a more precise rendering of the conversations in the corpus, so a narrow transcription of each conversation will also be included in the electronic versions (CD–ROM and diskette) of the CSAE. A narrow version of the same conversational fragment is given in (2). This example contains several additional transcription conventions beyond those mentioned above: parentheses surround non-verbal vocal noises (e.g. coughing, breathing); caret and raised stroke (or grave accent) indicate primary and secondary accent, respectively; equals sign indicates a lengthened or drawled sound; and slash, backslash and underscore at the end of a line indicate rising, falling and level pitch, respectively. (For other symbols, see Table 5.1.)

(2)
G: For ^most people it's ^celebration, \
   for ^me=, _
   it's .. it's a% ^ti=me, _
   to= - -
   (H) to 'get in ^be=d, \ /
   .. (H) to%- .. to 'put the 'mustard ^plaster 'o=n, \ /
   .. (H) a 'time to 'take ... (.8) (H) ^fifteen 'grams of vitamin 'C a
                                                    ^da=y, \ /
   ... (2.2) 'a=nd, _
   of course, _
   .. a 'lot of herb ^tea, \
   when I'd 'rather be drinking ^whisky. \
K: ... (1.3) @^You don't drink ^whisky. \ /
   ... (1.5) @N [(H)]
G: [I] 'would if I 'wasn't ^si=ck. \
K: @ (H)
   ... @'No you ^wouldn't. \ /
G: .. ^Yes I ^would. \ /
   I 'used to 'drink ^bourbon every 'Christmas. \

While this version is admittedly more difficult to read, it contains detailed prosodic information that many discourse researchers will find crucial. Users of the CD–ROM version will be able to toggle back and forth freely between the broad and narrow transcription of any given passage.

The next few illustrations show concorded text more or less as it will appear in the CD–ROM version of the corpus, as accessed by special data retrieval software. Table 5.2 shows a page of concorded text in broad transcription, and Table 5.3 shows a similar page in narrow transcription. (For this illustration we have concorded just one brief conversation; the concordances in the actual corpus will of course contain many more instances for each keyword.) It is worth noting that all words are alphabetized correctly, whether or not they contain prosodic markings (equals signs, carets, etc.), thanks to the sophisticated indexing software used (in this illustration, KWIC-

Table 5.2 Sample concordance page (broad transcription)

```
LEVELS
   107        D: ... So what about your titer *levels.*
   110                    G: My titer *levels,*
LIAR
   211              G: ...(1.7) You're a *liar!*
LIBRARY
   281                 K: [from the *library],*
LIGHT
   230        the one [2 you <X *light* it with X> 2]?
LIGHTER
   229   This is the– where the *lighter* one goes?
LIKE
     6             I would really *like* to have my ––
    10         G: ...(1.7) I'd *like* to have my lungs,
    35                  I had *like* a blowtorch,
    50   I [don't] normally sound *like* Lucille Ball.
   242        D:     [2 <X that's *like* the X> shammes 2]?
   252               ...(1.0) *like* a jack Mormon,
LITTLE
   234   What's the other– the *little* ones.
LOOK
    84           G: *[Look* at the bottom of my] feet
   264            <X *Look* at this X> [2 XXX 2],
LOOMING
   221        constantly *looming* over my head.
LOT
   172        G: [eat] a *lot* of candy,
   200             a *lot* of herb tea,
```

Table 5.3 Sample concordance page (narrow transcription)

```
NOTHING
    27                   K: [You have *'nothing* to ^complai=n about]. \
   101                   G: *[^Nothing],* /
NOW
    87       u has 'that right *@now].* \
    95                    [2 *'no=w* 2]. \
   229                       *no=w.* –
OF
    19          .. It's ^full *of* asbestos. \
    58      ^f=ierce .. case *of* ^rhinitis, \
    73   ecovered from all *of* them. \
    82       G: [That's ^one] *of* them. \
    88   ok at the 'bottom *of* my] ^ feet. \
   132    3] 'inflammation *of* the 'salivary ^gla=nds, \
   136    uses all sorts .. *of* 'other ^problems. \
   177       G: [eat] a ^lot *of* 'ca=ndy, \
   206  ) ^fifteen 'grams *of* vitamin 'C a ^da=y, \/
   208                     *of* course, _
   209        .. a 'lot *of* herb ^tea, \
   228    is the 'sight *of* that ^menorah, \
   231  t's ^not the 'end *of* ^Chanukah F>. \
   246         'each *of* the ^days, _
   263  I've never ^heard *of* it. \
OH
    85          .. *^Oh* 'no. \
   115          K: *Oh,* _
   275        D: <@ *'Oh,* \
   279    ... [2 *Oh* 2] ^that's nice. \
```

MAGIC).[3] All of these concordances will be linked to the corresponding audio, so that for any given keyword, users can listen to
the conversational exchanges that contain that keyword.

Tables 5.4 to 5.8 represent examples of computer screens as they
will be seen by users of the CD–ROM version of the corpus. Users
will be able to select the amount of context they wish to see when
they are searching for a set of keywords, and will also select the
desired delicacy of transcription. Table 5.4 shows a computer screen
illustrating a single line of context for each keyword in broad
transcription, while Table 5.5 shows the same amount of context in
narrow transcription. For research questions which require more
context – for example questions that hinge on an earlier turn in the
conversation – three lines of context can be selected, as in Table 5.6

Table 5.4 Sample computer screen (one-line context, broad)

Input: HYPO.BAS	Go	Parameters Filters	Hit CR to page
Output: SCREEN	List	DGTBSIFsUb Key S C	Merge C: Line# 150
KM~ eXport Special	Quit	+-----+# EXC 1 *	Drive C: Memory 375 K
Help?			

```
BED
    25                              I was in]  *bed,*
    29         G: [2 This year 2] I was [in  *bed]* on New Year's day,
   195                        to get in  *bed,*
BEEN
     1     G: ... My holiday season has  *been* marred,
    17              K: [It already] has  *been.*
    61          since since we've  *been* married,
BIG
   274                D:    [in] ...  *big* print,
BLOWTORCH
    35              I had like a  *blowtorch,*
    53      how did you have a  *blowtorch* up your nostrils.
BOOK
   255     Will you have to [consult the  *book?*
```

Table 5.5 Sample computer screen (one-line context, narrow)

Input: HYPO1.ASC	Go	Parameters Filters	Hit CR to page
Output: SCREEN	List	DGTBSIFsUb Key S C	Merge C: Line# 340
KM~ eXport Special	Quit	+-----+# EXC 1 *	Drive C: Memory 372 K
Help?			

```
   211             K: ...(1.3) @^You  *don't* drink ^whisky. \ /
   234              <Q ^Why  *don't* you 'put this ^away. \
   235              'Why  *don't* you 'put this ^awa=y Q>]. \
   248            D: ['They  *don't* have a ^word, /
DOWN
    58      .. I was 'coming  *^down* with a ^f=ierce .. case of
DRANK
   219      .. 'You haven't  *drank* 'bourbon at ^Christmas, \
   221              I  *'drank* it 'two ^years ago, \
DRINK
   164              and you  *^dri=nk,*/
   179     @ @it's a 'time that you  *'drink* and ^smoke. \
   211        K: ...(1.3) @^You don't  *drink* ^whisky. \ /
   217          I 'used to  *'drink* ^bourbon every
                            'Christmas.
```

Table 5.6 Sample computer screen (three-line context, broad)

Input: HYPO.BAS	Go	Parameters Filters	Hit CR to page
Output: SCREEN	List	DGTBSIFsUb Key S C	Merge C: Line# 450
KM~ eXport Special	Quit	+------+# EXC 1 *	Drive C: Memory 375 K
Help?			

25		
24		[two years ago,
25		I was in] *bed,*
26	K:	[You have nothing to complain about].
29		
28	K:	[2 You have noth– 2] ––
29	G:	[2 This year 2] I was [in *bed]* on New Year's day,
30	K:	[No you weren't].
195		
194		to ––
195		to get in *bed,*
196		to– to put the mustard plaster on,
BEEN		
1		
1	G:	... My holiday season has *been* marred,
2		by the same ... goddamn disease.

Table 5.7 Sample computer screen (three-line context, narrow)

Input: HYPO1.ASC	Go	Parameters Filters	Hit CR to page
Output: SCREEN	List	DGTBSIFsUb Key S C	Merge C: Line# 470
KM~ eXport Special	Quit	+------+# EXC 1 *	Drive C: Memory 372 K
Help?			

BARRE		
129		
128	D:	[2 What is 'that 2]. \
129	G:	'Epstein *'Ba=rre,* /
130	D:	.. What's 'cytomega[lovirus]. \
BE		
100		
99	D:	(0) What ˆis that. \
100	K:	ˆHe'll *be* 'over his leprosy [ˆsoo=n]. \/
101	G:	[ˆNothing], /
210		
209		.. a 'lot of herb ˆtea, \
210		when I'd 'rather *be* drinking ˆwhisky. \
211	K:	...(1.3) @ˆYou don't drink ˆwhisky. \/

Table 5.8 Sample computer screen (five-line context, broad)

Input: HYPO.BAS Output: SCREEN KM~ eXport Special Help?	Go List Quit	Parameters Filters DGTBSIFsUb Key S C + − − − − − + # EXC 1 *	Hit CR to page Merge C: Line# 600 Drive C: Memory 375 K

```
   217           ... @@
BECOME
   287
   285           what she's rejecting.
   286    D:     @
   287           Is he going to make her *become* a Catholic?
   288    K:     ...(1.0) Yes,
   289           he's going to, ((SPEAKERS_CHANGE _TOPIC))
BED
    25
    23    G:     ...(1.0) Well,
    24           [two years ago,
    25           I was in] *bed,*
    26    K:     [You have nothing to complain about].
    27    G:     on Christmas day.
    29
```

(broad) or Table 5.7 (narrow), or even five lines (Table 5.8) or more. Each way of accessing the concordance data serves a useful research function, and users of the CD–ROM version of the corpus will be able to choose freely between them. Whatever the amount of context that is requested, the corpus user will also be able to hear the corresponding audio.

Notes

[1] This article is based upon research supported in part by the Center for the Study of Discourse at the Social Process Research Institute, UCSB, and also by the National Science Foundation under grant number IST85–19924.

[2] We thank Danae Paolino for assistance with recording and transcription of the conversation cited.

[3] KWIC-MAGIC (from Dr. LST: Software, 545 33rd St, Richmond, California 94804) is a concordance program which has many capabilities specifically designed for linguistic and other discourse research.

6 The development of the International Corpus of English

SIDNEY GREENBAUM

6.1   Background

The concept of an international computerized corpus of English originated from a more modest proposal for the compilation of parallel computerized corpora of spoken English in Britain and the United States. My preliminary discussions to that end with Charles Meyer, a former colleague at the University of Wisconsin-Milwaukee, were appropriately held at the Reform Club in Pall Mall, London, the site of the fictional wager in *Around the World in 80 Days*.

The existing parallel computerized corpora of American and British English, the Brown Corpus and the LOB Corpus, are confined to printed material. Scholars wanting to compare speech and writing in British English can draw on the computerized London-Lund Corpus (derived from the Survey of English Usage (SEU)) for speech and the LOB Corpus for printed material, or they can consult the slips at the SEU premises at University College London, but they have no basis for similar comparisons between speech and writing in American English, nor can they compare British speech with American speech.

Our original idea was therefore for the compilation of corpora of spoken English in Britain and the United States to allow comparisons of speech across these two national varieties. The London-Lund Corpus could not serve as the British component, because we believed that it was important for the spoken corpora to be parallel in time. The texts in the London-Lund Corpus went too far back in time; they were assembled over a period of thirty years beginning in the late 1950s.

We were aware that computerized corpora were being developed for printed English in India (the Kolhapur Corpus) and in Australia (the Macquarie Corpus) on the model of the selection of samples in the Brown and LOB corpora, but (like the United States) these countries lacked a corpus of spoken English. Clearly, the value of our enterprise would be enhanced if scholars in other countries were willing to join us. We decided to investigate that possibility. The idea to develop an International Corpus of English (ICE) may be said to date from January 1988 when Charles Meyer accepted the invitation to compile a corpus of spoken English in the United States as part of an international effort.

The value of each national project as well as the international enterprise would be enhanced if the new corpora could be used for comparing spoken English with written English of the same period within each national variety and across national varieties. The existing Brown and LOB written corpora could not validly be used for such comparisons with the new spoken corpora for American and British English, since their texts were published in 1961. Most other national varieties did not have a written corpus. We accordingly decided to add written components, and (as in the SEU corpus) to include non-printed as well as printed material. We could then make international comparisons for written English as well as for spoken English.

Following discussions with Braj Kachru, an authority on international English, it was decided to invite participation in the ICE project from countries where English is not the first language for the majority of the population but an official additional language, despite the possible objection that in these countries the English language is not institutionalized. It seems odd, however, to exclude from an international project on the use of English at least half of those who use the language for communication with fellow speakers living in their country. In both first-language and second-language countries, there is a continuum of competence in English. Increasingly, second-language countries are developing their own linguistic norms. Sociolinguistically, this is an interesting period for investigating the growth of new institutionalized national varieties. Although independently conceived, the ICE project may be viewed as a belated partial reponse to Braj Kachru's call at the British Council's 50th Anniversary Conference in 1984 for an international institute for research on English across cultures (Kachru 1985: 25–7). As a commentator on his paper, I had welcomed the idea and had said that the Survey of English Usage would be happy to collaborate on a project for studying the progress of English as an international language (Greenbaum 1985: 32).

In the spring of 1988 I drew up a brief proposal for an international computerized corpus of English. It was published in *World Englishes* (Greenbaum 1988a) but circulated earlier in a preprint. The proposal envisaged the compilation of corpora sampling national varieties from first-language and second-language countries that would include both written (printed and manuscript) English and spoken English. The corpora were to be assembled along parallel lines and in the same period and were to be analysed in similar ways. I offered to initiate discussions with those interested in this proposal.

In November 1988 I issued the first ICE newsletter, in which I expressed willingness to coordinate the project. By that time three national teams (Nigeria, UK and USA) had committed themselves to the project and two others (Australia and Canada) had expressed interest. At the time of writing, there are thirteen regional teams; to the original five have been added East Africa (covering Kenya, Tanzania and Zambia), Hong Kong, India, Jamaica, New Zealand, the Philippines, Singapore and Wales.

In addition to the regional corpora, three international specialized corpora have been proposed: (1) written translations into English from languages used in the European Economic Community; (2) spoken international communication, in which the participants come from different countries and perhaps include people from countries where English is a foreign language; (3) texts used in the teaching of English as a foreign language. These specialized corpora can provide material for comparisons with relevant parts of the regional corpora.

Early in 1989 I established an international advisory board (which now has sixteen members) consisting of scholars that have expertise in the construction of English corpora, in computational techniques for the analysis of corpora, and in English as a world language. The ICE advisory board and participants met for the first time at the ICAME conference at Bergen in June 1989. That meeting resulted in some crucial decisions on the format of ICE. The ICAME conferences are expected to provide an annual venue for such meetings.

In April 1989 I submitted to the Economic and Social Research

Council a proposal for a research grant for the British contribution to the International Corpus of English, and subsequently a substantial grant was awarded for the first three years of the project. The proposal was made available to other ICE participants who requested it. Comments and questions from reviewers, to which I responded, proved valuable in directing attention to aspects of the international project that needed clarification.

For the rest of the paper I will outline the development of the ICE project by examining in turn the decisions that have been taken since the publication of the original proposal.

6.2   Date of texts

In the original proposal, one calendar year had been advocated as the period from which texts should emanate. It subsequently proved to be too restricted a period, partly because it might not be possible to record all the spoken material within such a time and partly because some research teams had other commitments that would prevent them from starting on the compilation when other teams were eager to get going. It is speech that is likely to cause difficulties in timing, since printed publications – and to a lesser extent manuscript material – can be collected years after they were produced. We allowed what we thought would be sufficient time for planning and settled on 1990 as the earliest date for the corpus texts and 1993 as the latest date. A three-year period seemed adequate for the collection of texts and constituted a reasonable (though arbitrary) period as a basis for synchronic comparative studies. The processing of the texts could, of course, continue for longer than three years, the length of time depending on the availability of funding and expertise and the extent of processing desired.

6.3   Size of corpus

Quite early in our discussions we agreed that the corpus should contain a total of one million words. This admittedly arbitrary figure simply follows the practice of the three earlier corpora (SEU, Brown and LOB) that attempt a systematic sampling of text varieties. Later discussions revealed that regional differences and preferences would require a more elaborate structure. We still envisage a *core corpus* of one million words for each region, and this is the corpus that would serve for international comparisons. In addition, we recognize that some regions would like to collect more material in certain text categories or to include additional categories. Each regional corpus serves independently as a resource for research into a regional variety of English, and the regional corpus can be extended for that purpose by additional material that will not be part of the international corpus. The core corpus can be extended by *specialized corpora* (e.g. business letters, student essays), some of which may constitute categories that are excluded from ICE because they are not significant for all regions (e.g. electronic mail, sermons) but are felt to be of value for researchers in a particular region. Research teams in some regions may decide to establish specialized corpora along similar lines for comparative purposes. In addition, a region may have a *monitor corpus* consisting of the core corpus, any specialized corpora, and material (perhaps already available in machine-readable form) that would not be subject to precise categorization and would not fit into the core corpus or specialized corpus. It is also possible that some national teams will want to investigate geographical differences in greater detail or perhaps even to collect data from those with lesser educational qualifications than the ICE threshold.

6.4   Size of texts and text categories

We agreed that each text in the core corpus should contain about 2000 words, as in the Brown and LOB corpora, the ending to come at a suitable discourse break. There will therefore be 500 texts in each regional corpus. Those wanting to retain a complete text (e.g. a book or lecture) for research on discourse could deposit the text in the monitor corpus and use an extract for the core corpus. We also decided on ten texts (20,000 words) as the minimum for each text category (e.g. business letters or news broadcasts) on the advice of those working at the University of Nijmegen on the TOSCA corpus project (cf. Oostdijk 1988a, b).

6.5   Text encoding

Our marking system is likely to be based on SGML (Standard Generalized Markup Language), the encoding system in wide use. In addition to the heavily annotated version required for computational processing, we expect to have more readable versions for concordancing and (displaying overlapping speech) for research in discourse analysis.

6.6   Prosody

In July 1988 a meeting was held at the Survey of English Usage with phoneticians at University College London and with those who had transcribed SEU spoken texts to discuss how we should transcribe the ICE spoken texts. The participants' views differed on how much information should be supplied on intonational and other spoken features and on what' prosodic system should be used. We also considered the degree of consistency we could expect in transcriptions. In subsequent discussions with ICE participants there was general agreement that the spoken material should be transcribed orthographically and not phonetically, since the project will not be concerned with pronunciation. At the 1989 ICAME meeting one member of the advisory board went so far as to propose that the spoken material be transcribed in orthographic sentences with punctuation (partly for ease of application of the word tagging and parsing programs), but this proposal was not accepted. My initial suggestion was to limit prosodic transcription to pauses, the location of tone-unit boundaries, and the location and direction of nuclear tones. At the ICAME meeting in June 1989 we agreed that only pauses should be marked, in a binary system of brief and longer pauses related to the tempo of the individual speaker. Our decision was partly economic, since prosodic transcription requires expertise and is costly in time, but we also recognized that intonation specialists differ in their preferences for prosodic analysis, that there were serious problems in consistency in transcription, and that international differences in English intonation make it difficult to apply one system that could be used for comparisons. However, the recordings will be available for those wanting to make their own prosodic transcription (or, indeed, phonetic transcription), and they can introduce the analysis and the degree of detail they prefer. It is hoped that for at least some of the corpora it will be possible to digitize the sound recordings to correspond with the computerized screen displays. The digitization can be used to resolve syntactic ambiguities and to study intonation or the relationship between syntax and intonation.

6.7   Population

We agreed that the population represented in the regional corpora should be adults of eighteen or over who had received formal education through the medium of English to at least the completion of secondary school. However, we recognized that we would need to be flexible and would admit others whose public status (e.g. as political leaders or as radio or television commentators) made their inclusion appropriate. The ICE project is restricted to educated English. Educated English is defined circularly by reference to the language used by educated people – in the sense given above. Our criterion is objective. We do not select the language; we select the people and we do not exclude any of their language on subjective criteria of correctness, adequacy or appropriateness.

We have discussed at length the range of population to be sampled in ICE as well as the text categories (cf. Schmied 1989). We agreed that we should not attempt to randomize our selection of texts. Rather, we should deliberately take account of population differences (as well as textual differences), though not necessarily in any predetermined quantities of material. We envision a multi-dimensional approach which will use text parameters to construct text categories and will introduce social variables for the participants who produce the texts. Through the text encoding system it will be possible to compare the social variables in a text category or across text categories. We have so far identified the following variables, some of which may be relevant to only some countries: age, sex, level of educational attainment, language use (e.g. first language, urban or rural locations, domains of language use, parental language), ethnic group, region, occupation and status in occupation, role in relation to other participants.

6.8   Text categories

Most discussion has focused on the selection of text categories and the number of texts to be assigned to each category. As a basis for discussion I circulated lists of the categories with word totals for the Brown, LOB and SEU corpora. A large part of the SEU spoken material consists of surreptitious conversations, i.e. the conversations were recorded without the participants being aware of the recording at the time. Such material can no longer be collected, on moral and legal grounds.

The major text parameters have been identified. We agreed that the corpus should be divided equally into *spoken* and *written* English. Within both halves a distinction is made between *private* and *public*, private denoting communication in the presence of only the participants (e.g. a conversation or letter, as contrasted with a lecture or a press news report). In speech we distinguish monologue from dialogue. In writing we have a three-way distinction: scripted (written to be spoken), non-printed (handwritten or typed) and printed. Additional parameters include, for speech, whether there is a distance between participants (e.g. face-to-face conversation versus telephone conversation), and, for writing, the particular subject matter (e.g. humanities or natural sciences). These parameters and others not mentioned here will be inserted into the set of identification tags for texts, which will also note the date and place of written composition or speech recording.

6.9   Processing

The minimum expectation is that the whole of the ICE will be computerized and concordanced for lexical strings by the end of 1995. Some texts may be available from the start in machine-readable form; others can be converted into machine-readable form through optical scanners; but most of the texts including all the speech recordings, will require keypunching. At present two concordance programs are available, each in two versions: the KAYE IBM and the WordCruncher programs. I hope that the Survey will be able to provide a program tailored to the needs of ICE. We expect that most corpora, if not all, will be subjected to further processing.

One possibility is that we will apply the CLAWS 2 program devised at the University of Lancaster to assign grammatical word tags from a repertoire of about 160 tags (cf. Garside *et al.* 1987: 30–56). The tagging program assigns the tags automatically with about 98 per cent accuracy, but post-editing is necessary to correct wrongly assigned tags. The program was devised for written material. We expect that we may need to make certain adjustments for our spoken material (for which we have permission from the author of the program, Roger Garside) and we assume that the spoken material will require a great deal more post-editing. The CLAWS 2 program is currently being applied to the SEU corpus.

We also intend to parse our texts. If we use the Lancaster tagging program, we will also use the Lancaster computer-assisted program for parsing our texts (cf. Leech and Garside 1991). It requires manual coding, but it is reported that the coding can be applied quickly. With the cooperation of Jan Aarts and his associates, we are experimenting on the SEU corpus with the automatic parsing program developed at the University of Nijmegen (cf. Aarts and van den Heuvel 1985). This program provides a more sophisticated level of parsing than the Lancaster program and includes word tags, but it requires a considerable amount of post-editing. If we find that it is possible to process material in a reasonable time, we will adopt the Nijmegen program. We expect major parsing problems to arise with our spoken material, which will have to be divided into sentence units. Both the tagged and the parsed texts will be concordanced.

6.10   Distribution

We agreed early on that distribution of computer disks and speech recordings will be entrusted to the Norwegian Computing Centre for the Humanities at Bergen, which is responsible for the International Computer Archive of Modern English (ICAME).

6.11   Prospects

ICE is a splendid example of international cooperation in English language research. The project will undoubtedly provide valuable information on the use of English in many countries, in most of which there have never been systematic studies, and it will provide the basis for international comparisons. It will stimulate insights into the sociolinguistics of English nationally and internationally, and offer data for sociolinguistic theory. The results of the project will have implications for the teaching of English and in some countries will be applied to language planning (cf. Greenbaum 1988b: 32–9). Phileas Fogg traversed the world in eighty days to win his wager. ICE encompasses the English-speaking world, but there is no deadline for its completion and no one is offering a wager. In any case, I must not press the analogy: Phileas Fogg never existed, whereas ICE has been conceived and is being propelled into existence.

Part 3

Exploration of corpora

7   *Between* and *through*: The company they keep and the functions they serve

GRAEME KENNEDY

7.1   Introduction

Between and *through* are among the hundred or so most frequently used words in English. Like most other structural words, they are semantically complex. In spite of their high frequency, however, it is not easy to explain how they are used and learners of English often confuse them. Indeed, when asked to explain how *between* and *through* are used, adult native speakers of English will often mention only the locative senses and suggest that the two words are not entirely discrete in meaning, giving responses such as the following:

(1)   You go between two things (*I passed between two trees*) but you go through one thing (*I passed through the house*).

(2)   *Between* is used when there are two objects with a third one in the middle, or passing through the middle (*Two people were standing outside the shop and I had to walk between them to go in*). *Through* is used when something penetrates a barrier or something (*water through a sieve*). We also go *through* a crowd of people or *through* a forest; but we go *between* two trees.

(3)   We seem to use *between* with numbers (*between 2 and 3 p.m.*), but I don't think we use *through* with numbers.

(4)   *Through* implies movement, but *between* doesn't to the same extent.

(5)   You can say *He looked through the telescope*, but you can't say *He looked between the telescope*.

(6)   Sometimes the two words seem very similar – *The sand ran between her fingers; The sand ran through her fingers*.

Native speaker intuitions such as these are not very different from those which often seem to inform many language teaching curricula and textbooks, which focus on or define the usage of quite diverse aspects of the meaning of *between* and *through*. Even a cursory examination of current syllabuses and language teaching textbooks will show considerable differences as to which uses of *between* and *through* are mentioned or taught and sometimes major uses listed in reference grammars or dictionaries are not included. Thus, for example, van Ek and Alexander (1975), in their influential syllabus, introduce these words as follows:

> *between*   We have a holiday between Christmas and Easter.
> We walked between two policemen.
> *through*   We drove through the centre of the town.

Eastwood and Mackin (1982) use illustrations to introduce *between* with 'The shoe shop is between the book shop and the pet shop' and *through* with 'through the water'. Swan and Walter (1984) introduce *between* with 'Temperatures in summer are between 30° C and 40° C', while *through* is introduced later with 'go through Customs'. Ellis and Ellis (1985) include the following sentences to define the use of *between* and *through*.

> She has lunch *between* ten past twelve and twenty to one.
> It costs *between* £5 and £10.
> Finally pour the tea *through* the strainer, into the cup, and stir.

Hall (1986) first introduces *through* as if it is closely associated with *between*:

> *through*: between the walls/parts of
> I didn't think I'd get the car through that narrow entrance.

The semantic functions of *between* and *through* on which Celce-Murcia and Larsen-Freeman (1983) focus in their pedagogical grammar are:

> *between* – at an intermediate point in relation to two entities (between the house and the street)
> – between 1 and 2 o'clock

- between 100 and 110 lb
- between you and me
through – penetrate: through the window; through the forest
- duration: through the years
- endurance: through thick and thin

That there can be such differences in the focus of pedagogy as is shown in these few examples should not be surprising given the lack of available statistical information about the functioning of these words in context. It may even be that the higher the frequency of words and the more complex their semantic structure, the less reliable our intuitions about their most important functions in text.

Statistical information on language in use has, of course, also not been a characteristic of most grammatical descriptions of *between* and *through*, because such descriptions are particularly concerned with systemic possibility. They have depicted *between* and *through* as exemplars of the word classes of preposition and what are variously called adverbs, prepositional adverbs or particles which behave in a similar way to other examples of these word classes. As prepositions, for example, *between* and *through* are described as preceding noun phrases to serve such syntactic functions as post-modifiers, adverbials, complements of verbs or adjectives (e.g. Quirk *et al*. 1985: 657), although each preposition has what are called its own prepositional meanings.

The most comprehensive lexical descriptions identify and classify these different meanings. For example, Collins' COBUILD diction-ary classifies some thirteen discrete meanings of *between* and twenty-four meanings of *through*. It is noteworthy that various meanings of the words sometimes overlap regardless of whether they function as prepositions or adverbs.

Although most clause-final occurrences of *between* and *through* are indeed adverbs, it is not always easy to assign words such as *between* and *through* to word classes, in spite of formal criteria. For example, because *through*, in *Proust comes through this test with flying colours* or *Go straight through the gate*, appears to collocate equally strongly with either the preceding or the following word, parsing is sometimes found to be difficult.

There has been an increasing literature arguing that patterned speech, routines or collocations are pervasive in English and that lexical grammars have not received the attention they deserve (e.g. Nattinger 1980, Pawley and Syder 1983, Peters 1983, Sinclair 1987b). There has also been significant corpus-based research on collocation (e.g. Sinclair 1989).

The purpose of the present study is to complement grammatical and lexical studies of *between* and *through* by exploring their linguistic ecology in a computer corpus as part of an empirical study of lexical grammar.

The one-million-word LOB (Lancaster-Oslo/Bergen) corpus of adult written British English, which is made up of 500 representative 2000-word samples from a wide variety of genres, is still one of the most readily accessible corpora of English on both mainframe and personal computers. While the texts it contains are now twenty-five years old and the corpus as a whole is too small for many purposes, the stability and high frequency of structural word usage continue to make it a valuable basis for computer-assisted text analysis.

The Oxford Concordance Program – OCP2 (Hockey and Martin 1988) – was used in the study to reveal collocational information about *between* and *through* in the LOB corpus. *Between* occurs 867 times and *through* 776 times in the corpus, and they clearly occur in different contexts.

7.2   Collocations with preceding word

A total of 345 tokens (40 per cent) of *between* are immediately preceded by the words listed in Table 7.1 and 274 tokens (35 per cent) of *through* are similarly listed. Table 7.1 shows a striking difference in the words which most frequently come directly before *between* and *through*. Nouns typically precede *between*, whereas verbs are the most common word class preceding *through*. Further, three out of the four commonest nominals preceding *through* are pronouns, and none appears to collocate strongly. Table 7.2 summarizes the proportion of the tokens of *between* and *through* which are preceded by major word classes.

Collocations, of course, frequently are more than two words in length. For example, on all four occasions *flashed through* occurs, it is in the wider collocation of *flashed through her/my mind*. Eight out of the nine occurrences of *way through* are preceded by a possessive (e.g. *tried to force his way through the foliage*).

A closer analysis of collocations in the corpus shows not only

Table 7.1 Words occurring four or more times immediately before *between* and *through* in the LOB Corpus

Before *between*	n	Before *through*	n
*difference	59	go	36
*relationship	25	pass	33
*distinction	19	come	20
*relation	16	be	15
*gap	12	and	13
*agreement	11	get	12
*contrast	11	break	10
*distance	11	*him	10
*place	11	run	10
be	10	*way	9
*comparison	9	*it	8
exist	9	fall	7
*meeting	9	lead	7
*contact	8	look	7
*link	8	out	7
and	7	in	6
in	7	live	6
as	6	only	6
*conflict	6	*them	6
*correlation	6	all	5
*gulf	6	carry	5
lie	6	cut	4
that	6	down	4
*time	6	flash	4
agree	5	*line	4
*connection	5	one	4
distinguish	5	or	4
*interval	5	right	4
pass	5	see	4
*border	4	shoot	4
*exchange	4		
make	4		
out	4		
*proportion	4		
*quarrel	4		
*similarity	4		
*space	4		
*struggle	4		
Total	345	Total	274

Note: Nouns are recorded in their singular form, verbs in their stem form; * = noun or pronoun.

differences in the particular words which tend to precede *between* and *through*, but also certain morphological features. For example, unmarked singular forms of nouns before *between* are overwhelm-

Table 7.2 Word classes occurring immediately before *between* and *through*

	Before *between*			Before *through*		
	Tokens	Types	% of tokens	Tokens	Types	% of tokens
Nouns or pronouns	570	272	65.7	221	162	28.5
Verbs	141	95	16.3	335	138	43.2
Adjectives	15	13	1.7	28	19	3.6
Other word classes	87	46	10.1	120	57	15.4
Clause initial	54		6.2	72		9.3
Total	867	426	100.0	776	376	100.0

ingly more frequent than the plural. Thus, of the fifty-nine occurrences of *difference(s) between*, forty-eight tokens (81 per cent) are singular; in the case of *distinction(s) between*, eighteen out of nineteen tokens (95 per cent) are singular; for *relationship(s) between*, twenty out of twenty-five (80 per cent) are singular, whereas for *contrast between* (eleven tokens), *conflict between*, *meeting between* and *correlation between* (six tokens each), all are singular. On the other hand, only six out of sixteen tokens (38 per cent) of *relation(s) between* are singular. There are also notable differences in the corpus in the verb morphology with *between* and *through*, although why these differences might occur is still not at all clear.

Of the 141 verb forms which precede *between*, 83 (59 per cent) are *-ed* forms (e.g. *passed*, *divided*). Of the 335 verb forms which precede *through*, 163 (49 per cent) are *-ed* forms (e.g. *caused*, *put*). A total of 72 per cent of the *-ed* forms before *between* are past participles in passive voice constructions, 22 per cent are finite past tense, and 6 per cent are past participles in perfect active voice constructions. In the case of *through*, only 31 per cent of the *-ed* forms are past participles used in the passive voice, 61 per cent are finite past tense, and 14 per cent are past participles used in perfect active voice uses.

Of the non *-ed* verb forms which constitute 41 per cent of the verb forms preceding *between*, 50 per cent are finite present tense and the remainder are infinitive or *-ing* forms. On the other hand, of the 51 per cent of the verb forms preceding *through* which are not *-ed* forms, only 20 per cent are finite present tense with the remaining 80 per cent being equally divided between non-finite *-ing* and infinitive forms.

Table 7.1 lists those words which occur in the LOB Corpus on four or more occasions immediately before *between* or *through*. However, many of the words which occur less than four times also seem to belong naturally with *between* or *through*, perhaps more naturally in some cases than some frequently recurring adjacent words such as *or through* or *that between*. Table 7.3 lists some of the words occurring before *between* or *through* on fewer than four occasions in the corpus but which nevertheless seem to have collocational bonds.

Table 7.3 Some key words occurring from one to three times before *between* or *through* in the LOB Corpus

---

Before *between*:

Nouns   *alliance, analogy, antagonism, argument, balance, barrier, bond, bridge, choice, clash, collaboration, communication, competition, compromise, controversy, conversation, cooperation, correspondence, discrepancy, discussion, dispute, division, fighting, frontier, harmony, ill-will, imbalance, inconsistency, interaction, line, love, merger, negotiations, nothing, partnership, period, problem, ratio, rivalry, showdown, talk, tension, trouble, trade, understanding, variation, vendetta, wall, war, year*

Verbs   *arbitrate, choose, come, differentiate, discuss, divide, fluctuate, go, mediate, sandwich, share, squeeze, suspend, vacillate, vary*

Other word classes   *halfway, midway, somewhere*

Before *through*:

Nouns   *break, current, door, echo, exit, flow, glance, journey, passage, procession, progress, route, stream, track*

Verbs   *burst, drive, flow, follow, glance, hurry, journey, march, pull, push, put, read, search, seep, shine, sort, travel, walk, wander*

Other word classes   *available, carefully, except, gently, gradually, halfway, straight, wet*

It can be argued that recording only the immediately adjacent word presents an inaccurate picture of collocations, and it is indeed the case that discontinuous collocations are not difficult to find in the corpus, sometimes several words apart. For example:

(7)   The *distinctions* we draw *between* better and worse...

(8)   ...*divide* my only loaf of bread equally *between* them

(9)   I found that I had *moved*, without realizing it, *through* the gateway.

In these examples the collocational associations are almost certainly stronger between the italicized words than between adjacent words. Computer software which is available to identify discontinuous collocations in text could therefore potentially enhance the number of tokens for some of those listed in Table 7.1.

7.3   Collocations with following word

Recurring patterns in the sequences of words which follow *between* and *through* are listed in Table 7.4.

Table 7.4 Words occurring four or more times immediately after *between* and *through* in the LOB Corpus

After *between*	n	After *through*	n
(number)	96	(clause final)	70
(pers. pronoun)	66	(pers. pronoun)	30
the two	37	(person's name)	17
(place) *and* (place)	22	the window	15
two ____	17	to	14
(date) *and* (date)	12	(number)	12
(clause final)	9	(place)	8
these two ____	6	(her) mind	7
the various ____	6	with	7
earnings	4	the door	6
		the house	5
		the trees	5
		her hair	4
Total	282	Total	217

It is apparent that there are fewer recurring collocations with following rather than preceding words. However, by treating different personal pronouns, numbers and place names, for example, as allomorphs of single collocations (Kennedy, in press), it can be shown that 282 of the tokens (33 per cent) following *between* occur in combinations appearing four or more times or in clause-final position. Similarly, 217 of the tokens (28 per cent) following *through* recur. *Between* and *through* tend to collocate more strongly with preceding words and show a tendency to collocate with particular following words only in a few cases in the corpus, notably in the case of *between* with *the two, two, these two* and *the various*, and in the case of *through* with *the window, (her) mind, the door, the house, the trees, her hair*.

Table 7.4 contains those words which immediately follow *between* or *through* on four or more occasions in the corpus. Some sequences occurring on one, two or three occasions in the corpus immediately after *between* or *through* seem, however, to collocate at least as strongly. These are shown in Table 7.5.

Table 7.5 Some key words occurring from one to three times after *between* or *through* in the LOB Corpus

---

After *between*:

now and ____, *any two* ____, *jobs, people, the lines, the parties, equals, friends, god and man, our two countries, the hours of* ____ *and* ____, *times, thumb and forefinger*

After *through*:

lack of ____, *the ages, the book, the day, the town, the years, a door, fear, his fingers, his teeth, life, negotiations, Parliament, prayer, several editions, the centuries, the doorway, the eyes of, the good offices of, the influence of, the meal, the motions, the street, the use of, the water; their eyes, the gate, a gap, a hole, a series of, a succession of*

Of course, not every recurring sequence of words in the corpus is a collocation. Thus, *between the India Office and the Foreign Office,* which occurred twice, was not listed in Table 7.5. Similarly, sequences of *between* or *through* and a determiner were not counted unless there was a common subsequent word.

Conversely, as in any corpus study, certain familiar collocations do not appear at all in the LOB corpus, reflecting perhaps both the written and regional sources of the texts, e.g. *between you and me, between the devil and the deep blue sea, between a rock and a hard place, through no fault of (his) own, through (her) own efforts.* The common American English collocation *(Monday) through (Friday)* is also absent in the corpus.

Patterning in the words which follow *between* or *through* can also be observed at other levels of analysis. For example, *between* is followed by two nominals about twice as often (65 per cent of occurrences) as by a single nominal (35 per cent of occurrences). That is, constructions such as (10)–(12) are twice as common as (13)–(15):

(10)   between boys and girls
(11)   between Falstaff and his followers

(12)   the partnership that exists between a rider and his horse
(13)   relationships between phenomena
(14)   in an interval between calls
(15)   the grill pan was suspended between runners

The personal pronouns which follow *between* and *through* differ markedly in their relative frequency, as Table 7.6 shows, with plural pronouns predominating after *between*.

Table 7.6 Personal pronouns which follow
between and *through*

Between		Through	
them	37	it	12
us	13	them	7
her	5	him	7
him	4	her	2
you	3	me	1
it	3	you	1
me	1	us	0

The relative pronoun *which* follows *between* only twice, but follows *through* on seventeen occasions in the corpus.

Thirty-six of the tokens which follow *through* (4.6 per cent) concern a part of the body (e.g. *he looked at her through flickering lashes*). They include *their eyes, their ears, a wisp of fair hair, every nerve, his body, his brain, his teeth, his fingers, his hands, his moustache, his open mouth* and *her tears*.

Through her/my mind occurs seven times in the corpus. On four of these occasions, *through* is directly preceded by *flashed*. Three out of seven instances of *through with* are preceded by *go*.

The differences noted in the words which collocate before or after *between* or *through*, if viewed only in terms of formal similarity, can mask important semantic distinctions of words in context. For example, *through the window* occurs fifteen times in the corpus. On two occasions a physical barrier is pierced (*the car crashed through the window of a shop*). On thirteen occasions, however, it is perception which is referred to – *I saw you through the window*.

7.4   Semantic functions of *between* and *through* in context

The possible semantic differences noted above in formally identical collocations functioning in different wider contexts illustrate the need for a complementary functional analysis of *between* and *through*. Accordingly, Tables 7.7 and 7.8 summarize the major semantic functions of the constructions in which *between* and *through* occur in the corpus. The functional categories in the tables are of course quite generalized. A more fine-grained analysis would have been possible, at a cost, however, of reduced reliability and probably of usefulness, since each use of a word is modified semantically, however slightly, by its own peculiar environment and the number of possible subcategories is thus potentially very large.

Each token of *between* or *through* was examined in a context of about ten preceding words and ten following words, and assigned to a category. Initially a small number of categories was established on an *a priori* basis and further ones were added when particular tokens did not fit the *a priori* categories. The tokens assigned to each category were then checked for consistency and the categories reorganized. Finally, further changes were made after a spot reliability check using other raters was undertaken. Agreement between the proposed categorization and those of the raters was at a level of just over 93 per cent. In many categories there was complete agreement. The categories in which least agreement occurred were for *through* Category 2 when metaphor was involved and Categories 5 and 6 involving the presence or absence of causation. In (16) below, for example, it is difficult to get agreement as to whether causation or agency is involved.

(16) . . . peaceful settlement of international disputes through negotiations.

Locative uses of prepositions or particles have often been characterized as being the basic or core uses with abstract or metaphorical extensions derived from them (cf. Quirk *et al.* 1985: 673–87). In Tables 7.7 and 7.8 both literal and metaphorical extensions are included within common categories. For example, *through* 2 (Penetration of a barrier or obstruction) includes both literal physical barriers, such as grids, and success in overcoming more metaphorical obstacles such as examinations, potential telecommunication failures and parliamentary opposition.

Table 7.9 contains words which occur in the corpus not necessarily immediately adjacent to *between* or *through* but in some proximity. The list is not exhaustive but includes the most obvious

Table 7.7 Major semantic functions in which *between* occurs

Function	Tokens	%
1 Location		
(a) Between two or more places, entities or states	216	24.9
e.g. the channel between Africa and Sicily		
let nothing get between her and her ambition		
(b) Between points on a scale or range	57	6.6
e.g. temperatures between 1000° and 1450°C		
earnings between £5 and £6 a week		
2 Movement		
(a) Going from one place or state to another	24	2.8
e.g. she ran between the dining room and the kitchen		
signals passing between them in free space		
(b) Going between entities	14	1.6
e.g. the lane curled off between its high hawthorns		
he was observed … walking between the metals		
3 Time		
(a) Occurring at some time between two events or points in time	40	4.6
e.g. anytime between November and late February		
98 changes of Cabinet between 1834 and 1912		
(b) Duration, occupying a period between two events or points in time	44	5.0
e.g. the time between pouring and knock out		
to keep myself going between terms at college		
4 Other relationships		
(a) Bond between entities, states or places	96	11.1
e.g. it had forged a bond between them		
an alliance between the Castilian and Leonese nobility		
(b) Interaction between entities or states	145	16.7
e.g. a row between Lawrence and Frieda		
communication between management and employees		
(c) Similarity	18	2.1
e.g. the resemblances between Lawrence's inner life and his own		
the important parallel between Handel and Beethoven		
(d) Difference	153	17.7
e.g. the distinction between ancient and modern		
the discrepancy between expected and observed scores		
(e) Comparison	18	2.1
e.g. a comparison between different car manufacturers' guarantees		
there is little to choose between the two		
5 Dividing or sharing	42	4.8
e.g. the division of the world between two ideological camps		
a balance has to be kept between the various denominations		
between them, fantasy and science have gobbled up the remainder		
Total	867	100.0

Table 7.8 Major semantic functions in which *through* occurs

Function	Tokens	%
1 Unimpeded motion		
(a) Through a hole or passage	75	9.7
e.g. they went along a lane, through a gate		
movement of blood through arteries		
(b) Through an area	72	9.3
e.g. when he was passing through London		
the footpath through the fields		
he went through to the bathroom		
(c) Through an entity or substance	44	5.7
e.g. she ran a comb through her hair		
Magda chugged through the dark		
(d) Through a point	36	4.6
e.g. through each point there pass three lines		
turned the knob through all the tuning points		
(e) Through a system or circuit	35	4.5
e.g. impurities pass through a heat exchanger		
the current through a series circuit		
a sweet thrill ran through every nerve		
a note of passionate idealism running through		
them		
(f) Searching through something	23	3.0
e.g. to look through the files		
he scrabbled through his drawers		
2 Penetration of a barrier or obstruction	138	17.7
e.g. shaken through a vibrating grid		
the sun burst through the blue-grey clouds		
he breaks through the Kantian dogma		
has survived its progress through Congress		
the call from Alastair came through		
3 Perception through an obstruction	56	7.2
e.g. to look through one of the windows		
his eyes met hers through the thin veil of smoke		
4 Time		
(a) Through a period of time	41	5.3
the longest days I have ever lived through		
going through the whole of his life		
(b) Through a process or event	22	2.8
e.g. go through the same routine		
what these poor people must go through		
5 Agent–intermediary–instrument	196	25.3
e.g. I should have met him through Robert Graves		
through the medium of the English language		
evidence obtained through the examination of stones		
secure cooperation through compromise		
6 Causation	38	4.9
e.g. time lost through the flooding of the workings		
her eyes were red through overmuch crying		
dilapidation through lack of maintenance		
Total	776	100.0

Table 7.9 Key words associated with various semantic functions of *between* and *through* in the LOB Corpus

---

A *Between*

1 Location:
  (a) *channel, gap, space, tunnel, distance, lie, border, line, barrier, frontier, gulf, margin, place*
  (b) (numerals), *estimate, values, cost, earnings, temperature, range, pressure, fluctuate, take, total*
2 Movement:
  (a) *go, run, sail, pass, trip, shuttle, alternate, oscillate, move*
  (b) *walk, passage, move, go*
3 Time:
  (a) *event, occur, begin, anytime, sometime,* (date) *and* (date)
  (b) *period, last, now and* ____, *stage, time, interval,* (date) *and* (date)
4 Other relationships:
  (a) *connection, alliance, meeting, agreement, point of contact, link, partnership, contact, union, cooperation, ties, collaboration, bond, merger, liaison*
  (b) *contest, struggle, interaction, conflict, showdown, love, tension, conversation, battle, row, trouble, competition, discussion, communication, exchange, problem, negotiation, argument, relation, relationship, trade, antagonism, quarrel*
  (c) *resemblances, parallel, overlap, similarity, analogy, same, similar*
  (d) *difference, imbalance, distinction, little in common, discrepancy, differentiate, distinguish, gulf, spread, gap, contrast, dissimilarity, rift, confusion, opposition*
  (e) *choice, comparison, little to choose*
5 Dividing or sharing:
  divide, share, balance, them, distribute, spread, division, split

B *Through*

1 Unimpeded motion:
  (a) *go, pass, move, put, send, travel, door, gate, tunnel, come*
  (b) *follow, route, journey, go, pass, town, village, room, world, park, city, way*
  (c) *water, darkness, air, space, area, crowd, spray, grass, dusk, run*
  (d) *pass, point, intersection*
  (e) *current, circuit, system, mind, body, brain, run, all, right*
  (f) *look, glance, go, list, files, book, pages, records, catalogue, papers, story, cupboard, drawers, pockets*
2 Penetration of a barrier or obstruction:
  barrier, grid, customs, break, burst, slip, cut, crack, get, scrape, help, go, test, examination, live, come, news, order, Bill, transaction, fall
3 Perception through an obstruction:
  look, peer, see, window, wall, hear, gap, listen, watch
4 Time:
  (a) *live, day, week, month, year, ages, life, meal, war, stage, period, phase*
  (b) *go, be, pass*
5 Agent–intermediary–instrument:
  meet, message, contact, operate, subsidiary, medium, available, planning, analysis
6 Causation:
  fear, neglect, flooding, cause, lack of, effort, struggle, negligence, ability

examples which occur, often on more than one occasion. The words
are organized according to the categories established in Tables 7.7
and 7.8. The functional analysis of *between* and *through* confirms
that locative senses of these words are quite frequent in the corpus.
However, other non-physical relationships are also very frequent
involving interaction, comparison, similarity, difference, agency,
causation and so on. In the case of *between*, non-locative uses
constitute a majority of the tokens. This finding is, of course,
consistent with the collocational information set out in Table 7.1.

The analysis also confirms that while both *between* and *through*
have static and dynamic literal locative senses, *through* is more
commonly used with a dynamic sense.

The proportions of the various subcategories identified in Tables
7.7 and 7.8 reflect the nature of one particular corpus. Spoken
English or other varieties might be expected to show differences in
the types and the relative proportion of tokens. However, a comparison with the semantic analysis of *between* and *through* contained
in West (1953), based on a completely different corpus, suggests
that the use of these words has been remarkably stable. West
divided the semantic functions into many fewer subcategories, and
his corpus was collected in the 1930s. When the proportions in
Tables 7.7 and 7.8 are reinterpreted in terms of West's analysis,
however, the results are comparable.

The analysis of the semantic functions in which *between* and
through occur in the LOB Corpus, and which are summarized in
Tables 7.7 to 7.9, suggests why these words may be difficult to learn
or use. For example, both are associated with movement, time and
with a variety of other relationships. The relationships differ but are
frequent and diverse. *Between* 4(b) (interaction) and *through* 5 and
6 (agent–intermediary–instrument; causation) together constitute
almost a quarter of all tokens and have complex semantic structures
involving abstractness and generalization.

Another source of difficulty may arise because *between* and
through can each function in contexts that appear to be semantically
contradictory. Examples include the following:

a similarity between	– *difference between*
a bond between	– *hostility between*
an understanding between	– *a split between*
get through (succeed)	– *fall through* (not succeed)

Similarly, although learners of English are sometimes told that *between* is used with two entities and is to be distinguished from *among* which is used with more than two, this distinction is often not made in the LOB Corpus. *Between* is frequently used where *among* might be expected, e.g.

(17)   We want it to obtain between non-graduates
(18)   [he] would help to establish an enduring peace between nations

The most comprehensive grammars and dictionaries already provide descriptively adequate accounts of the grammatical functions and possible meanings in context of *between* and *through*. The present corpus study goes beyond systemic possibility by adding to linguistic description a statistical dimension based on use in context. The use of such empirical information in contrast to the possible arbitrariness and unreliability of intuitive judgements is one contribution which corpus linguistics can make to language pedagogy. It is, of course, not easy to predict what particular quantitative information can be of pedagogical significance. Too much analysis can run counter to the necessary dynamic of language in use as a basis for pedagogy.

It would seem to be clear that *between* and *through*, like other structural words, are learnt not as representatives of word classes or as lexemes in isolation, but in association with other words. This corpus study demonstrates that while the two words share some functions, thus accounting in part for uncertainty in our intuitions or difficulties in learning, the company they keep and the major functions they serve differ very considerably. In making available such empirical information, corpus linguistics may thus both contribute to our understanding of psycholinguistic processes and also lead to improvements in pedagogical practices.

8 A mint of phrases

GÖRAN KJELLMER

8.1   'A mint of phrases' in Shakespeare

In *Love's Labour's Lost* Shakespeare introduces a character, Don
Adriano de Armado, who is described in the following words:

Our court, you know is haunted
With a refined traveller of Spain;
A man in all the world's new fashion planted,
That hath a mint of phrases in his brain;
One who the music of his own vain tongue
Doth ravish like enchanting harmony;
. . .
Armado is a most illustrious wight,
A man of fire-new words, fashion's own knight.
(Arden edition 1956, I, i, 161–77)

The Spaniard is bombastic and verbose; his letter to the King begins
'Great deputy, the welkin's vicegerent, and sole dominator of
Navarre, my soul's earth's God, and body's fostering patron' (I, i,
216–18). His language is ornate and overloaded and characterized
by a mixture of florid innovations, clichés and set phrases. In the
passage quoted, *mint* is used metaphorically in the sense 'place of
invention and fabrication' (Schmidt 1902). If Don Adriano has 'a
mint of phrases in his brain', this must mean that he is (exception-
ally) capable of producing and likely to use such rhetorical devices.
In what follows I shall attempt to demonstrate that any native
speaker of English (and, presumably, of any natural language) has
at his command 'a mint of phrases' in a much wider sense than
Shakespeare intended.

111

8.2   Types of set expressions

A large part of our mental lexicon consists of combinations of words that customarily co-occur.[1] The occurrence of one of the words in such a combination can be said to predict the occurrence of the other(s). Several types of combinations can be distinguished. If we attempt to establish a typology of the combinations, it must be realized, however, that the borderlines are often fuzzy, and that the categories will sometimes overlap.

First there are the fossilized phrases. One element of such a phrase will suggest the other(s) with great consistency. Unassimilated loans typically belong here, phrases like *Anno Domini, aurora borealis* and *nouveau riche*, but more genuinely English fossilized phrases also occur, such as *bubonic plague, Cocker Spaniel* and *be-all and end-all*. Variability in such phrases is exceptional. The only kind of variability that normally occurs in the predicted word (or 'collocate') is that represented by inflexional endings (*Cocker* suggests *Spaniel* or *Spaniels*). It will be noted that in all these phrases the first word is as 'predictive' as the last: *Anno* suggests *Domini* just as much as *Domini* suggests *Anno*, and *aurora* suggests *borealis* just as much as *borealis* suggests *aurora*, etc. Phrases of this kind could therefore be called 'right-and-left predictive'.

It is much more usual for fossilized phrases to be unidirectionally predictive. Consider the following combinations: *Artesian well, ballpoint pen, bonsai tree, boon companion, brussels sprouts, Gordian knot, Morse code, non-commissioned officer, pineal gland, sten gun, stumbling block, wellington boots. Artesian* suggests *well, ballpoint* suggests *pen* and *bonsai* suggests *tree*, but the process cannot be reversed; *well* can suggest a great many words with which it can co-occur, only one of which is *Artesian*, and similarly for the others. Phrases of this kind could therefore be called 'right-predictive'.

There is another kind of unidirectionally predictive fossilized phrases. *Ad infinitum, arms akimbo, deadly nightshade, from afar, full pelt, mint julep* and *open sesame* are fossilized in that one element suggests the other with great precision, but this time the last element suggests the first. For example, *ad* can be followed by a number of Latin nouns or pronouns in English (*absurdum, astra, hoc, lib, nauseam*, etc.), but *infinitum* can be preceded only by *ad*. This kind of phrase is hence 'left-predictive'.

What we have called fossilized phrases are thus sequences where the occurrence of one word almost unequivocally predicts the occurrence of another. In a second type of phrase, which we may call semi-fossilized, one word predicts a very limited number of words. The following sequences will illustrate the phenomenon: *Achilles heel/Achilles tendon, billy can/billy goat; by and by/by and large, caesarian operation/caesarian section, magnum bottle/magnum opus, moot point/moot question, nodding acquaintance/nodding terms, whipping boy/ whipping cream.* These are all right-predictive (*Achilles* predicts *heel* or *tendon*, etc.), but there are also occasional left-predictive cases, such as *go bail/ grant bail/ jump bail/ stand bail*, or *inferiority complex/ Oedipus complex/ persecution complex* (where *bail* thus suggests *go* or *grant* or *jump* or *stand*, etc.). It is essential here that the possible variants are lexically rather than functionally selected. If, say, the adjective *blue* can co-occur with any word answering a certain functional description (such as 'noun, concrete, . . .'), this is not enough to make the resulting combinations (*blue book, blue car, blue shirt,* etc.) semi-fossilized. The variants of a semi-fossilized phrase must make up a lexically specifiable and highly restricted set of words.

Idioms can be fossilized, but they characteristically belong to the semi-fossilized type. Typical examples are *have a weak/soft spot for, get off on the right/wrong foot, do badly/well for* (all discussed by Cowie and Mackin 1975: xix). Note that the traditional definition of idioms as 'groups of words with set meanings that cannot be calculated by adding up the separate meanings of the parts' does not set them apart from other phrases as a sharply defined subset. It is clearly more realistic to think of idioms in terms of a scale of idiomaticity, as is suggested by the discussion in Cowie and Mackin.

However, it is undeniable that our mental lexicon contains many more phrases than those belonging to the types discussed above. A third type, much more frequent than the ones we have discussed so far, consists of sequences of words that co-occur more often than their individual frequencies would lead us to expect. One of the words in such a sequence can be said to predict the other(s), as in the previous types, but 'prediction' will have to be interpreted more loosely. One word will tend to co-occur with one or a few out of a great number of words that can also co-occur with it. 'Tendency' is here a key concept. Such groups of words will here be called 'variable phrases'. In the fossilized and semi-fossilized types there is a high degree of cohesion between the members of a group; in this third type there is also cohesion, but of a less compelling kind. One set of such variable phrases consists of two or more lexical words, some of them also incorporating function words. Let us look at some examples: *glass of water, civilian clothes, classical music, loud and clear, close friend, go to college, in the years to come, feel comfortable, in the common experience of all.* For each of these, numerous sequences featuring one of the constituent members are possible both in theory and in practice, but unlike many of them the phrases just given can claim to be well established as groups and even enjoy lexemic status, simply by virtue of being more common. This is sometimes due to real-world circumstances – for instance, water is normally served in glasses rather than in mugs, cups, cans, goblets, beakers or tumblers in English-speaking countries, so *glass of water* can be expected to be better established in English than *mug of water, cup of water*, etc. for that reason alone. But just as often such factors are irrelevant: there is no real-world reason why *loud and clear* should always occur in that order (cf. ?*clear and loud*) or in that form (cf. ?*loud and manifest*, ?*loud and obvious*, ?*loud and intelligible*). It seems, then, that there is a tendency, independent of circumstances in the real world, for speakers of a language to arrange words in groups and to use the same arrangement whenever the need arises rather than to rearrange the words or to choose alternative ways of expression.

What could be regarded as a second set of variable phrases, although their variability is sometimes restricted, are established sequences of one lexical word and one or more function words. Although those combinations are mostly inconspicuous, they are a vital part of the lexicon, more so than the fossilized and semi-fossilized phrases. They help to lend structure to the lexicon, and are the ones that every learner of the language will need to learn before tackling the fossilized and semi-fossilized phrases. Such combinations are *a number of, a touch of, brought about by, for a change, his approach to, it appears that, it is obvious that, must admit that, out of action, their knowledge of, to apply to, to be appointed by*, and thousands of others. Their very inconspicuousness makes them fit for use in a variety of situations. The contrast in this respect with previous categories is striking; cf. *Anno Domini, artesian well* and *arms akimbo* on the one hand, and *a number of, a touch of, brought about by* on the other. It stands to reason that those in the latter category are more generally useful and more often called for than those in the former; they must be kept continually on tap by the speaker, as it were. Indeed, it is not until one considers this last type that the ubiquity and indispensability of set expressions become fully apparent.

8.3   Collocations in a prose sample

During the last few decades, large corpora of modern English text have been made available in computer-readable form. They represent many varieties of English and vary greatly in size. (For a survey of such corpora, see Taylor and Leech 1991.) The existence of these corpora enables anyone interested in ready-made phrases to investigate such aspects of their occurrence as their frequency, their distribution over text genres and their typology. It is important here that the individual character of each corpus is not lost sight of. Phrases occurring in a spoken corpus can be assumed to differ from those in a written one, and those in a British corpus may well differ from those in an American one, etc. One should also note, the lexical component of language being open-ended, that corpora inevitably supply only a sample of the words and phrases that are at the command of the language users as a group. The degree to which the phrases in a corpus are representative of those current in the language variety from which they are derived naturally increases with the size of the corpus.

However, if a corpus is to be used as a source of information about existing phrases each of which requires detailed analysis, very large corpora like the 20-million-word corpus assembled at Birmingham University under the direction of John M. Sinclair regrettably become unmanageable. It is fortunate, then, that more limited corpora, like the one-million-word American Brown Corpus or its British counterpart, the LOB Corpus, and even the London-Lund Corpus of Spoken English with about 500,000 words, although they are on the small side for a study of lexis, are none the less large enough to contain a considerable part of the English phrases in current use.

It was argued above that ready-made phrases are an important part of our linguistic make-up. Therefore it may not be unreasonable to hope that an inventory of such phrases drawn from one of the modern English corpora and established in a principled fashion will provide a window on our mental lexicon. On the other hand, it would be extravagant to claim that the inventory would be an accurate representation of (part of) the mental lexicon in any meaningful sense. This is partly because some of the items it contains are better established than others – there is a continuum from accidental combinations to universally recognized set phrases – and partly because the 'mental lexicon' will vary from one speaker to another. The inventory may nevertheless provide a rough sketch of the constitution of the mental lexicon in this general sense. It may therefore give an indication of the vital role set phrases or 'collocations' have to play in everyday communication.

In order to demonstrate the extent to which ordinary expository prose is dependent on ready-made phrases, a sample from a prose text will be examined below against the background of a corpus of collocations extracted from the Brown Corpus. In this collocational corpus, which I shall refer to as the Gothenburg Corpus of Collocations (GCC), collocations are defined as recurring sequences that have grammatical structure. Only those sequences that recur *in identical form* have been included. (Further information can be found in Kjellmer 1982, 1987 and 1990.) From now on, the term *collocation* will be used in the sense of structured patterns which recur in identical form. A total of 85,000 collocational types make up the collocational corpus. As the prose text I have chosen a passage from Jan Svartvik's *The Evans Statements* (1968), a fascinating linguistic suspense story. In his conclusion, Svartvik says (p. 46):

Summing up, we must consider at least three factors that will thwart all hope of reaching any firm conclusions for this study. The first is the small size of the material which imposes heavy restrictions on the choice of possible criteria; the second, the highly artificial linguistic situation which produced it: a policeman, probably of limited education and subject to all kinds of prescriptive pressures in his written English, giving a graphic rendering of the speech of an illiterate; the third, our inadequate knowledge of how language is used in different situations, which poses problems in the interpretation of our results.

In this piece there occur a number of the collocations in GCC. If we italicize them, the passage will look like this:

Summing up, we *must consider   at least   three factors* that will thwart *all* HOPE *of* reaching any firm conclusions for *this study*. *The first* is the small *size* OF *the material* which imposes heavy restrictions on *the choice of* possible criteria; *the second*, the highly artificial linguistic situation which *produced it: a policeman*, probably of limited education and *subject to all kinds of* prescriptive pressures in his written English, giving a graphic *rendering of the speech of* an illiterate; *the third*, our inadequate *knowledge of* how language *is* USED *in* different situations, which poses *problems in the interpretation of* our results.

(Capitalized words indicate overlap of collocations as they occur in GCC. For example, there is one collocational type *all hope*, and another type *hope of*; *all* HOPE *of* therefore represents *all hope* and *hope of*.)

It will be noticed at once that the italicized collocations are predominantly of the variable type. It is obvious that collocations play an important part in the linguistic build-up of the passage. One is left with the impression that the exposition moves from one set expression to the next in a hop, skip and jump fashion, the intervening elements being non-collocational and therefore freely variable. However, since the sequences marked as collocations derive from the one-million-word Brown Corpus, it should again be pointed out that the size of the Brown Corpus is rather small for a study of lexis. We may confidently assume that a collection of collocations extracted from a larger corpus of English would have been more representative of the collocational repertoire of an average speaker of English, who will be conditioned in his stringing together of lexical items to a greater extent than a list of collocations from a one-million-word corpus would suggest. This very largely explains why one's intuitions about what collocations there are in the piece may occasionally be at variance with the list of those included as collocations in GCC. Let us therefore take a look at the intervening (and, in the case of the first sentence, introductory) elements. How freely variable are they?

Summing up in the first sentence is not in GCC. The sequence (in that form) does occur in the Brown Corpus, but it is recorded only once and thus (because it is non-recurrent) does not qualify for inclusion as a collocation in GCC. However, other members of the same lexeme, *sums up* and *summed up*, are included as collocations. Further, a host of formally analogous collocations are represented in GCC, collocations such as *bounding up, breaking up, building up, catching up, clearing up, coming up*, etc., one of them being the semantically related *adding up*. If we take into account the principles inherent in the English verbal system as well as the fact that the other members of the same lexeme, *sums up* and *summed up*, occur as collocations (in addition to the fact that formally parallel and, in at least one case, semantically related collocations occur in the corpus), the chances that *summing up* also exists as a collocation in the mental lexicon of English speakers seem almost overwhelming.

Will thwart, a little further on in the sentence, is not in GCC but a great many combinations of *will* + infinitive are, among them *will prevent, will reduce* and *will stop*, which are all semantically related to *will thwart*. One might therefore assume that English speakers in general have *will thwart* as a variable collocation in their lexicon. (Note that we cannot describe the variable collocation simply as '*will* + infinitive', since collocations are lexically selected. With the present definition of collocation, a sequence representing a grammatical pattern is admitted as a collocation only if it meets certain lexical conditions.)

Although the next few words, *all hope of*, are accounted for in GCC (in the form of *all hope* and *hope of*), there is no *hope of reaching*. On the other hand, *hope of getting* is there (and so, incidentally, is the antonymous *fear of making*, a parallel construction of the antonym of *hope*). There is thus a pattern into which *hope of reaching* can fit.

It is doubtless an indication of the limited size of the Brown Corpus that *reach conclusions* is not attested as a collocation,[2] but there is a collocation in GCC, *reach a verdict*, which affords a semantic parallel.

As for *firm conclusions*, finally, which is not in GCC, there is a collocation *firm conviction* in the Brown Corpus, but it is doubtful if that phrase can be regarded as a model for *firm conclusions* because of the lack of semantic parallelism.

In this first sentence of our extract, the great majority of words thus belong to one collocational pattern or other, either because the groups in which they occur have already been classified as collocations on the basis of the criteria for inclusion in GCC, or because those groups have semantic and formal parallels among the groups accepted as collocations in GCC. If we indicate by means of superscript collocations, taken from GCC, the patterns and parallels that seem relevant to the whole of the passage, the result will be as follows (no parallels have been given for the collocations that already exist in GCC).

adding   up
summed   up
sums   up
Summing up, we *must consider at least three factors*

    will prevent   reach .... a verdict
    will reduce   fear of making
    will stop   hope of getting   (firm conviction)
that will thwart *all* HOPE *of* reaching any firm conclusions

                the ...... size of
      The other is   great size
for *this study*. *The first* is the small *size* OF *the material*

    imposed .... on   possible outcomes
          other restrictions   possible criteria
        similar restrictions   other   criteria
which imposes heavy restrictions on *the choice of* possible criteria;

      the .... military situation
      the .... political situation
      the .... present situation
      highly individualistic
      highly sensitive
      highly speculative
the second, **the highly artificial linguistic situation**

                    of higher education
                    of vocational education
                    limited knowledge
                    limited application
which *produced it: a policeman*, probably of limited education

    subject to .... limitations
            economic   pressures
            normal   pressures
            social   pressures
            strong   pressures
and *subject to all kinds of* prescriptive pressures

written notice   of

in the written language   of THE LANGUAGE of

in .... English gave .... evidence of

his .... English given a .... demonstration

in his written English, giving a graphic *rendering of the speech of*

our .... knowledge

an individual(ist)   their   .... knowledge of

an intellectual   limited   knowledge of

an invalid   through   knowledge of

an illiterate; *the third,* **our inadequate** *knowledge of*

under different circumstances

in   some   situations

how language *is* USED *in*   **different situations, which poses**

of our experience

of the results

problems in the interpretation of **our results.**

Our first impression, that the text consists of freely variable words between fixed combinations, will clearly need to be modified. Even the words occurring between those combinations constitute groups whose form and order are likely to be conditioned in varying degrees by patterns of collocability. Note that this does not mean that the analogical force of existing patterns is irresistible. Analogy is a forceful factor but, for one thing, its presence or absence is not a plus or minus affair. Analogy may be variably present and may be felt more acutely by some speakers than by others (cf. *firm conviction* vs *firm conclusions* above). The concept of 'semantic parallelism', which I believe is operative here, is in itself relative in character. For another thing, the force of well-established collocational habits regularly counteracts the force of analogy: we neither clean our hands nor wash our teeth, though analogy might suggest both.[3] However, it is eminently plausible to regard existing collocational patterns as holding out the possibilities from which the language user can make his final choice. The chances are that less well-established groups of words will be made to conform to those patterns.

So it seems that collocations cannot be said to make up a well-demarcated category in the same way as single-word lexemes. As in the case of the idioms above, we will do well to think in terms of a continuum. At one end of such a collocational continuum we would find the established collocations (including a great many idioms). Examples from the Svartvik passage could be *subject to* and *all kinds of*. At the other end we would find sequences of doubtful cohesion, like *possible criteria* or *linguistic situation*. As we move towards the latter end of the scale, a productive element comes increasingly into play. At this end we no longer merely reproduce set phrases, we rather operate productively within certain lexical limits. The limits are there because as long as we stay within the collocational continuum the selection of collocates is lexically restricted; in other words, the combination of the items of a sequence is conditioned by non-structural factors in addition to the structural ones that generally regulate our linguistic behaviour. At the productive end of the scale the distinction between collocational and non-collocational sequences of words will be blurred from the point of view of the language system although perhaps clear from the point of view of the individual speaker – different speakers will have different intuitions here depending on their linguistic experience, their professional training, reading habits, social life, etc.

8.4 A driving analogy

The concept of predictability was seen to be important, if not crucial, to the discussion of a collocational typology above. Some recent work in this field is relevant here. In two articles, Jean Aitchison and John Sinclair both deal with questions of cohesiveness and predictability in language. In Aitchison (1987) the focus is on the representation of words in our mental lexicon: do we make them up from an inventory of discrete morphemes or are they stored in the lexicon as units to be used when the occasion arises? Her interest thus centres on the question of whether, and if so how, morphemes combine to form words in the mental lexicon. Sinclair (1987a) is concerned with larger entities and distinguishes two principles – the open-choice principle on the one hand, where the language user makes a series of choices, the only restraint being grammaticalness, and the idiom principle on the other, where the user 'has available to him or her a large number of semi-preconstructed phrases that constitute single choices, even though they might appear to be analysable into segments' (p. 320). Sinclair is therefore interested in whether, and if so how, words combine to form higher units in the mental lexicon. In their different fields, Aitchison and Sinclair arrive at strikingly similar views. Aitchison makes use of a bus-or-taxi analogy, buses representing speakers using ready-made combinations of linguistic elements (morphemes in her case) and taxis representing speakers using discrete elements capable of being combined into larger structures. She concludes that 'the evidence outlined here suggests that people try to be buses. They turn into taxis only if the bus-route is unsatisfactory. Humans start by using memory, and routine possibilities. If this proves inadequate, they turn to computation' (p. 14). Sinclair says, 'For normal texts we can put forward the proposal that the first mode [of interpretation] to be applied is the idiom principle since most of the text will be interpretable by this principle. Whenever there is good reason, the interpretive process switches to the open choice principle, and quickly back again' (p. 324). To develop the vehicular analogy somewhat, I will here suggest that an act of speaking or writing is like driving a car. When we are driving a car, we have a goal most of the time (although we may occasionally drive for the sake of driving). To get to our goal we have to abide by the traffic rules and follow certain stretches of road. If we know the lay of the land reasonably well, we do not stop at every street corner to make fresh decisions, but we do have to make minor decisions at most crossroads and major decisions at main junctions. There is only a limited number of ways of reaching a given goal, and few personal variations ordinarily occur (like driving across a lawn, or on the pavement). In a similar fashion we normally have a goal in speaking or writing (although again we may speak for the sake of speaking). We have to obey the rules laid down by the grammar of our language and we normally follow certain 'lexical stretches', i.e. well-established sequences of words. If we speak the language reasonably well, we do not stop at every word or every few words to get our bearings; a lexical stretch will often link up or overlap with other lexical stretches that will take us further along our chosen path. Decisions will of course have to be taken, minor ones at the 'crossroads', at breaks between lexical stretches, and major ones at the 'main junctions', where one train of thought succeeds another. Again, few personal deviations from the established pattern occur, such as choosing unexpected words or ungrammatical forms. So, just as in driving, we use semi-automated routines in speaking and writing; both traffic rules/grammatical rules and a road network/a set of lexical stretches are essential to ensure adequate communication.

8.5 Collocations manipulated

If as speakers of a language we thus very largely make use of chunks of prefabricated matter that allow us to move swiftly through the discourse, and if as listeners we expect other speakers to behave in the same way, this implies that anyone who happens to manipulate this mechanism of language will create something of a surprise effect. That effect may be both unintentional and unwelcome, as when learners of English piece together perfectly grammatical but totally un-English sentences (Pawley and Syder 1983), or when native speakers of English take the wrong turning and produce, for example, *an arduous lover* for *an ardent lover* or *the electric roll* for *the electoral roll* (Aitchison 1987: 9). On the other hand, deviations from a collocational norm can be used intentionally with a definite end in view. 'How every fool can play upon the word!' says Lorenzo in *The Merchant of Venice* (III, v, 40), to quote Shakespeare again, and it is true that such manipulations are mostly used for humorous purposes. Shakespeare's own clowns and fools make abundant use of the trick, but it seems to be equally popular with the authors, journalists and copywriters of today. For example, a West End farce in the mid-1980s by Ray Cooney was called *Run for your Wife* (advertised with a critic's comment: 'Should run for life'). In *Changing Places*, David Lodge describes 'the transformation of the dim Rummidge lecturer into Visiting Professor Philip Swallow, member of the academic jet-set, ready to carry English culture to the far side of the globe at the drop of an airline ticket' (p. 37). Journalists are fond of the device: an article in *The Times* describing a blunder committed by Neil Kinnock and involving Michael Foot was headlined 'Neil put Foot in it' (8 March 1985), and a feature article in *The Observer* about Mexico was called 'Not exactly my cup of tequila' (12 November 1989). Advertisements abound in this kind of facetiousness. A slogan for season tickets in the London Underground in 1985 ran 'A ticket every day is money down the tube', and a book about the use of a Macintosh computer, which is operated by means of a so-called mouse, is described as a 'comprehensive and systematic compilation of "word of mouse" Macintosh information' in an advertisement in *MacUser* (1986/9: 7).

As these examples show, the result can be startling or comical or both, if relatively stable collocations are modified so as to include other elements than those which normally make up the collocations, or to substitute unexpected for expected elements. (The substitution of the unexpected for the expected is, of course, the essence of comic art.) In the examples above, the readers' familiarity with the collocations *run for one's life, at the drop of a hat, put one's foot in it, (not) one's cup of tea, money down the drain* and *word of mouth* is taken for granted. The use of the device can therefore be seen as an indication both of the extent to which the collocations in question are stable and predictable and of the unquestioned position of collocations as an integral part of an English-speaker's proficiency.

8.6   Collocations and the language learner

The 'collocational' way in which large parts of the native speaker's vocabulary are organized has important implications for second and foreign language learners. It is instructive to compare the output of only moderately fluent native speakers – diffident, uncertain or hesitant speakers – with that of only moderately fluent learners of the same language. While the typical moderately fluent native speaker makes considerable hesitation pauses between often quite long sequences of words (cf. Pawley and Syder 1983: 200ff), the typical moderately fluent learner pauses after every two or three words. It seems reasonable to believe that the difference between them in this regard can be ascribed largely to a difference in the automation of collocations. The native speaker has acquired an automatic command of substantial portions of speech and uses his pauses to plan one or more thought units ahead. In building his utterances he makes use of large prefabricated sections. The learner, on the other hand, having automated few collocations, continually has to create structures that he can only hope will be acceptable to native speakers; he, too, will of course have to plan his thought units, but we can assume that his pauses are to a great extent used for decision-making at this fairly trivial word-structure level. His building material is individual bricks rather than prefabricated sections. So even if he is not diffident, uncertain or hesitant he will inevitably be hampered in his progress, and his output will often seem contrived or downright unacceptable to native ears. Analogous phenomena can be observed in his written output.

One obvious solution to the learner's problems would seem to lie in a new approach to the teaching and learning of foreign languages: lexical items should not be taught and learnt in isolation but only in their proper contexts. This means shifting the emphasis from individual words to the collocations in which they normally occur. Some teachers, schools and maybe even school systems have already done this, but I would suggest that a radical change from conventional methods is needed in a great many places. It is essential that vocabulary learning, from a very elementary level and upwards, should focus on how the words of the target language are actually used. 'Lexical phrases are in fact basic to language performance,' insist Nattinger and DeCarrico (1989: 119), who propose ways in which they could be taught.[4] As our brief investigation of the extract from *The Evans Statements* has shown, most words, however inconspicuous, are structured collocationally in one way or another, which indicates that a collocational approach to word learning is desirable in every sector of the vocabulary and at every stage of learning. This may be particularly important even at fairly elementary levels of vocabulary learning, when the learner is still chiefly preoccupied with high-frequency words.[5]

Pupils and students who have acquired 'collocational learning habits' at an early stage can be expected with some confidence to pursue their further studies of lexis in a more fruitful way than would otherwise have been the case. It is only when the student has acquired a good command of a very considerable number of collocations that the creative element can be relied on to produce phrases that are acceptable and natural to the native speaker.

8.7   Summary

The mental lexicon of any native speaker contains single-word units as well as phrasal units or collocations. Mastery of both types is an essential part of the linguistic equipment of the speaker or writer and enables him to move swiftly and with little effort through his exposition from one prefabricated structure to the next. A decisive characteristic of collocations is the predictable nature of their constituents: the presence of one of them will predict the presence of the other(s). While predictability is thus an important element of collocations, it is not unconditional. It varies from being total or near-total, and recognized as such by all speakers, to being only partial and recognized by some speakers but not by others. By the same token, collocations range from well-established and integrated phrases to doubtfully cohesive sequences of words. There is therefore no generally valid cut-off point between collocations and accidental groupings of words. At the total predictability end of this spectrum there is little or no room for manoeuvre by the language user – each collocation has a given form which he has to accept if he is to use it – but at the other end a creative or productive element comes into play, all the time conditioned by the selectional restrictions that are defining factors of collocations. Contraventions of those rules are not normally tolerated, except for humorous or artistic purposes, which should be a caveat for learners and teachers of a second language.

So anyone who can be said to be proficient in a language has command of a great number of set phrases as well as skill in producing acceptable variants within the limits drawn up by the selectional rules. To come back to Shakespeare once again, Don Adriano de Armado is not alone in having a mint of phrases in his brain.

Notes

[1] The problems involved in defining 'word' are notorious (see for instance Carter 1987: 3–14). In their discussion of the concept, Sinclair and Renouf (1988: 146f) make the point that treating word forms in a language course in terms of lemmas (e.g. discussing *go, goes, going, went, gone* in terms of the lemma GO) may well be misleading since the individual forms often differ with regard to meaning and behaviour. This point is clearly relevant to a study, such as this, of the combinatory properties of lexis. In the present paper a 'word' is seen as any one of the manifestations a lemma may have.

[2] There is one instance of *reached a conclusion* and another of *reached some predictable conclusions*, neither of which hence achieves collocational status.

[3] Cf. the following word groups (quoted from Bolinger 1975: 103–4):

good likelihood	strong likelihood	*high likelihood
*good probability	strong probability	high probability
good possibility	strong possibility	*high possibility
good chance	*strong chance	*high chance

We are common enemies.
?We are mutual enemies.
*We are common friends.
We are mutual friends.

4 'Lexical phrases' is the term used by Nattinger and DeCarrico (1989: 118) for 'multi-word lexical phenomena that exist somewhere between the traditional poles of lexicon and syntax'.

5 Cf. Sinclair and Renouf (1988: 155) on a suggested lexical syllabus:

Almost paradoxically, the lexical syllabus does not encourage the piecemeal acquisition of a large vocabulary, especially initially. Instead, it concentrates on making full use of the words that the learner already has, at any particular stage. It teaches that there is far more general utility in the recombination of known elements than in the addition of less easily usable items. . . . Other languages may be different; English makes excessive use, e.g. through phrasal verbs, of its most frequent words, and so they are well worth learning.

9   Collocational frameworks in English

ANTOINETTE RENOUF and JOHN McH. SINCLAIR

9.1   Introduction

In the OSTI Project (Sinclair *et al*. 1970) it was demonstrated that grammatical words have collocates, and in our 1988 paper on the Lexical Syllabus we went on to observe that common grammatical words also combine with each other in various ways. At that stage, we briefly pointed to the discontinuous pairings, or 'frameworks', in which they occurred, and to the tendency of these frameworks to 'enclose' characteristic groupings of words. In this paper we should like to move on to investigate aspects of the framework phenomenon in a more detailed and, where appropriate, quantitative way, and to raise questions that seem to us to warrant future attention.

Göran Kjellmer has defined collocation in a 1987 paper as follows: 'a sequence of words that occurs more than once in identical form . . . and which is grammatically well-structured'. In this paper we are also looking at collocations of a type, although our definition differs from Kjellmer's. Our 'frameworks' consist of a discontinuous sequence of two words, positioned at one word remove from each other; they are therefore not grammatically self-standing; their well-formedness is dependent on what intervenes. At this early stage of enquiry we are also considering single occurrences of completed frameworks, in order to be able to spot generalities that might otherwise be lost. A group of single occurrences may been seen to be constituting a class, and in frameworks of this kind, classes are to be expected.

Co-occurrences in the language most commonly occur among grammatical words, far more commonly than among combinations

128

of grammatical and lexical words. So it would seem justifiable to study their patternings with a view to understanding more about the phenomenon. The 'framework' is an integral part of the language, yet it is currently not accounted for in descriptions of the language. In grammar, it lies somewhere between word and group; in lexis, it is missed by conventional definitions of collocation, lexical item and phrase; semantics has no means of dealing with such grammatical co-occurrences, either as two individual items or as a unit with interdependent meaning.

Our focus of study will be on the framework and its intermediate word, or 'collocate'. The frameworks that we have selected consist of different pairings of high-frequency grammatical words:

$$a + ? + of \qquad be + ? + to \qquad for + ? + of$$
$$an + ? + of \qquad too + ? + to \qquad had + ? + of$$
$$many + ? + of$$

The first two, $a + ? + of$ and $an + ? + of$, have been chosen because we know them to be very productive, and the remainder represents a range of lexical combinations.

Our investigation will be based on two sections of the Birmingham Collection of English Text: a one-million-word corpus of spoken British English, and a 10-million-word corpus of written British English.

9.2 Analysis

We shall begin by looking at a profile of the frequencies of occurrence of the different frameworks and their collocates.

Table 9.1 Frequency of occurrence of frameworks

Framework	Spoken corpus			Written corpus		
	Tokens	Types	Ratio	Tokens	Types	Ratio
$a + ? + of$	3830	585	6:1	25416	2848	8.9:1
$an + ? + of$	208	94	2.2:1	2362	479	4.9:1
$be + ? + to$	790	216	3.6:1	5457	871	6.3:1
$too + ? + to$	59	36	1.6:1	1122	367	3:1
$for + ? + of$	127	56	2.3:1	1230	332	3.7:1
$many + ? + of$	63	36	1.8:1	402	159	2.5:1

The data shown in Table 9.1 allow us to make two observations. The first relates to the type–token ratio for each framework. There is, on average, a very high rate of recurrence of types in proportion to the number of framework tokens. This indicates that the frameworks are highly selective of their collocates. It is, of course, also consistent with the frequent usage of the words involved, and the fact that shorter word combinations, such as triplets, are proportionally more recurrent in text than longer ones (cf. Altenberg 1990b and Renouf, forthcoming).

The second noticeable feature is the differing degree of productivity of the different frameworks. This is not attributable simply to the absolute frequency of the individual collocate types. If we find that the *a* + ? + *of* and *an* + ? + *of* frameworks attract nouns as their middle element, the fact that these frameworks, taken together, are the most productive may be explicable in grammatical terms, with reference to Kjellmer's observation (1990: 167) that nouns have a high 'constructional tendency'.

To shed further light on this, we shall look at the commonest triplets formed by each of these frameworks. Tables 9.2 to 9.6 present the top twenty types in each case (twenty is chosen as a matter of convenience).

Table 9.2 Collocational types for frameworks *a/an* + ? + *of* in the written corpus

a + ? + *of*		*an* + ? + *of*	
1322 lot	320 pair	125 act	38 image
864 kind	302 member	77 example	33 examination
762 number	293 group	73 average	31 account
685 couple	268 result	71 expression	29 atmosphere
550 matter	222 part	66 air	29 idea
451 sort	216 variety	58 element	28 instrument
438 series	205 state	54 understanding	27 age
415 piece	175 bottle	45 extension	23 indication
379 bit	174 man	39 area	22 impression
356 sense	174 quarter	38 hour	22 object

These frameworks attract a range of collocates that are both similar and different. They are all nouns in the broadest sense, but of different types, and we shall look at the classes that are represented a little later on. Within these particular frameworks, the order of

Table 9.3 Order of occurrence of the top twenty *a/an* + ? + *of* collocates as
items in the written corpus

a + ? + *of*				*an* + ? + *of*			
10639	man	1996	bit	2826	air	770	image
4412	part	1322	result	2499	idea	716	understanding
4212	kind	1138	piece	2402	age	686	object
2836	state	1105	couple	1814	act	550	impression
2731	sense	1019	bottle	1802	example	429	atmosphere
2727	matter	900	member	1596	area	421	examination
2646	group	766	series	1578	hour	352	element
2540	number	615	variety	872	account	217	extension
2505	lot	589	pair	849	expression	190	instrument
2150	sort	490	quarter	813	average	131	indication

frequency in which the collocates occur does not correspond with
their ranking in the same corpus as individual items, which is shown
in Table 9.3.

The discrepancy in the ordering of the lists in Tables 9.2 and 9.3
is informative. It indicates the hierarchy of attraction between
the collocates and the *a/an* + ? + *of* framework; for instance, the
promotion of *lot* to the top of the list indicates that *a lot of* is the
tightest collocation, and so on. To see how significant the triplets
are in the language as a whole, we turn to Table 9.4. Here we
indicate the proportion of corpus occurrences accounted for by the
words in their function as collocates in the *a/an* + ? + *of* framework.

Table 9.4 Proportion of occurrences in the written corpus contributed by
words as *a/an* + ? + *of* collocates

a + ? + *of*				*an* + ? + *of*			
%	Collocate	%	Collocate	%	Collocate	%	Collocate
62	couple	21	sort	21	extension	5	image
57	series	20	matter	18	indication	4	account
54	pair	20	result	17	element	4	example
53	lot	19	bit	15	instrument	4	impression
36	piece	17	bottle	9	average	3	object
36	quarter	13	sense	8	examination	2	area
35	variety	11	group	8	expression	2	hour
34	member	7	state	8	understanding	2	air
30	number	5	part	7	act	1	idea
21	kind	2	man	7	atmosphere	1	age

These percentages show how central to the language the *a* + ? + *of* framework is. For instance, they show that the triplet *a couple of* accounts for 62 per cent of all the occurrences of *couple* in the corpus, that *a series of, a pair of* and *a lot of* each account for over 50 per cent of the total corpus instances of *series, pair* and *lot*, and so on.

We also see that *an* + ? + *of* makes a significant impact in somewhat different areas of the lexis, such as nominalization. The triplet *an extension of* accounts for 21 per cent of the total corpus instances of *extension,* while *an indication of, an element of* and *an instrument of* each contribute 15 per cent, or more of the total corpus occurrences for the individual words. However, these percentages do not quite match the high degree of influence exerted by the previous framework. It is not clear why this is so – whether the selection of this framework is governed by phonological, lexical, psycholinguistic or other factors. Whatever the reason, other frameworks will doubtless prove to be more or less central according to this statistical criterion.

It might be interesting at this point to move on and compare the triplets in Table 9.2 with those created by other types of frameworks. It is predictable, perhaps, that *a* and *an*, on the one hand, and *of*, on the other, will attract nouns in their immediate environment, and Sinclair (1989) has endorsed this in a study of corpus data relating to *of*. We shall look at the *be/too* + ? + *to* frameworks to see which types of items fill their slots and what grammatical explanation there might be for the selection of those items. In the left-hand environment of *to*, the items shown in Table 9.5 occur at the top level. Again, only the top twenty types are provided in each case.

Table 9.5 Collocational types for *be/too* + ? + *to* in the written corpus

be + ? + to		too + ? + to	
1108 able	56 forced	67 late	17 early
171 allowed	53 necessary	65 much	16 hard
119 expected	50 glad	40 young	15 busy
91 said	48 given	38 easy	15 ready
79 put	47 done	27 small	14 dark
74 made	46 ready	26 close	13 big
71 prepared	45 seen	25 tired	12 long
70 possible	40 better	22 weak	12 poor
67 used	40 brought	21 good	12 proud
57 unable	39 difficult	18 old	11 far

Both lists in Table 9.5 contain a preponderance of adjectival items, but only one of these is shared, namely *ready*. In the first list, several of the adjectives are of the verbal kind, such as *prepared*, whereas those in the second, with the exception of *tired*, are, non-verbal. The difference in these selections shows that they are not governed by *to* alone but by the combined influence of the framework pair. In some cases, however, there seems to be a closer collocational pull exerted by one of the pair on some items rather than others. For example, in the framework *too* + ? + *to, to* would be able to collocate in the absence of *too* with *easy, hard, good, close, ready* and *proud*: (a) *easy to, hard to, good to, close to, ready to and proud to,* but not with the other items, except in a marked way: (b) ? *late to,* ? *much to,* ? *young to,* ? *small to,* ? *tired to,* etc.

A number of overlapping grammatical categories occur in the environment of Group (a), so that a grammatical explanation is hard to find. It seems that Group (b) combinations do not take cataphoric *it*, whereas *easy, good* and *hard* do in Group (a) (e.g. 'it is easy to do it' corresponding to 'to do it is easy'); that *close* has a different complementation pattern, and so on. A semantic explanation might be that the word *to* in Group (b) has a 'condition of purpose' sense of 'for this purpose to be achieved', so that *It's too late to save him* can be paraphrased as 'It's too late for the purpose of saving him to be achieved', whereas *He's too proud to ask for help* does not paraphrase as 'He's too proud for the purpose of asking for help to be achieved'. More study is needed to establish the precise set of constraints operating here, but one begins to get a feeling that it is the collocational frameworks that dominate, and that somehow the grammar has developed to accommodate their use.

By way of comparison with the framework extracts offered in Tables 9.2 and 9.5 above, three others pairing *of* with high-frequency words are offered in Table 9.6. Grammatically speaking, these three frameworks attract collocates of the word classes that one would expect: nouns for *many* + ? + *of*, verbs for *had* + ? + *of*, and quantifiers or nouns for *for* + ? + *of*. However, there is a degree of overlap that is perhaps surprising. The common elements are chiefly quantifiers and abstract, 'support' nouns (see Sinclair's classification later). This is partly indicative of the influence of *of* in its specifying function, and also that these frameworks share some high-frequency items which, by definition, collocate widely. Actual items that occur

Table 9.6 Collocational types for *for/many/had* + ? + *of* in the written corpus

for + ? + *of*		*many* + ? + *of*	
118 most	28 much	28 thousands	8 ways
65 all	26 each	28 years	7 aspects
65 one	26 those	24 kinds	7 species
57 fear	24 want	24 parts	6 hundreds
41 both	23 thousands	19 millions	6 types
40 some	19 any	9 cases	6 varieties
39 lack	17 signs	9 hours	5 others
32 many	14 control	9 members	4 details
31 reasons	13 purposes	8 examples	4 forms
28 hundreds	11 out	8 more	4 points

had + ? + *of*	
31 enough	8 dreamed
30 plenty	7 said
29 thought	7 something
23 heard	7 visions
20 one	6 lots
19 died	6 seen
17 spoken	5 made
15 been	5 moments
12 none	5 read
10 some	4 hundreds

in all three of these top-frequency listings are shown in Table 9.7.

At the top levels of frequency, there is generally quite a high degree of correspondence between the framework listings from the written and spoken corpora. A fairly representative sample of those we have examined is *many* + ? + *of*, shown in Table 9.8 (with shared items in italics).

Table 9.7 Shared collocates for *many/had/for* + ? + *of* in the written corpus

Collocate	*many* + ? + *of*	*had* + ? + *of*	*for* + ? + *of*
one		20	65
some		10	40
lots		6	3
many	1	1	32
hundreds	6	4	28
thousands	28	1	23
millions	19		7
all		3	66

Table 9.8 The·commonest collocational types within the framework
           many + ? + of

(a) *The spoken corpus*

7 *members*	2 *sort*	1 *heads*	1 out
6 *hundreds*	2 *tens*	1 *historians*	1 *people*
4 *parts*	2 *thousands*	1 languages	1 *pieces*
3 *examples*	2 *ways*	1 *layers*	1 *schools*
3 *millions*	1 acres	1 lessons	1 sources
3 *aspects*	1 *cases*	1 *many*	1 *things*
2 *branches*	1 *citizens*	1 *men*	1 *units*
2 facets	1 *countries*	1 *more*	1 varieties
2 *kinds*	1 er	1 *other*	1 *years*

(b) *The written corpus*

28 *thousands*	2 *schools*	1 dozens	1 perils
28 *years*	2 scores	1 echoes	1 periods
24 *kinds*	2 sheets	1 elements	1 photographs
24 *parts*	2 teachers	1 even	1 pictures
19 *millions*	2 variants	1 evidences	1 portraits
9 *cases*	2 volumes	1 expressions	1 possibilities
9 hours	2 walks	1 families	1 programmes
9 *members*	1 accounts	1 feet	1 qualities
8 *examples*	1 activities	1 fewer	1 races
8 *more*	1 advertisements	1 fields	1 rains
8 *ways*	1 advocates	1 foreigners	1 relatives
7 *aspects*	1 ambiguities	1 frames	1 relics
7 species	1 attitudes	1 friends	1 reports
6 *hundreds*	1 bales	1 gardeners	1 reservations
6 types	1 bands	1 glimpses	1 results
6 varieties	1 bells	1 gradations	1 scraps
5 others	1 billions	1 *heads*	1 shades
4 details	1 bottles	1 herds	1 *sort*
4 forms	1 boxes	1 hues	1 spheres
4 points	1 brands	1 imprints	1 springs
4 problems	1 busloads	1 institutions	1 studies
4 stories	1 calabashes	1 investors	1 subvarieties
4 weeks	1 categories	1 items	1 tablets
3 areas	1 centuries	1 kilos	1 taken
3 *branches*	1 characteristics	1 laws	1 tales
3 changes	1 children	1 lighthouses	1 *tens*
3 features	1 cities	1 *many*	1 *things*
3 *layers*	1 *citizens*	1 matters	1 think
3 *people*	1 clones	1 *men*	1 thoughts
3 sections	1 colours	1 methods	1 times
2 as	1 communes	1 miles	1 town
2 causes	1 components	1 mistakes	1 treasures
2 discussions	1 copies	1 modes	1 tricks
2 gallons	1 *countries*	1 moons	1 *units*
2 months	1 courses	1 necklaces	1 uses
2 opportunities	1 days	1 opponents	1 variations
2 pairs	1 descriptions	1 pages	1 victims
2 permutations	1 disapproved	1 paintings	1 virtues
2 *pieces*	1 discomforts	1 parents	1 works
2 portions	1 divisions	1 patrons	

Obviously the written corpus data are more extensive and make use of a wider range of lexis, the precise nature of which depends on the particular framework pair.

At this point we return to one of our first frameworks, *an* + ? + *of*, as a focus for further investigation. This framework offers a more manageable body of data than does its *a* + ? + *of* counterpart. A first observation concerns the kinds of words that complete the triplet *an* + ? + *of*. We have already noted, in Table 9.2, that the commonest of them are nouns, and the remainder are also. We shall attempt to classify all of them that occur ten times or more, in a tentative way. For this purpose we shall draw on Sinclair's provisional, and largely functional, classification of nouns preceding *of* (1989). The collocates in the *an* + ? + *of* framework are obviously a subset of these, and all fall within Sinclair's subcategory of 'N1 in a double-headed nominal group'. Sinclair divides this subcategory again, into classes of noun 1(a), 1(b), 1(c), in which the N1 is in some sense subordinate to the N2 (in which case Sinclair argues that the N2 is functionally the head of the nominal group), and classes of noun (2), (2a), (2b), in which neither N1 nor N2 seems to be 'pivotal or dominant', and the nominal group is truly double-headed. The classes of noun that are applicable in this study are as follows.

(1)   N1 in nominal group of which N2 is head
(1a)   *Measurement* of the second
        noun in a nominal group
        (1aii) lexically rich quantifiers   – *ounce, article*
(1b)   *Focus* on the second noun in a
        nominal group
        (1bi)   lexis naming part of N2   – *edge, end, part*
        (1bii) lexis specifying part of
                N2   – *evening, hour*
        (1biii) lexis specifying attribute
                of N2   – *array, index*
(1c)   *Support* to the second noun in a
        nominal group
        (1ci)   'delexicalized' noun   – *act, example*
(2)   *First head* in double-headed
        nominal group
(2b)   Propositional relationship
        with N2

(2bi)   Nominalization (of V in
V–S, V–O)   – *extension, explanation*
(2bii) Complement (N2 as
quasi-subject)   – *absence, awareness*
(2c) other types of N1 in double-headed nominal group

Given these categories, the list in Table 9.8 can be classified as shown in Table 9.9.

Table 9.9 Classes of noun within the *an* + ? + *of* framework

1a) *Measurement*	1b) *Focus*	1c) *Support*	2) *First head, nom. grp*
73 average	38 hour	125 act	54 understanding
18 attack	14 end	77 example	45 extension
18 ounce	13 assortment	71 expression	33 examination
17 army	12 index	66 air	31 account
17 inch	11 array	58 element	28 instrument
15 acre	10 arrangement	39 area	27 age
10 article		38 image	23 indication
		29 atmosphere	21 analysis
		29 idea	20 explanation
		22 impression	19 awareness
		22 object	18 increase
		20 attitude	16 enemy
		16 agony	14 absence
		16 aspect	14 illusion
		14 effect	13 agent
		13 issue	12 acceptance
		11 aura	12 officer
		11 inkling	11 invasion
			11 order
			10 appearance
			10 appreciation
			10 era
			10 exchange
			10 indictment
			10 injection
			10 upsurge
Tokens 168	98	677	492
Types 7	6	18	26

The type count in this analysis indicates that the core collocates in the *an* + ? + *of* framework are predominantly Class (2) and that within this class, the commonest subclass, (2bi), is that of nominalization; that the second and third commonest classes in the hierarchy are (1ci) and (1aii) respectively; and that the fourth class is (1b), of which the commonest subclass is (1biii) and contains 'attribute' nouns. The token count, meanwhile, tells us that, while most nouns belong to Class (2), Class (1ci) actually contributes more instances to the language (or corpus).

Sinclair's set of classes is based on his observation of a modest, random sample of concordance lines for the word *of*. To apply them to all of the top 1435 instances that we have for *an* + ? + *of* presents difficulties, but these are informative in themselves.

The first problem is that the classes postulated by Sinclair are not mutually exclusive; this is acknowledged in his paper (1989). Problems of assignation expose the overlap and dual interpretation that is possible for some words. For example, the collocates *illusion, instrument, area, effect* and *image* can be seen at the same time as being support nouns and *bona fide* emancipated first noun heads in the double-headed nominal group. Similarly, *assortment* could be a noun of measurement or focus, depending on interpretation. *Age* and *era* seem to fit almost all classes. The second problem of classification is that, when viewed in their range of contexts in the corpus, many of the collocates prove to have more than one meaning or function. This is different from the matter of overlap, and interesting; it tells us that many triplets seem to hold good over a range of functions, for some reason. *Agent* is one example, which occurs in text as shown in Table 9.10.

Another case in point is *issue*, shown in Table 9.11, which also serves to exemplify the tendency towards fixed phraseology that makes word classification irrelevant for some aspects of the collocate. Many collocates have this phrasal inclination, including *idea, agony, inkling* and *order*.

A number of other interesting observations can be made on the basis of the *an* + ? + *of* data. For instance (in contrast perhaps to the *too* + ? + *to* triplets in Table 9.5), most of its triplets lie clearly within a unit; only rarely is there a boundary within them, as in:

   . . . a continuous output over *an hour of* up to one litre of sweat
   . . . seen that the cost to *an employer of* laying off workers
   . . . the secession did not come to *an end of* its own accord

On the other hand, it is perhaps not surprising to discover that some triplets function more or less typically as part of a larger lexical unit, often an idiomatic one, for example:

Table 9.10 Multi-functionality of the noun collocate *agent*

(a) *Focusing noun*

does not attempt revolution: it is	an agent of democratic change. One ca
's greatest resource, will then be	an agent of destruction, in accordance
business, because he was a demon,	an agent of destruction. His job was to
ancing of the welfare state itself	an agent of redistribution (in addition
ribution element has not been made	an agent of redistribution of wealth. A
instream of the Labour movement as	an agent of revolution. Related to the

(b) *N1 in double-headed nominal group*

elf employs, in the unlikely event	an agent of equal courage and dexterit
t was the name? – all the time was	an agent of M16.' 'She didn't know it h
uch clerk to hand over the mail to	an agent of R.3 had failed. The man ha
er Uncle Nick thought that she was	an agent of the 'enemy'. (She <P 22>
planned if it had been the work of	an agent of the government. Hours, da
lican Army. It has just been ruled	an agent of the IRA by a federal judge.
sed, and in the heated discussions	an agent of the landlords was killed. S

Table 9.11 Multi-functionality of the noun collocate *issue*

(a) *Measurement noun*

The General Chen Cheng dominated an issue of Time as the Defender of Ch

(b) *Support noun*

volt on what they considered to be	an issue of confidence, and announced
But Wilson turned the strike into	an issue of confidence. He accused 'a t
up Poll sample thought immigration	an issue of national importance; afterw
the first time that Man has faced	an issue of this kind. At the beginning

(c) *Verbal noun*

raise about another $200m through	an issue of common stock to sharehold

(d) *Phrasal component*

et some adoptive parents make such	an issue of adoption, of the fact that
as you know.) Children rarely make	an issue of day-time urination. It seem
but wasn't prepared, yet, to make	an issue of it. 'Cecilia, you eat the
rom their fat child without making	an issue of it. They can cut out rich
or even months. If you don't make	an issue of them, the chances are grea
frica. If Mr Muldoon wants to make	an issue of this he could make the Melb
ing up. It isn't necessary to make	an issue of this. He'll get the idea so

---

(*come*/*came*/*been*)	+ *within an ace of* +	(verb *-ing*)
(verb)	+ *in an agony of* +	(noun; semantics of negative emotion or sensation)
(verb + obj)	+ *with an air of* +	(noun)
(*we live*)	+ *in an age of* +	(abstract noun)
(seen/considered)	+ *as an instrument of* +	(verbal noun)
	[*give*] *an account of* +	(noun)
	[*make*] *an issue of* +	(noun, often pronoun)
(noun, pronoun)	+ [*have*] *an inkling of* +	(*what, it*)
(*to give*/*get*/*have*)	+ *an idea of* +	(*what, how,* determiner)

Another way of viewing this phenomenon is perhaps to see it as a series of collocational units flowing into each other – that in fact, the last element or elements of one frame form the beginning of the next.

Such a model, in which the linguistic unit for selection is a series of words rather than a single word, and the units blend into each other, is quite different from the 'slot-and-filler' models of old. Given that frequent grammatical words very roughly alternate with lexical ones in text, we can represent this patterning as follows:

G L G L G L G L G L G

where L is lexical and G is grammatical. This can be split into frames which, in the case of successive triplets, might look as follows:

G1 L1 G2
　　　G2 L2 G3
　　　　　　G3 L3 G4
　　　　　　　　　G4 L4 G5 … etc.

If we move on and undertake a brief investigation of the literal and non-literal meanings of triplets, we discover that there is a range, from the primarily literal *an injection of* or *an ounce of* (Table 9.12),

Table 9.12 An ounce of – literal and figurative meaning

(i) *Literal*	
elpful to have the baby drink half	an ounce of boiled water, or suck it fr
farms a thousand acres with never	an ounce of chemicals, and whose yield
poonfuls of each. And so on, up to	an ounce of each. Then gradually decre
in them. Fat is rich in calories;	an ounce of it has twice as many as an
ts into energy. A horse wastes not	an ounce of its food: what it doesn't c
example, in terms of carbohydrate,	an ounce of jam is equivalent to 1 oz o
0 oz of milk. And in terms of fat,	an ounce of lard equals l oz of butter,
till 15 months or even later. Put	an ounce of milk in a small glass that
Cheese is a useful form of milk.	An ounce of most varieties contains ab
For breast-fed babies, pour half	an ounce of pasteurized milk into a cup
empty can that had once contained	an ounce of pipe tobacco, Three Nuns E
n ounce of it has twice as many as	an ounce of starch, sugar or protein. B
milk comes in cups, too. Four half	an ounce of the formula into a small cu
mployed when they were deprived of	an ounce of their threepenny bar of soa

(ii) *Figurative*	
irly brainless I should think. Not	an ounce of education. She wouldn't sa
cottage producers, and so forth?	An ounce of practice is generally worth
made me feel better." "She hadn't	an ounce of spite in her, she shouted
ounds rather like you." "I haven't	an ounce of talent as a painter." "Ross

to the triplets that are equally literal and figurative, like *an army of*, *an ingredient of*, to those that are essentially figurative as in *an agony of*, or primarily so, as in *an avalanche of*, shown in Table 9.13.

This shift from literal to figurative meaning can be said to reflect the productivity of the individual word. To what extent the surrounding framework is also integral to the process needs further study. One of the most powerful arguments for studying the framework phenomenon is, in fact, the degree to which it seems to be productive in the language. As an example, we note that certain measurement nouns – those relating to parts of the body or buildings/ containers – can become partitives by the addition of certain suffixes.

(a) *–ful*
    a man came in with an armful of cardboard boxes
    he began to whimper with an eyeful of sand
    with a noise like an officeful of typewriters

Table 9.13 An avalance of – literal and figurative meaning

(i) *Literal*	
s landed on the cliff top, sending	an avalanche of earth and stones in thr
o one – a roller coaster ride down	an avalanche of white water. We were al

(ii) *Figurative*	
volutionary path is buried beneath	an avalanche of containment mechanisms,
anted children disappeared beneath	an avalanche of dirty dishes, stale tak
am looking for! I step inside and	an avalanche of memory, loosened by the
she loaded her daughter down with	an avalanche of peripheral data. Rather
reness began to grow and grow into	an avalanche of thought and awareness o

(b) *–load*

entered the barred room with an armload of clothes

These cases are supported by a more substantial number of instances from the *a + ? + of* framework, including those in Table 9.14.

Another local observation concerns triplets containing measurement nouns relating to 'time'. These occur within a distinctive patterning, i.e. *an* + (time noun) + *of* + (verb *–ing*), as follows:

. . . after half an *hour* of circl*ing* and backtrack*ing*. . .
. . . about an *hour* of cook*ing* to produce one pan of. . .
. . . after an *hour* of crawl*ing* on hands and knees. . .

Table 9.14 Productive suffixes

(a) *-ful*		(b) *-load*	(c) *-worth*
handful	thimbleful	wagonload	pennyworth
fistful	bucketful	boatload	ha'porth
mouthful	pailful	barrowload	
spoonful	barrelful		
teaspoonful	spadeful		
tablespoonful	pocketful		
scoopful	drawerful		
plateful	classful		
saucerful	choirful		
glassful	roomful		
jugful	houseful		
panful			

. . . we still had an *hour* of flounder*ing* in front of us. . .
There's at least an *hour* of scrap*ing* and blow*ing* in. . .
After an *hour* of wrangl*ing* and snapp*ing* at one another. . .
. . . in the cafeteria after an *evening* of study*ing*. . .
. . . faced with an *evening* of social tight-rope walk*ing*. . .
. . . ordered an *afternoon* of wrestl*ing*. . .

As a final example of the value of studying the framework phenomenon and of the productive potential of frameworks, we draw attention to the fact that a triplet within a conventional idiomatic nominal phrase can function as an idiomatic platform from which to diversify. A case in point is the triplet *an accident of*, which allows linguistic movement from conventional to creative use:

to a whole way of life, not simply	an accident of birth. Appro
was forgotten. It was, of course	an accident of history at wh
ated traditions. The peerage was	an accident of history or bir
t is that the town's appearance is	an accident of history, creat
of minor members of staff, and by	an accident of fate exactly
person who got into high office by	an accident of post-war poli
were stretched to breaking, it was	an accident of war, the Cou

9.3   Conclusion

Linguists are accustomed to seeing the language as divisible into coherent units such as phrase, group or clause. The simple frameworks proposed here are intended to raise consciousness of the many different and eminently sensible ways we might develop to present and explain language patterning.

We have sought to demonstrate that two very common grammatical words, one on either side, offer a firm basis for studying collocations. We have shown that the choice of word class and collocate is specific, and governed by both elements in the framework; and we have pointed to the high type–token ratio as a clear indication that the frameworks are statistically important.

We have also offered evidence in support of a growing awareness that the normal use of language is to select more than one word at a time, and to blend such selections with each other (Sinclair 1987a; cf. Altenberg 1990b).

10   The modals of obligation and necessity in Australian English

PETER COLLINS

10.1   Introduction

The semantic category of modality has attracted the interest of a large number of linguists. Despite widespread recognition that the category is realized by items from a range of grammatical classes (adjectives such as *likely* and *necessary*, adverbs such as *perhaps* and *possibly*, nouns such as *ability* and *probability*, and so on), most scholars have restricted their attention to the subset of auxiliary verbs known as the modals.[1] The complexity of the meanings expressed by the modals has presented a challenge to both semantic theory (see for example the different theoretical approaches of Boyd and Thorne 1969, Halliday 1970, Marino 1973) and descriptive grammar (for recent descriptions of modal semantics based on textual data, see Coates 1983, Hermerón 1978, Palmer 1979). In addition to their semantic complexity the modals display a significant amount of regional variation (as noted by Trudgill and Hannah 1982) and register variation (see for instance Coates 1983, Hermerén 1978, Collins 1988a) in Standard English. It is appropriate that the extent and nature of such variation should be explored via large-scale comparative corpus study.

Within Australia the lack of a sample corpus comparable to the standard corpora of British English (the Lancaster-Oslo/Bergen and London-Lund corpora) and American English (the Brown Corpus) has hindered research into the distinctive grammatical features of Australian English (henceforth AusE). However, a million-word corpus of written AusE is currently under preparation. Designed as a parallel to Brown and LOB, it is intended to match their text categories as directly as possible except where local differences necessitate some reweighting, but differs from them in the choice of 1986 rather than 1961 as the sampling year.[2] The corpus used in the study reported in this article includes all the texts from Category A (Press reportage) of the Australian Corpus, the only category which was available at the time the study was initiated.

10.2   The modals of obligation and necessity

This paper reports a corpus-based investigation of the set of modals and quasi-modals in AusE which express meanings associated with obligation and necessity (*must, should, ought, need* and *have (got) to*).[3] Findings are systematically compared with those derived from comparable studies of British English (henceforth BrE) and American English (henceforth AmE).

There are several reasons why few linguists have extended their attention to non-modal forms expressing obligation and necessity (such as *presumably, be imperative that* and *be required to*). One is theoretical: as Perkins (1983: 24) notes, 'The fact that the modals are systematically distinct from other modal expressions clearly suggests that they may be semantically distinct as well.' Another reason is practical: the present focus enables comparisons to be drawn with previous quantitative studies of the modals. The inclusion of *have (got) to* is defended on the grounds of its close semantic relationships with the modals of obligation and necessity (as noted by Leech 1971, Palmer 1979). In fact *have got to*, as Coates (1983: 52) observes, unlike *have to*, exhibits most of the formal properties of modal auxiliaries (as defined, for example, by Huddleston 1976 and Palmer 1979), as indicated in Table 10.1.

Each of the items under review has two main meanings, epistemic ('necessity' – alternatively referred to in its different nuances as 'inference', 'certainty', 'conclusion', and so on) and root ('obligation' – also 'compulsion', 'requirement', and so on). The epistemic meanings indicate the speaker's convictions or assumptions about the truth of the proposition expressed, with *must* and *have (got) to* typically expressing a greater degree of certainty than *should* and *ought*. The epistemic category is syntactically distinctive: negation affects the proposition rather than the modality, past tense forms are rare, and it co-occurs with the perfect and progressive aspects.

Table 10.1 Formal features of modal auxiliaries: a comparison of have got to
and have to

	have got to	have to
Negative form with -n't (e.g. I mustn't leave)	+	–
Inversion with subject (e.g. Must I leave?)	+	–
Ellipsis/substitution constructions (e.g. I must leave and so must you)	–	+
Emphatic affirmation (e.g. She's not here. She must be.)	+	–
No -s form for third person singular (*musts)	–	–
No non-finite forms (*to must, *musting)	+	–
No co-occurrence with modals (*will must)	+	–

By contrast with epistemic necessity, root necessity is a somewhat indeterminate category. Palmer (1979) recognizes, and attempts to handle, the range of root necessity meaning by positing two sub-categories: 'deontic' (which he had called 'discourse-oriented' in Palmer 1974), where the speaker is generally the source of the obligation, and 'dynamic', where the speaker is not the source of the obligation. Palmer admits (1979: 91) that 'there is no clear dividing line between the two meanings', but claims that the distinction facilitates description of the relationship between *must* (which he claims may be either deontic or dynamic) and *have (got) to* (which he claims may be only dynamic). Not only does Palmer's distinction obscure the essential unity of root necessity meanings (all para-phraseable as 'it is necessary for'), but also there is corpus evidence to suggest that the alleged difference between *must* and *have (got) to* does not obtain, at least in contemporary AusE (see Section 6).

The complexity and indeterminacy of modal meaning provide challenges to analysts, challenges which are effectively confronted in the theoretical approach which has been developed by Leech and Coates (1980) and Coates (1983), and which is used in the present study. A central concept is that of the fuzzy semantic set, whose members range from the 'core' (representing the prototypical mean-ing: culturally stereotyped and ontogenetically prior, though not necessarily more statistically common) to the 'periphery' of the set, with continually graded degrees of membership (the phenomenon of 'gradience', as explored by Quirk 1965). As an illustration, consider the gradience of meaning associated with root *must*, extending from the core of strong compulsion to the periphery of weak obligation, with the relative ordering of examples between these extremes being subject to a good deal of fuzziness. (Abbreviations used to refer to text categories of the corpus, which is described in the next section, are: A01–A44 (Australian Corpus: Category A), Horv (Horvath), B & D (Bernard and Delbridge), and Sen (Senate Hansard).)

(1) You *must* come over for dinner one night. (Horv, p. 40)
(2) P: Yes you're better to get a mask with a nose piece on it in it that you can grab your nose.
     R: Yes.
     E: Oh you *must*, you *must* (. . .) so that you get hold of it. (Horv, p. 54)
(3) No, I *must* catch her. If I see her around the hospital again I'll catch her and ask her about it. (Horv, p. 28)
(4) Just as [ə] occurs only in weakly stressed positions most other vowels occur only in stressed ones, and we *must* remember this when transcribing words like 'bútter'. (B & D, p. 21)
(5) and the only thing that, that she knows that to, you know, knows to say, no that's a joke, and she learnt this from me I *must* admit is 'I do piss'. (Horv, p. 20)
(6) In this case the law says your benefits *must* be reduced and you will have to meet part of the cost. (A43, p. 148)
(7) It is clear that anyone who wants to discuss how language works *must* have an easy and reliable way of referring to the basic units of language, the phonemes. (B & D, p. 16)

Examples (1) and (2) are regarded as representing the core, even though neither corresponds to the 'psychological stereotype' of root *must*, an essentially performative use in which the speaker clearly takes responsibility for the imposing of the obligation. There were no examples in the Australian data; an example from BrE (quoted in Coates 1983: 34) is:

(8) 'You *must* play this ten times over,' Miss Jarrova would say, pointing with relentless fingers to a jumble of crotchets and quavers.

Whereas the utterance containing *must* in (8) could be described as a 'command', those in (1) and (2) are more appropriately described as 'exhortation' and 'exhortation/advice' respectively, the difference with (8) deriving mainly from the speaker's lack of authority over the listener in these two cases. Cases where the speaker is directly involved as the source of the obligation are labelled 'subjective' by Lyons (1977: 792) and Coates (1983: 32), and 'discourse-oriented' by Palmer (1979: 58).

Whereas core uses of root *must* typically involve second person subjects, examples (3) and (4) have first person subjects. Example (3), lying just outside the core, involves self-exhortation: the speaker urges himself to do something. The 'impersonal' construction in (4) exemplifies the pseudo-exhortative use of root *must* commonly found in rhetorical forms of discourse. Weaker still are formulaic holophrases of the type *I must admit* in (5). These involve such verbs of saying as *confess, say* and *admit*, and are common in spoken language.

In examples (6) and (7) the source of the obligation is not the speaker but some external body or phenomenon. As is usual in such cases, the subject is third person, and the sense of obligation is less strongly felt than it is in cases with direct speaker involvement. In (6) the requirement derives from legal regulations. In (7), which represents the periphery of the set, the stative main verb *have* ensures that the sense of obligation is extremely weak, paraphrase-able as 'it is important that' or 'it is necessary for'.

The type of indeterminacy involved in gradience pertains to set membership. Indeterminacy may also be associated with individual tokens. In (9) below the failure of the context to determine whether *must* is to be understood in a root or epistemic sense results in ambiguity.

(9)   In cases of doubt it sometimes helps to pronounce the word deliberately with two sounds and then with one to see which is really intended. Thus 'meanness' *must* be [minnəs] because [minəs] suggests the improbable word 'me-ness'. (B & D, p. 20) (= 'it's necessary for "meanness" to be ...' or 'it follows logically that "meanness" is ...')

10.3   The data

The composition of the database, totalling 225,000 words and comprising four genre categories, is summarized in Table 10.2. The Press reportage texts from the Australian Corpus, representing what might be broadly described as 'semi-formal writing', were com-

Table 10.2 Composition of the material

Genre categories	Speech or writing	Degree of formality	Approx. no. of words
Australian Corpus (Category A: Press reportage)	writing	– formal	88,000
Luncheon/dinner party conversations (B. Horvath)	speech	– formal	81,000
Learned writing (Bernard and Delbridge 1980)	writing	+ formal	28,000
Hansard: Senate questions without notice (Sept. 1987)	speech	+ formal	28,000
Total			225,000

plemented by informal spoken data (transcripts of luncheon and dinner party conversations kindly lent to me by Dr Barbara Horvath). The remainder of the database comprised a smaller amount of formal writing (from a textbook, Bernard and Delbridge's *Introduction to Linguistics: An Australian Perspective*, 1980) and relatively formal speech (Hansard of Senate Questions without Notice, 15 September 1987). All the texts represent contemporary AusE, having been produced within the last decade by Australians in Australia.

The genre selection was deliberately skewed towards informal/semi-formal usage on the grounds of its greater frequency of production and reception. Conversation is undeniably the spoken genre that people engage in more often than any other, and circulation figures indicate that newspapers are read more widely than any other type of publication.

The primary source of information on the modals in BrE used here is Coates (1983), the first full-length account of modal semantics to be based on an adequate corpus. Coates's corpus comprised over a million and a half words (1,000,000 from the LOB Corpus of written BrE and 545,000 from the spoken and non-printed written sections of the Survey of English Usage Corpus). From this database Coates extracted a 'representative sample of each modal' (1983: 2), each sample consisting of approximately 200 cases. The only other study to use British corpus data is Palmer (1979), but he uses material from the Survey of English Usage merely for heuristic purposes and to exemplify theoretical claims.

For information on the modals in AmE we lack any study that rivals that by Coates in scope. A major drawback for the corpus research of AmE has been, and still is, the lack of any corpus of spoken AmE. Two corpus studies of the modals in AmE have been reported, both based on the million-word Brown Corpus (which contains written – in fact printed – material only). Ehrman (1966) uses one third of this corpus (but supplies no frequency findings), while Hermerén (1978) is based on four of the fifteen categories of Brown. It is the latter that is used as a source of frequency figures on AmE in the present study.

When comparisons are made in this paper between Coates's, Hermerén's and my own findings, several sources of non-comparability between the corpora used in the three studies need to be borne in mind. This problem is compounded by the selective presentation of frequencies by Coates and Hermerén, which often renders comparisons difficult. The corpus used in the present study contains approximately equal proportions of spoken and written data. By contrast LOB, as used by Coates, contains printed texts only (e.g. press reportage and editorials, biography, government documents, scientific writing, fiction), while the Survey material she uses is heterogeneous as to formality and medium: one half private speech, one quarter public speech, and one quarter writing of a type not included in LOB (namely texts written to be spoken, such as BBC news scripts and plays, and handwritten texts, such as letters and diaries). These facts need to be borne in mind when in my tables Coates's figures for LOB are characterized as 'BrE writing', and those for the Survey (unfortunately rarely broken down by Coates) as 'BrE speech'. Hermerén's figures are based on printed texts only, representing a narrower variety of genres than in the Coates study and a wider range than in my own. An additional difficulty arises from Hermerén's use of a different form of semantic classification (based on a categorical componential approach) from those of Coates and me. Some manipulation of the figures given in Hermerén's tables (1978: 174–8) – essentially, combining figures for separate categories – has thus been necessary in order to align them with those for the present study.

A further source of non-comparability between the corpora is the chronological gap between the British and American material (from the late 1950s and early 1960s) on the one hand, and the Australian material (from the 1980s) on the other. One can therefore not be certain about the relative importance of chronological and regional factors in specific cases of dialectal divergence.

10.4   Distribution of forms in AusE

The distribution of items investigated is presented in Table 10.3. In order to compensate for the unevenness in size of the genres, relative frequencies (tokens per 10,000 words) are given in Table 10.3 and subsequent tables. In Table 10.3 absolute frequencies are given in parentheses.

Table 10.3 Distribution of *must, should, ought, need, have to* and *have got to* in Australian English

	Press reportage (Category A)	Conversation (Horvath)	Learned prose (Bernard and Delbridge)	Parliamentary debate (Senate)	Total
must	4.3 (38)	12.0 (97)	12.1 (34)	2.5 (7)	7.8 (176)
should	8.7 (71)	3.5 (28)	5.7 (16)	16.1 (45)	7.1 (160)
ought	0.1 (1)	0.4 (3)	0.7 (2)	2.1 (6)	0.5 (12)
need	0.1 (1)	0.0 (0)	1.4 (4)	0.0 (0)	0.2 (5)
have to	3.2 (28)	10.1 (82)	1.8 (5)	12.1 (34)	6.6 (149)
have got to	0.1 (1)	12.0 (97)	0.0 (0)	0.0 (0)	4.4 (98)
Total	15.9 (140)	37.9 (307)	21.8 (61)	32.9 (92)	26.7 (600)

If *have to* and *have got to* are treated as variant forms of a single lexeme, then this is clearly the most popular of the items (11.0 per 10,000 words), and markedly so in the conversation genre (22.0 per 10,000 words – the highest incidence of any of the items in any genre). The only modal whose frequency in a particular genre rivalled that of *have (got) to* in conversation is *should* in parliamentary speech, where its popularity stems from its usefulness in offering advice, making recommendations and encoding expressions of propriety. Numbers for *ought* and *need* are extremely small. However, the claim which one occasionally encounters that *ought* is obsolescent (cf. Svartvik and Wright 1977) needs to be balanced against the evidence that it occurs considerably more often in speech than writing (as noted also by Coates 1983: 24 for BrE). Worthy of note, finally, is the comparatively low frequency of the modals examined in newspaper reportage. It would seem that journalists, committed as they are to a factual, non-speculative mode of discourse, have less occasion to produce assertions modalized in terms of obligation (at least of a subjective type) and necessity than those engaged in the production of the other three genres represented here.

10.5   Comparison between AusE, BrE and AmE

Table 10.4 compares the frequencies of the modals of obligation and necessity in Australian speech and writing, British speech and writing (the source of the figures being Table 3.1 in Coates 1983: 23) and American writing (figures being taken from Francis and Kučera's 1982 frequency analysis of the Brown Corpus). Unfortunately Coates does not indicate whether her figure for *have to* includes *have got to*.

Table 10.4 Frequencies of *must, should, ought, need, have to* and *have got to* in Australian, British and American English

| | AusE | | | BrE | | | AmE |
	Speech	Writing	Total	Speech	Writing	Total	Writing
must	9.5	6.2	7.8	11.6	11.3	11.4	10.2
should	6.7	7.5	7.1	11.2	12.9	12.0	9.2
ought	0.8	0.3	0.5	2.6	1.1	1.8	0.7
need	0.0	0.4	0.2	0.3	0.7	0.0	—
have to	10.6	0.4	5.3	—	7.0	—	—
have got to	8.9	0.1	4.3	—	—	—	—

A considerably lower frequency of *must, should, ought* and *need* is in evidence in AusE than in the other two dialects. The differences may be attributable to the chronological gap between the two corpora and/or the differing range of genres represented therein. With *have (got) to* the unavailability of figures for BrE and AmE renders dialectal comparisons impossible and thus deprives us of the opportunity to test what may be a plausible hypothesis: that *have (got) to*, already established as the main exponent of root obligation in informal spoken AusE (see below), is increasing its sphere of influence in BrE and AmE as well. In all three dialects *ought* has a comparatively low frequency of occurrence, while for *need* (no figures are available for AmE) they are even lower. Accordingly, the forms which will be discussed at greatest length below are *must, have (got) to* and *should*.

10.6   Results

(i)   Must

Table 10.5 presents figures for the root and epistemic meanings of *must* in the three dialects.

Table 10.5 Must: meanings in Australian English, British English and American English

		AusE			BrE			AmE
	Speech	Writing	Total	Speech	Writing	Total	Writing
Root	16 (9.1%)	47 (26.7%)	63 (35.8%)	106 (24.3%)	153 (35.1%)	259 (59.4%)	51 (75.0%)
Epistemic	88 (50.0%)	18 (10.2%)	106 (60.2%)	92 (21.1%)	74 (17.0%)	166 (38.1%)	16 (23.5%)
Indeterminate	0 (0.0%)	7 (4.0%)	7 (4.0%)	2 (0.5%)	9 (2.1%)	11 (2.5%)	1 (1.5%)
Total	104 (59.1%)	72 (40.9%)	176 (100.0%)	200 (45.9%)	236 (54.1%)	436 (100.0%)	68 (100.0%)

The striking figures here are those for *must* in Australian speech, with over five times more epistemic than root uses (compared with a fairly even balance in BrE). The proportionality between root and epistemic uses of *must* in AusE is undoubtedly affected by the extreme differences in the spoken material. The relative infrequency of root uses in Australian speech is probably explicable in terms of the 'democratic' dinner party conversations between equals which account for the bulk of the spoken data and in which obligations are occasionally reported but rarely imposed (unless self-imposed). It is suggested below that *have (got) to* has taken over from *must* as the main exponent of root obligation, at least in informal genres.

The relative frequency of epistemic uses in Australian speech may have been influenced by differences in the composition of the databases, with inferencing on the basis of known facts being a common practice in dialogue between intimates but less common in spoken genres of a more 'public' kind.

As noted in Section 2 above, root *must* covers a considerable range of meanings, and yet its meaning is more suitably described in terms of a single (albeit fuzzy) category than in terms of subcategories. The examples in (1)–(8) illustrate the semantic continuum from strong, subjective, almost performative uses ('it is imperative/compulsory') to weak requirement ('it is important/necessary'). The

Australian data do not evidence the 100 per cent association of root *must* with negation found in Coates's (1983: 39) study. The *mustn't* in (10) is one of only two examples of negated root *must*, as against five examples of negated epistemic *must* (see (15) below):

(10)   Now she said um Rose *mustn't* post it to the post office this Christmas, you know because (...) is closed. (Horv, p. 16)

With negated root *must* the negation affects the proposition and not the modality ('it was important that Rose should not post it ...').

As (10) indicates, *must* can be used in reported speech. Elsewhere *had (got) to* operates as the past of *must* (see below).

Epistemic *must* expresses the speaker's conviction (ranging from strong to weak) about the truth of the proposition, as warranted by deductions from the available facts. Some examples follow.

(11)   Mr Cain *must* have a very painful and tender private region from the amount of time he has spent sitting on the fence in recent weeks. (Sen, p. 75)
(12)   I think they *must* be disturbed a lot though by what ... erm ... that there's not much ahead for ... for their employment. (Horv, p. 32)

In (11) the grounds upon which the deduction is made are specified ('from ...'). In (12) the epistemic nature of *must* is reinforced by the hedge *I think*.

In the majority of cases epistemic *must* refer to states or activities in the present, as in (11) and (12), or in the past, as in (15) below. Occasionally, however, it is used to refer to a future state or activity, as in (13).

(13)   Tithing is a very ancient principle of prosperity. Whatever we give away *must* come back to us – even money. (A42, p. 146)

Epistemic *must* exhibits a strong tendency to occur with the perfect aspect in the Australian data, as in (15) below, with stative verbs, as in (11) and (12) above, and with the progressive aspect, as in (14).

(14)   Some of them *must* be still waiting in line to go in. (Horv, p. 43)

It has been claimed by some writers that epistemic *must* lacks (or 'normally' lacks) a negative form (e.g. Leech 1971: 72, Coates 1983: 46, Quirk *et al.* 1985: 225). The claim has been challenged by

Jacobson (1979), who quotes ten examples of epistemic *must not* from contemporary British and American writings, and Tottie (1985), who reports an elicitation experiment in which 17 per cent of American undergraduates tested used epistemic *must not* in their responses, compared with a negligible 0.2 per cent of British subjects. Tottie's findings cast some suspicion on Trudgill and Hannah's (1982: 47) claim that 'the most common negative of epistemic *must* is *must not*', and support Quirk *et al.*'s claim (1985: 225, note b), which is presented as a qualification of their assertion that '*must* [= logical necessity] cannot normally be used in interrogative or negative clauses', that:

Occasionally, *must* [= logical necessity] does occur with negations:
  His absence must not have been noticed.
This has the same meaning as *His absence can't have been noticed*. Such sentences have been regarded by many commentators as impossible but are increasingly accepted and used, especially in AmE.

My Australian corpus contains six examples of epistemic *mustn't*, identical to the number of examples of epistemic *can't* with which it is semantically parallel. However, the genre distribution of the forms is not identical. Whereas epistemic *can't* tokens are spread evenly across speech and writing, all six epistemic *mustn't* tokens occur in conversation. Given that linguistic change typically originates in casual spoken genres before spreading to more formal and conservative genres, this distributional pattern suggests that epistemic *mustn't* is fairly recent in origin. An example follows.

(15)   He *mustn't* have wanted the coupons because he came up and give them to me. (Horv, p. 30)

(ii)   Need

Auxiliary *need* can express both root and epistemic meanings, although only the former is represented in the small number of examples in the Australian data.

(16)   It also meant that unlike other juries, only a majority of them, that is twelve, *need* be satisfied one way or the other. (A15, p. 51)

As Coates (1983: 50) observes, the primary function of *need* seems to be to provide a negative form in which the modality is within the

scope of the negation ('it is not necessary for/that...'), whereas
with negative *must* the modality is outside the scope of the negation
('it is necessary for/that... not...'). Four of the five examples were
negative.

(17)   Note that although the manifestations of paralanguage and
       the minutiae of language proper are usually unconscious, they
       need not be. (B & D, p. 6)

(iii)   Have (got) to

As noted in Section 2, *have got to* (but not *have to*) is modal-like in
its formal properties. Semantically, too, *have got to* is indistinguishable from *must*, as we shall see. Figures for the meanings of *have got
to* and *have to* in AusE are presented in Table 10.6. Unfortunately
no comparative figures for BrE or AmE are available.

Table 10.6 Have (got) to: meanings in Australian English

	have got to			have to		
	Speech	Writing	Total	Speech	Writing	Total
Root	97	1	98	109	33	142
	(99.0%)	(1.0%)	(100.0%)	(73.2%)	(22.1%)	(95.3%)
Epistemic	0	0	0	6	0	6
	(0.0%)	(0.0%)	(0.0%)	(4.0%)	(0.0%)	(4.0%)
Indeterminate	0	0	0	1	0	1
	(0.0%)	(0.0%)	(0.0%)	(0.7%)	(0.0%)	(0.7%)
Total	97	1	98	116	33	149
	(99.0%)	(1.0%)	(100.0%)	(77.9%)	(22.1%)	(100.0%)

Have got to may express both root and epistemic meanings in AusE,
although there are no examples of the latter in the data (see Table
10.6). An invented example is:

(18)   Have you seen my keys? They*'ve got to* be here somewhere.

As the following examples show, root *have got to* covers a similar
range of meaning to root *must*.

(19)   Well this little old lady, they'd tuck her into bed you know
       and they'd have her all nice and comfortable you know and
       'You stop there' the nurse'd say. 'You *gotta* stop there, love,

don't you get out because you worry the other patients.'
(Horv, p. 11)

(20)   M: Oh they've got some lovely things in the case. They've
       got these big blankets there, big woolly blankets and
       everything, which I'm looking out (. . .) Wednesday.
       R: You've got to win a jackpot though Maisie.
       M: Yeah but next Tuesday.
       R: You've got to get 100 coins. (Horv, p. 30)

(21)   she's brought a nice peanut brittle bar there and well I've got
       to keep my mind above that. (Horv, p. 46)

(22)   Well she's got to be able to do all that before they'll let her go
       back. (Horv, p. 9)

No semantic ill-effects would result from substituting *must* for *have
got to* in these examples, merely a degree of stylistic awkwardness
(all examples are from conversation, the genre which accounted for
100 per cent of root *have got to* tokens, but only 18 per cent of root
must). As with *must*, *have got to* ranges in meaning from strong
subjectivity (core) to weak objectivity (periphery). Example (19)
provides counter evidence to Coates's (1983: 53) claim that root
have got to is never performative. This claim may have been valid
for Coates's BrE data, now three decades old, but it does not obtain
for contemporary AusE. In (19) the nurse's position of authority
entitles her to issue commands to her patients; her modalized
utterance *You gotta stop there*, flanked on either side by the imperatives *you stop there* and *don't you get out*, carries the force of an
order. In (20) the subject of *have got to* in each case is generic *you*,
its meaning therefore objective ('[the regulations are such that] it is
necessary for you to . . .'). Closer to the core than (20) is (21), which
involves self-exhortation by the speaker. Closer to the periphery is
(22): the speaker is minimally involved, the verb non-dynamic, and
the sense of obligation consequently weak.

   Another claim by Coates (1983: 54) concerning the behaviour of
have got to which is not supported by the present study is: 'Root
HAVE GOT TO like MUST cannot be habitual in meaning, unlike HAVE
TO.' That her starred example **I've got to get up at 7 a.m. every day*
would be quite acceptable in AusE is indicated by the following (not
untypical) corpus example.

(23)   You've got to be on their backs all the time, haven't you?
       (Horv, p. 22)

With negative *have got to*, like negative *need* but unlike negative *must*, the modality falls within the scope of the negative. The paraphrase 'it is not necessary for...' is applicable to the following example.

(24) And she said 'No, you *haven't got to* give it to me.' (Horv, p. 25)

Have got to is realized variably in non-standard Australian usage, sometimes with *be* rather than *have* (in (25)), and in one corpus example, (26), with *and* rather than *to* (cf. *try and*).

(25) Cause you*'re gotta* come back in again. (Horv, p. 36)
(26) Yes, that's the trouble. You*'ve got and* ask. (Horv, p. 22)

Like *have got to, have to* has both root and epistemic meanings. Unlike epistemic *have got to*, examples of epistemic *have to* are available in the corpus (albeit a small number – six). It is Coates's impression that epistemic *have to* is 'still felt to be an Americanism, and its usage is, for the most part, associated with the teenage sub-culture' (1983: 57). While there are undoubtedly many Australians who also feel that epistemic *have to* is an Americanism, its use in AusE extends beyond the 'teenage sub-culture'. In fact, all six corpus examples were produced by middle-aged speakers. An example is:

(27) Ma: And this Babette, she's Pakistani, is she?
      Pe: She'd *have to* be, she'd *have to* be, yes. (Horv, p. 62)

The present study suggests that in AusE (as Coates 1983: 57 notes to be the case for BrE) the normal way of expressing epistemic necessity is by *must* (60 per cent of *must* tokens are epistemic, as against 8 per cent of *should* and 3 per cent of *have (got) to*).

A number of writers have contrasted *must* and *have to* in terms of speaker authority. Leech (1971: 73), for instance, claims that where-as the authority of the speaker is involved with root *must*, root *have to* 'conveys obligation generally, without specifying who does the compelling'. This distinction is maintainable only in a probabilistic sense in AusE, where examples of subjective root *have to*, though not common, are certainly to be found. In each of the following corpus examples it is clearly the speaker who is the source of the 'obligation'.

(28) Ed: I love persimmons.
      R: Yes.
      Ma: You'll *ave to* come when they're in... in full blast...
           you'll *ave to* come in. (Horv, p. 19)
(29) And I thought well I'll *have to* get out. I can't stop here no
      longer now that door's open, so I fled behind Maiv. (Horv, p.
      18)

More typical are examples of root *have to* where the source of the
obligation is external to the speaker (and referred to explicitly in
(30)).

(30) When I look back over the last year or perhaps two years as
      to the number of occasions on which I would *have to* produce
      the Australia Card under this legislation, I can think of three
      or four instances where I have *had to* obtain a Medicare
      benefit. (Sen, p. 71)

Negative root *have to* involves negation of the modality.

(31) 'We got our equipment from another senator who had lost in
      the primary, so we really didn't *have to* do any shopping
      around.' (A01, p. 2) (= 'it was not necessary for...')

Have to, unlike *must*, has a past tense form (*had to*). Coates
(1983: 57) suggests that *had to* provides a suppletive past form for
must. However, it is unclear why we should want to regard *had to* in
(32) as suppletive to *must* rather than simply the past of *has to*.

(32) Today, a man *had to* be held back by police and coastguards
      from plunging in after the boy. (A08, p. 27)

More plausible is Coates's (1983: 57) claim that *have to* supplies
missing non-finite forms for *must* and *have got to*. The latter could
certainly not be substituted for *have to* in (27), (28), (29), (30) or
(31).

(iv)   Should

In addition to its use as a modal expressing epistemic necessity and
root obligation, *should* functions as a quasi-subjunctive and (rarely
in AusE: no corpus examples found) as a first person variant for
hypothetical *would*: *I should take an umbrella if I were you*; *I should*

Table 10.7 Should: meanings in Australian English, British English and American English

	AusE			BrE			AmE
	Speech	Writing	Total	Speech	Writing	Total	Writing
Root	66 (41.3%)	69 (43.1%)	135 (84.4%)	84 (23.0%)	117 (32.0%)	201 (54.9%)	56 (72.7%)
Epistemic	3 (1.9%)	13 (8.1%)	16 (10.0%)	36 (9.8%)	28 (7.7%)	64 (17.5%)	4 (5.2%)
Quasi-subjunctive	1 (0.6%)	5 (3.1%)	6 (3.8%)	19 (5.2%)	38 (10.4%)	57 (15.6%)	12 (15.6%)
Indeterminate	3 (1.9%)	0 (0.0%)	3 (1.9%)	20 (5.5%)	24 (6.6%)	44 (12.0%)	5 (6.5%)
Total	73 (45.6%)	87 (54.4%)	160 (100.0%)	159 (43.4%)	207 (56.6%)	366 (100.0%)	77 (100.0%)

imagine so, etc. The hypothetical use is irrelevant to the present discussion. Frequencies for *should* in AusE, BrE and AmE are presented in Table 10.7. Notable findings are the dominance of root *should* in AusE speech and writing, the rarity of quasi-subjunctive *should* (though it must be observed that the bureaucratic genres in which this use is common were not represented in the Australian corpus), and the unpopularity of epistemic *should* in Australian speech. (Figures in Table 10.7 for hypothetical *should* and for *should* used as the past of *shall* presented by Coates (1983: 58) for BrE are excluded because these two uses did not occur in the Australian data. The AmE figures for quasi-subjunctive *should* are slightly inflated because Hermerén (1978: 147) includes certain main-clause uses of *should* in this category.)

As with root *must* and *have (got) to*, root *should* ranges in meaning from strongly subjective (a forceful suggestion – but not a command, as with *must* – often with moral or legal overtones) to weakly objective (a reference to appropriate or proper behaviour). Consider the following examples:

(33) 'Mr White *should* come here and work for a couple of weeks and then maybe he will change his mind,' Mr Ainalis said. (A15, p. 50)

(34) Because of our ability to combine census and political information, we can tell you where you *should* be concentrating your broadcasting money. (A01, p. 2)

(35) Through the 1960s and most of the 1970s the conventional wisdom was that governments *should* impose limits on foreign equity holdings in Australian business. (Sen, p. 47)

(36) A householder is adopting this means of communication when he or she places two empty milk bottles in a particular place so that the milkman knows that he *should* leave two full ones. (B & D, p. 3)

Examples (33) and (34) are subjective: the suggestion derives from the speaker. Example (33) is strong in force (Mr Ainalis considers Mr White to be under a moral obligation); (34) is weak in force ('we consider it advisable'). Examples (35) and (36) are objective: the source of the requirement is external to the speaker. Example (35) is strong in force (the source is conventional wisdom); (36) is weak in force (the source is the milkman's acquaintance with a customary procedure).

Root *should*, being itself historically a past tense form, has no past form. Rather, it occurs with the *have* V–*en* construction, expressing a past, normally contrafactive meaning, as in (37).

(37) Pe: (. . .) I sometimes don't know if I got my money worth out of the Commodore.
      ?   Oh it's not that bad, it's all right.
      Neil: *Should*'ve kept the 323.
      Ma: We *should* have, actually, but we didn't. (Horv, p. 34)

Epistemic *should* expresses a less certain assumption than epistemic *must* and *have (got) to*. In each of the following examples *should* could be paraphrased as 'I assume that. . .' or 'It is likely that. . .'

(38) 'It *should* be a fantastic race for the public with three drivers fighting for the title,' said Prost. (A40, p. 139)

Quasi-subjunctive *should* occurs as a semantically empty form in nominal clauses, as in (39).

(39) However, Gorbachev had recently decreed that shift work *should* be implemented to use idle production capacity. (A32, p. 112)

Occasionally the quasi-subjunctive use of *should* merges with the root meaning.

(40) The chief executive of Qantas, Mr John Menadue, has again

endorsed at least some of the benefits of airline privatization, but stopped short of urging it *should* happen in Australia. (A18, p. 61)

(v)   Ought

Ought, like *must, have (got) to* and *should*, expresses both root and epistemic meanings. As Table 10.8 shows, the root meaning greatly outweighs the epistemic meaning in AusE and BrE (no figures are available for AmE because Hermerén excludes *ought* from his analysis).

Table 10.8 Ought: meanings in Australian English and British English

	AusE			BrE		
	Speech	Writing	Total	Speech	Writing	Total
Root	8 (66.7%)	3 (25.0%)	11 (91.7%)	119 (48.6%)	87 (35.5%)	206 (84.1%)
Epistemic	1 (8.3%)	0 (0.0%)	1 (8.3%)	12 (4.9%)	13 (5.3%)	25 (10.2%)
Indeterminate	0 (0.0%)	0 (0.0%)	0 (0.0%)	10 (4.1%)	4 (1.6%)	14 (5.7%)
Total	9 (75.0%)	3 (25.0%)	12 (100.0%)	141 (57.6%)	104 (42.4%)	245 (100.0%)

Root *ought* may be subjective (a recommendation or piece of advice from the speaker), as in (41), or objective (asserting the desirability of an activity or state of affairs), as in (42).

(41)   He said 'Oh, look, I'm sorry about this,' and I said, 'Well you *ought* to see the flak that's been firing, firing around over you.' (Horv, p. 43)

(42)   ... we are not going to be given the opportunity to debate the amendments which the government itself accepts are correct and proper and which *ought* to be made. (Sen, p. 78)

Epistemic *ought*, like *should*, expresses an assumption based on logical inference (rather than the more confident conclusion expressed by epistemic *must* and *have (got) to*). *Ought* in (43) is paraphraseable by 'I assume that...' or 'presumably'.

(43)   The ID card will not catch illegal immigrants. Who said that? The Department of Immigration, Local Government and Ethnic Affairs said that and it *ought* to know. (Sen, p. 68)

10.7   Conclusion

While *must, have (got) to, should* and *ought* all express both root and epistemic meanings, *must* is the only form in which the epistemic meaning dominates (the root–epistemic proportions being: *must* 0.6:1; *should* 8.3:1; *ought* 10:1; *have (got) to* 33.3:1).

If we may assume that the genre of casual conversation provides the most reliable indicator of current developments in a dialect, then it seems clear that in AusE *must* is the primary modal of epistemic necessity, and *have (got) to* the primary exponent of root obligation. In the Australian material root *must* is about three times more common in writing than speech, and relatively more frequent in formal learned writing than semi-formal writing (newspaper reportage). *Should* is also a regular exponent of root obligation in conversation, differing from *have (got) to* in terms of subjectivity. Whereas *should* is generally (in 75.0 per cent of cases) subjective – typically used to express the speaker's advice or recommendation – *have (got) to* is generally objective (in 78.9 per cent of cases; 85.2 per cent for *have to*, and 75.5 per cent for *have (got) to* – typically used to express an obligation or duty which is binding on the subject and derives from a source other than the speaker.

A similar picture emerges if we focus on newspaper reportage, a genre which may be assumed to reflect recent developments in the written language. Once again *must* is the only significant exponent of epistemic necessity (65.8 per cent of *must* tokens in the Australian press sample expressed this meaning, but only 12.7 per cent of *should* and none of *have (got) to*.)

Several advantages of the corpus-based approach are suggested by the present study. The requirement that all tokens, no matter how recalcitrant, be accounted for has necessitated the use of a model capable of handling the range, complexity and indeterminacy of modal meanings. The exploitation of an Australian corpus has enabled quantitative statements to be made on the distribution of forms across a variety of genres and dialects. The use of 'real' data has provided a safeguard against the danger of idiolectal bias present in studies based on introspectively derived examples. The future availability of large, up-to-date corpora, particularly those incorporating spoken language material, will undoubtedly facilitate further studies of this kind.

Notes

[1] A notable exception is Perkins (1983).

[2] For details on the Australian Corpus, which is due for completion in 1990, see Collins and Peters (1988) and Collins (1988b).

[3] The present investigation forms part of a larger study of the modals in AusE. See also Collins (1988a).

11 A corpus-based study of apposition in English

CHARLES F. MEYER

11.1 Introduction[1]

In the past, to study the usage of grammatical constructions in English a researcher not only had to compile a corpus to serve as the basis of the study but had to spend much time extracting by hand the relevant information from it. Otto Jespersen, for instance, spent much of his life collecting and analysing the examples he used to serve as the basis of his multi-volume work *A Modern English Grammar on Historical Principles*. The introduction of computer corpora, however, has greatly eased this process. Because a variety of corpora is now available on computer tape or diskette (see Taylor and Leech 1991 and Meyer 1986), researchers no longer have to compile their own corpus; the drudgery of analysing a corpus by hand has been greatly facilitated by the introduction of programs (discussed in Jones 1987, Kaye 1989 and 1990) that can automatically search corpora for a variety of different kinds of grammatical constructions. In short, grammatical studies that in the past took years to complete can now be conducted in a relatively short span of time. In this article I will discuss how I used three computer corpora to study a much-neglected area of English grammar: apposition. After briefly defining apposition, demonstrating that it is a grammatical relation having specific syntactic, semantic and pragmatic characteristics, I will describe some of these linguistic characteristics as they occurred in the computer corpora I studied.

Because research has shown that the use of a grammatical construction will vary from context to context (Biber 1988), I analysed three corpora containing samples of English used in a variety of different contexts: the Survey of English Usage Corpus (SEU), the Brown Corpus (Brown), and the London–Lund Corpus (LLC). Approximately 120,000 words of text from each of these corpora were investigated, making the corpus on which this study was based 360,000 words in length. Three kinds of variation were investigated in the corpora. First, SEU and Brown were compared to determine whether appositions were used differently in written British and American English. Second, to study variation by genre, equal proportions of very different kinds of writing in SEU and Brown were investigated: journalistic writing, which included both press reportage and editorials; learned writing, which consisted of writing from both the humanities and the natural and social sciences; and fictional writing, which comprised samples taken from both novels and short stories. Third, LLC was used to investigate variation in speech and writing and also to study variation by speech genre. In LLC, equal proportions of spontaneous conversation between various kinds of speakers were investigated: disparates, such as students and teachers who stand in an unequal social relation to one another; equals, individuals of an equal social standing; intimates, such as husbands and wives who have a very close relationship with one another; and intimates and equals, combining the categories described above.

11.2   Defining apposition

In the literature on the subject it is often not clear whether apposition is a construction type or a grammatical relation. Fries (1952), for example, describes apposition as a specific type of grammatical construction, namely two noun phrases that are coreferential and juxtaposed. Other works (such as Sopher 1971) view apposition not as a specific grammatical construction but as a grammatical relation on the same level as modification, coordination and complementation. Unless one is willing to admit only juxtaposed noun phrases as appositions, it makes little sense to say that apposition is a particular construction type. Instead, apposition is best viewed as a grammatical relation having various realizations. These realizations, in turn, have specific syntactic, semantic and pragmatic characteristics that both define the relation of apposition and distinguish it from other grammatical relations. In the remainder of this article I will first discuss the realizations of apposition I found in the corpora I investigated, and then describe some of their syntactic, semantic and pragmatic characteristics.[2]

11.3   The realizations of apposition

As Table 11.1 shows, the three corpora contained a total of 2841 constructions which I have counted as appositions.

Table 11.1 Distribution of appositions in the three corpora

Brown	LLC	SEU	Total
1026 (36%)	778 (27%)	1037 (37%)	2841 (100%)

Approximately three-quarters of the appositions in the corpora were evenly distributed among the written samples of British and American English. A smaller percentage (27 per cent) occurred in the spoken samples. This distribution indicates that overall there is little difference in the occurrence of appositions in written British and American English but that there is considerable variation in their use in spoken and written English. This variation has a pragmatic explanation: appositions are communicatively more necessary in writing than in speech, a point discussed in greater detail in Section 8.

11.4   The syntactic structure of apposition

Syntactically, apposition is a grammatical relation between two or more units that can be analysed in terms of their syntactic form, their syntactic function and their contiguity. As Table 11.2 indicates, the appositions in the corpora had the following syntactic realiza-tions: two noun phrases (example 1); a noun phrase followed by a clause (example 2); two units (most frequently noun phrases) joined by an obligatory marker of apposition (example 3); or two units one or both of which was a clause or a phrase other than a noun phrase (example 4).[3]

(1)   *Alacrity, the Podger cat*, came by the hammock, rubbed her
       back briefly against it, and then, sure of a welcome hopped up.
       (Brown B09 680–700)

Table 11.2 Structural types of apposition

Types	Brown	LLC	SEU	Total	
Nominal apposition	647	282	637	1566	(55%)
NPs in apposition with clauses or sentences	150	100	162	412	(15%)
Appositions with obligatory marker of apposition	102	151	124	377	(13%)
Non-nominal apposition	127	245	114	486	(17%)
Total	1026 (36%)	778 (27%)	1037 (37%)	2841	(100%)

(2) The first speaker was Amos C. Barstow who had been un-animously chosen president of the meeting. He spoke of *his desire to promote the abolition of slavery by peaceable means* and he compared John Brown of Harper's Ferry to the John Brown of Rhode Island's colonial period. (Brown J58 1420–60)

(3) *About 40 representatives of Scottish bodies*, including *the parents of some of the children flown to Corsica*, were addressed by an English surgeon and doctor and by M. Naessens. (SEU W.12: 1–40)

(4) This circumstance in the patient's case plus the fact that his tactual capacity remained basically in sound working order constitutes its exceptional value for the problem at hand since the evidence presented by the authors is overwhelming that, when the patient closed his eyes, he had absolutely no *spatial* (that is, *third-dimensional*) awareness whatsoever. (Brown J52 100–50)

Even though apposition is realized by a variety of syntactic forms, it is predominantly a relation between two noun phrases. As Table 11.2 demonstrates, over half the appositions in the corpora consisted of two noun phrases.

Table 11.3 lists the syntactic function of appositions in the corpora for which a syntactic function could be determined for at least one of the units in apposition. Because apposition is a relation in which at least one of the units is usually a noun phrase, it is not surprising that nearly 88 per cent of the appositions in the corpora had

Table 11.3 The syntactic functions of the units in apposition

Functions	Brown	LLC	SEU	Total	
Subject	331	141	327	799	(33%)
Non-existential	312	120	308	740	
Existential	19	21	19	59	
Object	155	156	172	483	(20%)
Direct	155	155	171	481	
Indirect	0	1	1	2	
Prep. complement	344	142	343	829	(34%)
Complement	67	73	63	203	(8%)
Subject	64	71	61	196	
Object	3	2	2	7	
Adverbial	20	32	38	90	(4%)
Verb	1	2	0	3	
Total	918	546	943	2407	(100%)

functions associated with noun phrases: subject (example 5), object (example 6) and prepositional complement (example 7).

(5)   On the shores north and south, *the fishers and mooncursers – smugglers –* lived along the churning Great South Bay and the narrow barrier of sand, Fire Island. (Brown K16 80–3)

(6)   These are few and seemingly disjointed data, but they illustrate *the important fact that fundamental alterations in conditioned reactions occur in a variety of states in which the hypothalamic balance has been altered by physiological experimentation, pharmacological action, or clinical processes.* (Brown J17 1420–60)

(7)   Vital secrets of *Britain's first atomic submarine, the Dreadnought,* and, by implication, of the entire United States Navy's still-building nuclear sub fleet, were stolen by a London-based soviet spy ring, secret service agents testified today. (Brown A19 1110–1140)

In addition, appositions had functions associated with positions in the clause or phrase that are explained by Quirk *et al.*'s (1985) principle of end-weight: the lengthier and more complex a noun phrase, the less likely it is to occur in the subject position of a clause (see also Aarts 1971, de Haan 1987). Because appositions typically consist of two noun phrases or a noun phrase and a nominal clause, they are relatively heavy constructions. Consequently, 64 per cent of the appositions in the corpora had functions associated with end-weight: direct object (example 6), prepositional complement (example 7), subject complement (example 8), and subject of sentences containing existential *there* (example 9):

(8)   I'm S\URE# that J\ACK# is is in S\OME ways *a B/\ETTER man to work with#* an /\EASIER *man to work with#* than Dan R/OSS# (LLC S.1.2:245–9)

(9)   There is *a marked tendency for religions, once firmly established, to resist change, not only in their own doctrines and policies and practices, but also in secular affairs having religious relevance.* (Brown J23 1790–810)

Despite the fact that the two units of an apposition create a relatively heavy construction, 31 per cent of the appositions in the corpora occurred in a position that is not associated with end-weight: the pre-verbal subject position (as in example 5). However, a large number of appositions in subject positions (359, or 49 per cent) occurred in the press genre, a genre containing a high number of relatively short and non-complex appositions such as the following:

(10)   *Comic Gary Morton* signed to play the Living Room here Dec. 18, because that's the only time *his heart, Lucille Ball,* can come along. (Brown A16 1140–60)

As Table 11.4 demonstrates, most appositions in the corpora contained units that were continuous (example 11) rather than discontinuous (example 12):

(11)   she   she   was   {\ABSOLUTELY}   \/OBSTINATE#   self-W/ILLED# and and determined to do her TH\ING# (LLC S.1.12.948–50)

(12)   *Cavendish* stood there, *a maypole round which the others executed a three-step.* (SEU W.16.4:55–62)

There were various reasons why units in apposition were not continuous. Some factors are indicated in Table 11.5. In the written corpora, two reasons predominated. First, a number of units were separated for reasons of end-focus and end-weight. In examples (13) and (14) the appositives are separated to place the second unit in the emphatic end-position of the sentence.

Table 11.4 Continuous and discontinuous apposition

Form	Brown		LLC		SEU		Total	
Continuous	950	(93%)	598	(77%)	973	(94%)	2521	(89%)
Discontinuous	76	(7%)	180	(23%)	64	(6%)	320	(11%)
Total	1026 (100%)		778 (100%)		1037 (100%)		2841 (100%)	

Table 11.5 Factors favouring discontinuous apposition

Factors	Brown		LLC		SEU		Total	
End-focus/weight	32	(42%)	7	(4%)	27	(42%)	66	(21%)
Syntactic constraints	35	(46%)	64	(36%)	30	(47%)	129	(40%)
Right dislocation	9	(12%)	52	(29%)	6	(9%)	67	(21%)
Pragmatic expressions	0		57	(32%)	1	(2%)	58	(18%)
Total	76 (100%)		180 (100%)		64 (100%)		320 (100%)	

(13)   *The following possibilities* exist for achieving this [improving the efficiency of plasma generators]: *1. The use of high voltages and low currents by proper design to reduce electron heat transfer to the anode for a given power output. 2. Continuous motion of the arc contact area at the anode by flow or magnetic forces. 3. Feed back of the energy transferred to the anode by applying gas transpiration through the anode.* (Brown J02 480–540)

(14)   What is the use of propounding this definition? *Its use* is that of any valid definition: *to enable us to agree what comes into our discussion and what does not.* (SEU W.9.4:56–62)

Units were also separated because of syntactic factors influencing the placement of words in a sentence or clause. In example (15) the units are separated because it is natural in this context to place the adverbial *however* between the units.

(15)   They [the dishes] looked *so formidable*, however, *so demanding*, that I found myself staring at them in dismay and starting to woolgather again, this time about Francesca and her husband. (Brown R02 350–80)

   In the spoken corpus there were two additional reasons for discontinuity. First, appositives in examples such as (16) and (17) were separated as a result of the spontaneous, unplanned nature of speech.

(16) *she*'s a SH\OCKER you know# *L\/IZZIE*# (LLC S.1.13: 669–70)

(17) I was S\URE# *that* would be one of the most difficult TH\INGS# *buckling down to Anglo-s\AXON*# (LLC S.3.1: 142–6)

The appositions in the above examples, also known as 'right dislocations,' are found primarily in speech where they serve the function of 'postponed identification' (Quirk *et al.* 1985: 1310).

A second feature in speech accounting for discontinuity was the insertion of 'pragmatic expressions' (Erman 1986), such as *you know* or *I mean*, between the appositives.

(18) *the political reasons INV\\/OLVED*# I mean *the ones of national PREST\/IGE*# are entirely ones of T\IMING# (LLC S.2.8:49–51)

(19) it [the beer] tasted *so W\ATERY*# you know *L\IFELESS*# (LLC S.1.7:239–40)

11.5   The semantic structure of apposition

When discussing the semantics of apposition, most writers note that units in apposition are typically coreferential. However, as I argue in Meyer (1987), many units that are considered appositions in the literature are not coreferential at all. To describe more fully and accurately the semantic structure of appositions, I have classified them along two semantic parameters. First, I have expanded the number of semantic relations that can exist between appositives to include not only coreferentiality but also other relations, such as synonymy and hyponymy. Second, I have postulated a number of semantic classes determined by whether the second appositive provides information about the first that is more specific, less specific or equally specific.

11.6   The semantic relations existing between the appositives

Table 11.6 shows the frequency of the semantic relations between the elements in apposition. As this table illustrates, the relationship between the appositives can be either referential or non-referential.

Table 11.6 Semantic relationships between units in apposition

Relationship	Brown	LLC	SEU	Total	
Reference					
Coreference	366	263	469	1098	
Part/whole	64	90	78	232	
Cataphoric reference	153	111	162	426	
Total	583	464	709	1756	(62%)
Synonymy					
Clausal	87	195	74	356	
Absolute	26	16	34	76	
Speaker	53	47	35	135	
Total	166	258	143	567	(20%)
Attribution					
Phrasal	238	15	153	406	
Clausal/phrasal	12	2	15	29	
Total	250	17	168	435	(15%)
Hyponymy					
Syntagmatic	20	30	7	57	
Non-syntagmatic	7	9	10	26	
Total	27	39	17	83	(3%)
Total	1026	778	1037	2841	(100%)

Examples (20)–(22) illustrate three kinds of referential relations holding between the appositives. Examples (20) and (21) exhibit two types of coreference. In example (20) the units are strictly coreferential: they have identical referents. In example (21), on the other hand, the units are not strictly coreferential. Instead, the reference of the second unit is included within the reference of the first, a type of semantic relation that Lyons (1977: 311) terms a part–whole relation.

(20)   could we return to *a play that you say you know pretty* W\ELL# MACB\ETH# (LLC S.3.5:1106–7)

(21)   In the last eight years, *all Presidential appointments*, including *those of cabinet rank*, have been denied immediate action because of a Senate rule requiring at least a 24 hour delay after they are reported to the floor. (Brown A03 1830–60)

To account for the relationship between the units in (22), one must distinguish, as Cornish (1986) argues, between constructions which corefer and constructions in which one unit simply refers to a second unit. In (22) the first unit refers cataphorically forward to the second unit.

(22)   It was then that Picasso and Braque were confronted with *a unique dilemma: they had to choose between illustration and representation.* (Brown J59 1200–10)

Examples (23)–(29) illustrate various kinds of non-referential relations holding between appositives. In examples (23)–(25) there exist relations of clausal and lexical synonymy between the appositives.

(23)   it's like a C\UBE# that is either it can be CONV/EX# or it can be CONC\AVE# (LLC S.1.8:934–6)
(24)   Most laboratory workers are familiar with *'devitrification', the appearance of crystals in old glass that is heated slightly.* (SEU W.9.9:33–5)
(25)   [Steinbeck's style is] *rather ABR\UPT# ECON\OMICAL* I should TH/INK# (LLC S.3.5:656–7)

The clauses in (23) are linked by the optional marker of apposition *that is*, a marker that indicates that the clauses express the same meaning. In (24) and (25) the units are lexically synonymous. Following Cruse (1986), I have distinguished between various degrees of synonymy. In (24) there is 'absolute' synonymy between the two units: the units, as Cruse (1986: 268) observes, have identical meanings because their 'contextual relations' (i.e. their meanings in any context) would be identical. In (25), on the other hand, there is what I have termed 'speaker' synonymy. That is to say, the units are not synonymous in the dictionary sense but rather in the sense that the speaker intends them to be synonymous. The meaning of one word in this type of synonymy, Cruse (1986: 267) maintains, serves 'as an explanation, or clarification, of the meaning of another word'. And, as Table 11.6 indicates, appositions whose units exhibited this kind of synonymy were quite common.

In appositions of the attributive type illustrated in (26) and (27), the units do not corefer but rather, as Burton-Roberts (1975: 395) observes, have an 'ascriptive, descriptive or classificatory role'. This role can exist between two noun phrases (26) or a clause and a noun phrase (27).

(26)   West Police believe they have caught *Raffles, one of Britain's most wanted men.* (SEU W.12.7:f–2)
(27)   *Mercantile's growth is far more broadly based than before, a factor* which has enabled the group to live with high interest

rates and still keep a firm grip on margins. (SEU W.12.6:a–5, a–6)

Examples (28) and (29) contain appositives related by hyponymy. The majority of these appositions, as Table 11.6 demonstrates, were instances of what Lyons (1977) terms 'syntagmatic' hyponymy: the second appositive becomes a hyponym through the addition of a pre- or postmodifier.

(28)   what I think we N/\EED# you see is rooms with *a T\ABLE# a table which students can sit R\OUND#* (LLC S.3.4:47–9)

Only a few examples consisted of hyponymous units in a non-syntagmatic relation.

(29)   The nitrogen in *organic matter (dead roots and shoots, manure soil humus, etc.)* is changed during decomposition to an ammonium form . . . (SEU W.9.6:19)

11.7   The semantic classes of apposition

Table 11.7 contains a listing of the semantic classes into which appositions can be classified and the frequency with which these classes occurred in the corpora.

Table 11.7 The semantic classes of apposition

Semantic class	Brown	LLC	SEU	Total	
More specific					
Identification	323	239	451	1013	
Appellation	212	21	124	357	
Particularization	49	49	40	138	
Exemplification	42	80	55	177	
Total	626	389	670	1685	(59%)
Less specific					
Characterization	208	37	205	450	(16%)
Equally specific					
Paraphrase	165	258	143	566	
Reorientation	26	32	13	71	
Self-correction	1	62	6	69	
Total	192	352	162	706	(25%)
Total	1026	778	1037	2841	(100%)

Many of the classes in this table are adapted from Quirk *et al.*'s (1985: 1308–16) discussion of apposition. However, I have had to modify or add to Quirk *et al.*'s classes to account for all of the appositions I found in my corpora. As Table 11.7 indicates, the majority of appositions in the corpora (59 per cent) consisted of constructions whose second unit contained information that was more specific than the first unit; the remaining appositions contained second units that were either less specific than the first units (16 per cent) or equally specific (25 per cent).

Identification and appellation contain second units that identify (30) or name (31) the first unit.

(30)   Consider *the features of Utopian communism: generous public provision for the infirm; democratic and secret elections of all officers including priests; meals taken publicly in common refectories; a common habit or uniform prescribed for all citizens; even houses changed once a decade.* . . . (Brown J57 1640–80)

(31)   *this chap Robbe GR/ILLET#* starts from N\OTHING# at \ALL# (LLC S.3.1:321-3)

Particularization (32) has the effect of singling out some aspect of the first unit.

(32)   Upon receiving the news [of the slave rebellion of 1859], Northern writers, editors, and clergymen heaped accusations of murder on *the Southern states*, particularly *Virginia*. (Brown J58 300–10)

Exemplification (33) is similar except that the second appositive provides an example of the first.

(33)   you might read *a a a a N/EW {and OR/IGINAL piece#} of CR\/ITICISM#* such as */ELIOT#* on *H/AMLET#* (LLC S.3.5:1014–16)

Only one kind of apposition provides information that is less specific than the first unit. Characterization (examples 34 and 35) provides information that attributes some general characteristic to the first unit.

(34)   About 45,000 people would lose their homes as a result of the Greater London Council's 1000 million road plans, *Mr Douglas*

*Jay, Labour MP for Battersea North and former President of
the Board of Trade*, said last night. (SEU W.12.4:61–2)

(35)   The Association of Head Mistresses warmly welcomed *the
Newsom report* – '*a vital and moving human document*' – but
was convinced that a 'crash' programme of recruitment was
essential to provide teachers who were alert to new ideas and
adaptable to changing times. (SEU W.12:1–46)

Three semantic classes provide information that is equally specific
as the information in the first unit. In the class illustrated in (36) the
second appositive provides a paraphrase of the first.

(36)   In this puddled soil the exchange of air between atmosphere
and soil is minimized, so creating an *anaerobic (oxygen-
deficient) environment for roots, the so-called reduced zone.*
(SEU W.9.6:16–17)

Reorientation (37) provides an alternative way of viewing the first
appositive.

(37)   And it was *Greaves', that master goal scorer, that masterful
taker of the half-chance*, who put Tottenham in that happy
position. (SEU W.12.5:c–3)

Appositions resulting from self-correction (38) occur primarily in
speech. They contain a second unit that corrects some inadequacy in
the first unit.

(38)   C\ECILY# *his new w\IFE#* or *his s\ECOND wife#* she
T/EACHES# (LLC S.1.13:638–40)

11.8   The information structure of apposition

From the point of view of information structure, apposition is a
relation in which the second unit provides new information about
the first unit and 'adds' to the flow of discourse (Meyer 1987). This
characteristic of apposition explains two tendencies that were present
in the corpora: appositions were especially common in some genres,
and certain semantic classes of apposition occurred much more
frequently in some genres than in others.

Table 11.8 outlines the uneven distribution of appositions in the
various genres of the corpora. This skewed distribution indicates

Table 11.8 Total number of appositions per genre.

Genre	Number of appositions	Appositions per 1000 words
Fiction (SEU)	201	5.0
Intimates (LLC)	158	5.3
Equals (LLC)	169	5.6
Fiction (Brown)	244	6.1
Learned, scientific (Brown)	132	6.6
Disparates (LLC)	223	7.4
Intimates/equals (LLC)	228	7.6
Learned, humanistic (Brown)	180	9.0
Learned, scientific (SEU)	197	9.9
Press (SEU)	394	9.9
Press (Brown)	470	11.8
Learned, humanistic (SEU)	245	12.3
Total	2841	7.9

that appositions were communicatively more necessary in some genres than in others. Specifically, appositions are most necessary in genres characterized by a low degree of shared knowledge. In general, as Biber (1988: 46) observes, spontaneous speech is produced by speakers possessing a great deal of shared knowledge, written texts by discourse participants with a low amount of shared knowledge. As Table 11.8 illustrates, this difference between speech and writing is reflected in the genres of the corpora: the spoken genres tended to contain fewer appositions, the written genres more.

But this spoken/written dichotomy does not give the entire picture. Within the spoken genres, fewer appositions occurred in the speech of equals and intimates – individuals who would possess a high degree of shared knowledge – than in the speech of disparates – individuals who would not possess a high degree of shared knowledge. Within the written genres, fewer appositions occurred within the fiction genre than within the press genre. It is not surprising that the press genre contained such a high density of appositions: journalistic writing, particularly press reportage, must appeal to a very wide and diverse audience, and consequently, journalists must assume little shared knowledge with the audience for whom they are writing. It is somewhat more surprising, however, that the fiction genre contained relatively few appositions. One possible explanation is that as a fictional world unfolds in a novel or short story, the

Table 11.9 Select semantic classes per genre

Genre	Appellation	Characterization
Press (Brown)	179 (4.4)	147 (3.7)
Press (SEU)	89 (2.2)	147 (3.7)
Learned, scientific (Brown)	2 (0.1)	6 (0.3)
Learned, scientific (SEU)	6 (0.3)	17 (0.9)
Learned, humanistic (Brown)	12 (0.6)	15 (0.8)
Learned, humanistic (SEU)	5 (0.3)	6 (0.3)
Fiction (Brown)	19 (0.4)	40 (1.0)
Fiction (SEU)	24 (0.6)	35 (0.9)
Disparates (LLC)	8 (0.3)	4 (0.1)
Equals (LLC)	7 (0.2)	9 (0.3)
Intimates/equals (LLC)	5 (0.2)	13 (0.4)
Intimates (LLC)	1 (0.03)	11 (0.4)
Total	357 (1.0)	450 (1.3)

Figures in parentheses indicate number of appositions per 1000 words

writer (or narrator) and reader come to share much personal knowledge about characters and events. As a result, there arises little communicative need in a fictional text for appositions to be used.

While appositions are in general communicatively more necessary in some genres than in others, particular types of appositions have communicative functions that are better suited to some genres than to others. Table 11.9 provides a breakdown of the frequency of occurrence of two semantic classes – appellation and characterization – having communicative functions most appropriate in the press genre. Because individuals are the primary focus of press reportage, it is not surprising that the semantic class of appellation figured so prominently in this genre, a class in which the second unit of the apposition names the first unit.

(39)   A pastoral letter from *the Bishop of Bristol, Dr Tomkins*, was read today in churches throughout the diocese. (SEU W.12: 1–48)

In addition, it is important in the press genre, particularly in reportage, to provide descriptive information about individuals presented in articles. Consequently, appositions in the class of characterization are well suited to this style, since the second units of these appositions provide descriptive information about the first units.

(40) *Skinny Brown and Hoyt Wilhelm, the Flock's veteran knuckle-ball specialists*, are slated to oppose the American League champions in tomorrow's 8 p.m. contest. (Brown A11 1010–30)

The other semantic classes (identification, exemplification, particularization, etc.) were similarly distributed differently across the various genres of the corpora (see Meyer, forthcoming).

11.9   Conclusion

I have demonstrated in this article that a clearer understanding of apposition can be obtained if it is viewed as a grammatical relation whose realizations have specific syntactic, semantic and pragmatic characteristics. I have also shown that the study of a grammatical category (in this case apposition) can be greatly enhanced by text corpora: they provide researchers with a wealth of linguistic data upon which to base their explanations, and they allow these explanations to include information on the actual use of the construction being studied. As the development of text corpora continues, they ought to play an increasingly important role in linguistic description and linguistic theory.

Notes

[1] I am indebted to David Chin (Computing Services, University of Massachusetts at Boston) for computational assistance and to Sidney Greenbaum for the many helpful comments he has given me on my work on apposition.

[2] For more detailed information on the syntactic, semantic and pragmatic characteristics of appositions, see Meyer (1987, 1989 and forthcoming).

[3] Not all of these constructions are fully appositional; some are partially appositional and on gradients between apposition and other relations, such as coordination or complementation. For a more detailed discussion of the gradable nature of apposition, see Meyer (1989 and forthcoming).

12 Syntactic evidence for semantic distinctions in English

DIETER MINDT

12.1 Syntax and semantics

Semantic distinctions are very often arrived at intuitively and described accordingly. For this reason there is often no operational criterion for assigning a certain meaning or a set of meanings to a certain linguistic element.

However, it is a well-known fact that the specific meaning of a linguistic element is to a large extent determined by the syntactic context in which it occurs. This leads to the question of whether it is possible to discover syntactic regularities that correlate with the semantics of certain linguistic elements. This article is concerned with describing areas of English where such dependencies between syntax and semantics can be found.

The study is based on the assumption that the meaning of an element is either unambiguously revealed by its form or clarified by a contextual signal. Within the sentence this signal can be either prosodic, morphological or syntactic.

During the history of English there has been a severe reduction of morphology. As a result, syntactic devices have taken over the functional role of morphological disambiguation in many areas. The fact that syntactic devices very often serve this purpose has frequently been overlooked in the past.

The aim of the following study is to establish a systematic link between syntax and semantics. In order to achieve this link we have to look for areas of English grammar where there are clearly observable surface correlates of semantic distinctions.

There will be three examples to illustrate this:

182

- specification and futurity
- subjects and intentionality
- negation and the semantics of *any*

The first case deals with indicators of future time that occur in connection with verbal constructions which express futurity in English. The second concerns the dependencies between subjects and verbal constructions which signal future time. The third deals with syntactic correlates of various functions of *any* in English.

12.2   Specification and futurity

Since the majority of English verbs have only two inflectionally marked tense forms, present and past, temporal differences are in a considerable number of cases indicated by elements that co-occur with the verb. An early study of how co-occurring elements account for the temporal interpretation of certain verb forms was undertaken by Crystal (1966), who introduced the term 'specification' for this phenomenon.[1]

Future time reference in English is expressed by a number of constructions (cf. Carstensen 1972: 20–1, Mindt 1987a: 44–5). The four most frequent ones are:

will	*I will do my best*[2]
be going to	*I'm going to buy a new kit tomorrow*
the present progressive	*Well, I'm quitting for a promotion*
the simple present[3]	*His birthday is next week*

Of these constructions it is generally assumed that *will* and *be going to* do not normally need a specification (i.e. a temporal reference outside the verb which signals future time). On the other hand, most grammars claim that both the present progressive and the simple present are invariably accompanied by an adverbial or some other contextual element that refers to the future (e.g. Alexander 1988: 163, 165).

Futuric specification can be achieved in several ways, as illustrated by the following examples.

(1)   I'm starting another class in May.
(2)   We have a stunner for you in a moment.

(3)   Tomorrow's going to be an extraordinarily good day.
(4)   He'll burn himself out if he goes on at this rate.

In (1) the specification of the present progressive is performed by the prepositional phrase *in May*; in (2) the future time reference is established by the prepositional phrase *in a moment*; in (3) the temporal reference of *be going to* is specified by the adverb *tomorrow*; in (4) the reference of *will* is specified by the conditional clause.

For a systematic study of specification, fifteen classes were established on the basis of the co-occurring element that signals future time reference (adverbs, noun phrases, conditional clauses, etc.; see Mindt 1987a: 98ff). These were subsequently conflated into a single class (called *spec*) which is contrasted with *zero*. The class *zero* contains all those cases where no specification of a verb form can be found in the context.

Two corpora were selected for a comparative study of specification: *The Corpus of English Conversation* (Svartvik and Quirk 1980, abbreviated CONV) and a corpus consisting of twelve contemporary plays (abbreviated PLAYS).[4] The absolute and relative frequencies of specification in these sources are given in Table 12.1.[5] Figure 12.1 presents the percentages in graphic form.

The data reveal that specification varies in a very systematic way for the different verb constructions. Four conclusions can be drawn from the data.
– The simple present has clearly the lowest inherent futuric value, since it has the greatest frequency of specification in both corpora. On the other hand, *be going to* has the highest inherent futuric value of the four constructions, even though there is a specifying element in more than 60 per cent of the cases. The present progressive ranges lower in terms of inherent futuric value than

Table 12.1 The distribution of specification with constructions for future time reference in CONV and PLAYS

	CONV		PLAYS	
	n	%	n	%
Simple present	61	95.3	56	86.2
Present progressive	70	86.4	102	79.1
will	330	79.7	710	74.6
be going to	117	73.6	159	68.0

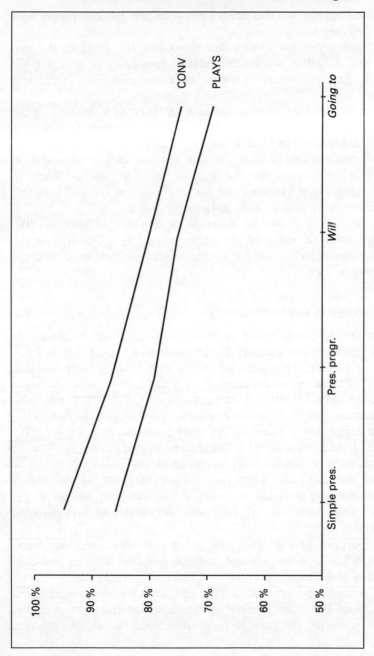

Figure 12.1 Percentages of specification with constructions for future time reference in CONV and PLAYS

the simple present. *Will* ranges between the present progressive and *be going to*.

- The rank order for specification is exactly the same in the two corpora. In other words, the relative frequency of specification for the four constructions shows the same tendencies in the text types.
- The degree of specification can also be taken as a measure of the degree of redundancy. Figure 12.1 shows very clearly that there is more redundancy in CONV than in PLAYS. This does not come as a surprise if one considers that in genuine spoken conversation there is no chance for the listener to stop and go back to something which has been said earlier. Speakers seem to take this subconsciously into account in their production.
- Specification is clearly an indicator of semantic distinctions (the inherent futuric value of the constructions in question). At the same time it can be used for an operational distinction of different text types.

12.3   Subjects and intentionality

The traditional classification of subjects is based on the categories person, number and gender. These categories are obviously irrelevant for a study of subjects and verbs with future time reference. Instead what seems to be relevant is a distinction between intentional and non-intentional subjects (see Leech 1971: 59, who mentions the factor 'conscious human agency' when referring to the present progressive). However, in many examples (e.g. *I'll get a lift*) it is very hard or impossible to decide whether an intentional subject is consciously or intentionally involved in the event or state. To simplify the task and still capture something of the distinction intentional/non-intentional a crude distinction was made in the present study between subjects with personal and non-personal reference.

The purpose of the study was to see if there are systematic dependencies between personal and non-personal subjects and constructions which express future time reference in English.

Again the two corpora CONV and PLAYS were used for a comparison. The study is based on the same constructions as above: *will, be going to,* the present progressive, and the simple present.

Table 12.2 The distribution of personal subjects with constructions for future time reference in CONV and PLAYS

	CONV		PLAYS	
	n	%	n	%
Present progressive	76	93.8	122	95.3
will	321	77.5	807	85.1
be going to	119	74.8	196	83.8
Simple present	39	60.9	43	66.2

The frequencies (per cent) of personal subjects in CONV and PLAYS are given in Table 12.2. Figure 12.2 presents the percentages in graphic form.

The following conclusions can be drawn from the material:
- Personal subjects occur most frequently with the present progressive. This is clearly in accordance with the observations in the linguistic literature (cf. Quirk *et al.* 1985: 215).
- The lowest number of personal subjects is found with the simple present. This contradicts other grammatical statements (Close 1975: 255).
- The constructions *will* and *be going to* do not differ very much with respect to personal/non-personal subjects, although in each case *will* is slightly more common with personal subjects than *be going to*.
- The rank order for the distribution of personal subject is the same in the two corpora. There is no variation in the frequency of the category 'personal subject' between the two text types.
- As with specification, there is a systematic difference between the text types: the figures for personal subject are in each case higher in PLAYS than in CONV.

The distribution of subject types indicates a semantic distinction among the four different constructions which can be expressed in the form of a gradience. The present progressive can be classified as a construction which in the overwhelming majority of cases has a personal subject and thus an association with intentionality. On the other hand, the simple present shows the least correlation with a personal subject and intentionality. *Will* and *be going to* occupy a middle position with respect to subject type and intentionality.

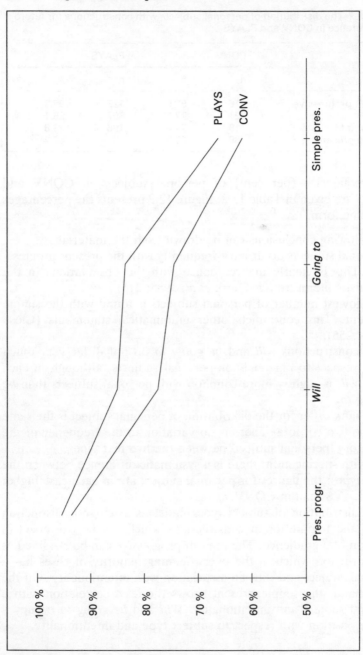

Figure 12.2 Percentages of personal subjects with constructions for future time reference in CONV and PLAYS

12.4   Negation and the semantics of *any*

In the description of the indefinite pronouns *some* and *any* there has been a strong tendency to stress a clear-cut relation between syntax and semantics. This is especially true of school grammars, where it is often claimed that *any* and its compounds *anyone, anything*, etc. normally occur in negative or interrogative contexts, whereas *some* is used in affirmative and non-interrogative sentences (Bald and Schwarz 1984: 20, 113; Eastwood 1989: 110).

A description of *some* and *any* which is based on the semantic distinction 'assertive' and 'non-assertive' is given by Quirk *et al.* (1985: 782ff). *Some* is assigned to the class of assertive items and *any* to the class of non-assertive items. For non-assertive items there are characteristic non-assertive contexts such as clause negation, questions, conditional clauses, etc. Thus the authors establish a direct link between semantics and syntax (see also Ungerer *et al.* 1984: 80–1, who make the same distinction; for a detailed discussion of previous research, see Tesch 1990: 17–49).

This analysis, however, is taken one step further in Quirk *et al.* (1985: 390). Negative, interrogative or conditional contexts are described as 'superficial' and the choice of *some* or *any* is shown to depend on the basic meaning of the whole sentence in which either occurs. This explains the use of *some* in questions like *Did somebody telephone last night?* (basic sentence meaning assertive), or the use of *any* in statements such as *Freud contributed more than anyone to the understanding of dreams* (basic sentence meaning negative and non-assertive). In the latter case, the basic sentence meaning of *any* is said to appear in the paraphrase *Nobody contributed as much to the understanding of dreams as Freud*.

The shift of focus to the meaning of the whole sentence still leaves unresolved the question of the meaning of *any* in these cases. To find out the meaning of individual lexical items, one has to turn to the dictionary. For a case like *They're all free – take any (of them) you like*, the *Longman Dictionary of Contemporary English* (1987) supplies the meaning: 'every (of more than two), no matter which', which is clearly an assertive interpretation.

The observation by Quirk *et al.* (1985) and statements in dictionaries on the meaning of *any* raise the question of whether there is a correlation between the uses of *any* and observable surface syntactic elements. A corpus-based study by Tesch (1990) can shed some new light on the syntax and semantics of *some* and *any*.

To be able to deal with the meaning of *any* taken on its own she introduced a pragmatic–semantic category which refers exclusively to the indefinite pronoun. This category is concerned with the speaker's assumption about the actual presence or existence of the object or person referred to by *some* or *any*. There are two manifestations of this category:

(a) 'supposed to be present', and (b) 'not supposed to be present'. Sentences like *She spoke as fast as any Frenchwoman* are cases of (a) because the speaker presupposes the existence of Frenchwomen. Sentences like *I mean I haven't had any results* are cases of (b) because the speaker does not presuppose the existence of results (see Tesch 1990: 117).

In addition to the pragmatic components 'supposed to be present' and 'not supposed to be present' there is a semantic feature present in *any*. This becomes evident by a translation into German of affirmative sentences. For *you'd better get rid of any other ideas you might have*, which is a case of 'supposed to be present', the German translation of *any* is *irgendwelche*. For *have you any money?*, which is a case of 'not supposed to be present' because the speaker does not assume the existence of money or is not sure about it, the German translation of *any* is *zero*: *hast du Geld?* (i.e. absence of a determiner preceding the noun *Geld*).

It is now possible to check if there are systematic syntactic combinations with which these pragmatic–semantic categories occur. Two pairs of syntactic distinctions were used for this purpose, the variable AFNEG with the two values 'affirmative' and 'negative' (Tesch 1990: 99–102) and the variable DECINTR with the values 'declarative' and 'interrogative'.[6]

The question is how the two pragmatic–semantic categories 'supposed to be present' and 'not supposed to be present' relate to the syntactic values 'affirmative' and 'negative' and 'declarative' and 'interrogative' with the types of *any*. A cross-tabulation of the pragmatic categories with the syntactic values 'affirmative' and 'negative' is presented in Table 12.3.[7]

Of all cases of *any* in CONV, 342 or 43.3 per cent have the meaning 'supposed to be present' and occur in affirmative contexts. This type of *any* is called any_1.[8] Example: *I thought any fool would know*.

Table 12.3 The distribution of *any* in CONV in affirmative and negative
contexts with different presuppositions

	Supposed to be present		Not supposed to be present	
	n	%	n	%
Affirmative	342	43.2 (*any₁*)	69	8.7 (*any₃*)
Negative	33	4.2 (*any₄*)	347	43.9 (*any₂*)

The second type of *any* (making up 347 cases or 43.9 per cent of
all occurrences of *any* in CONV) conveys the presupposition 'not
supposed to be present' and is syntactically marked by negative
contexts. This type of *any* is called *any₂*. Example: *I shan't get any
scripts from the assistants before then.*

The third type, called *any₃*, occurs in affirmative contexts with a
percentage of 8.7 of all occurrences of *any*. Example: *But is there
any truth in it?*

A fourth type (*any₄*) is far less frequently used (4.2 per cent of all
cases of *any* in CONV). It conveys the presupposition 'supposed to
be present' and occurs in negative contexts. Example: *Vera had
decided not to confide any of her business affairs to her.*

In order to be able to make comparisons, two sub-corpora were
chosen from the LOB Corpus: (1) a selection of fictional texts
(LOB_f), and (2) a selection of expository texts (LOB_s). (On the
choice of texts, see Tesch 1990: 67–9.) Although there are certain
differences between LOB_f and LOB_s there is no significant difference
in the distribution of the features studied here (Tesch 1990: 226).[9]
For reasons of space the following comparison will therefore be
restricted to LOB_f. The data for LOB_f are presented in Table 12.4.
Figure 12.3 presents the percentages from CONV and LOB_f in
graphic form.

Table 12.4 The distribution of *any* in LOB_f in affirmative and negative contexts
with different presuppositions

	Supposed to be present		Not supposed to be present	
	n	%	n	%
Affirmative	170	43.5 (*any₁*)	41	10.5 (*any₃*)
Negative	29	7.4 (*any₄*)	151	38.6 (*any₂*)

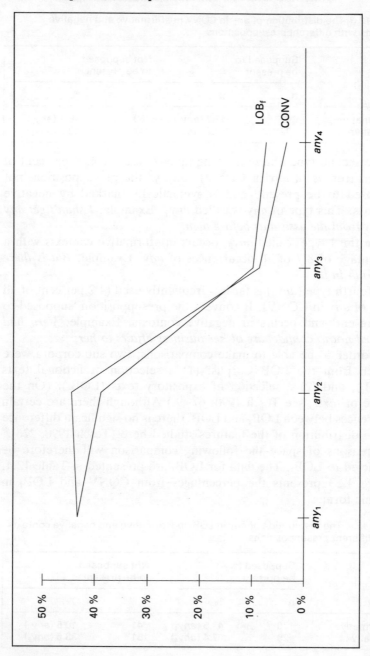

Figure 12.3 Percentages of the combined categories 'supposed to be present', 'not supposed to be present', 'negative' for the four types of *any* in CONV and LOB$_f$

The results can be summarized as follows.

- The distribution of the four types of *any* is very similar in the two corpora. There is very little difference in the distribution of the two most important types any_1 and any_2. The same is true of the less common types any_3 and any_4.

- Contrary to statements in most grammars, the most common syntactic environment of *any* is affirmative. This syntactic environment is clearly connected with a very important pragmatic–semantic feature ('supposed to be present'). This combination of a pragmatic–semantic feature with a corresponding syntactic environment accounts for an important part of the use of *any* in contemporary English (any_1).

- The traditional description of *any* ('not supposed to be present' in negative contexts = any_2) is equally important. It would, however, be incorrect to describe this combination of pragmatic–semantic and syntactic features as the only or characteristic use of *any*.

In a second step, the three main types of *any* (any_1, any_2 and any_3) were correlated with the two values 'declarative' and 'interrogative'.

For any_1 in spoken English and in fictional texts the distribution of the categories 'declarative' and 'interrogative' was 80 per cent and 20 per cent respectively. Since this distribution can be assumed to be the general proportion of these categories in spoken English (Tesch 1990: 231f),[10] any_1 does not seem to have a preference for either declarative or interrogative contexts.

Any_2 occurs almost exclusively in declarative contexts (more than 96 per cent in all corpora; Tesch 1990: 232–3). There is no significant difference between the figures for the spoken and written corpora.

For any_3 the rate of interrogative contexts is about 50 per cent in the written texts. In spoken English (CONV) interrogative contexts make up about 75 per cent of all occurrences of this type. Obviously, any_3 is much more frequently used in interrogative contexts than the other two main types of *any*.

The distribution of the syntactic features 'declarative' and 'interrogative' again differs in a systematic way for the three types of *any*. This means that for *any* a further link between syntactic and pragmatic–semantic categories can be established.

12.5   Conclusion

For the three areas of English grammar investigated here it could be shown that there are syntactic correlates which correspond to semantic distinctions. Specification, which has a clear syntactic correlate, can obviously serve as an indicator of the inherent futuric value of verbal constructions used to refer to future time in English. Another factor which can be taken as a syntactic marker of futurity is subject type. The degree to which verbal constructions referring to future time in English are combined with personal subjects makes it possible to assign them certain positions relative to each other on a gradience scale.

Both specification and personal subject show a clear parallelism in terms of rank order. This indicates that the relative distribution of specification and personal subjects is an invariant feature of English and possibly holds for different types of texts. At the same time, systematic text type differences could be found in both cases, which, however, do not affect the rank order of the constructions.

For *any* it could be shown that the traditional description (non-assertive meaning with a syntactic environment which is basically marked by negation) is true for less than 50 per cent of the occurrences of *any*. The majority of cases of *any* occur in a syntactic environment which is affirmative. From these observations a new classification of the meanings of *any* can be worked out which is again marked by clear syntactic correlates on two different levels.

The interdependencies between syntactic regularities and semantic distinctions that have been put forward in this article shed some new light on the way in which syntax is related to semantics. By studying correlations of this kind it is possible to establish new and operational syntactic criteria for semantic distinctions. As a result, the traditional domain of intuitive methods in the analysis of semantics can be replaced by more objective methods.

The close correspondence between syntax and semantics has very often been neglected in the past. This is mainly due to the fact that the analysis of syntax poses a number of very intricate problems. With traditional methods it is not possible to perform analyses of language data which are large enough to permit empirically founded generalizations.

After the first steps of data collection it very often becomes necessary to redefine linguistic classes, regroup cases or reclassify items.

This may be prohibitive if the researcher has to rely on the traditional manual procedures of linguistic analysis. The computer, on the other hand, makes it easy to rearrange, regroup or reclassify items or groups of items by means of sorting and/or recoding procedures. For this reason it is possible to arrive at generalizations inductively from the data rather than look for examples that confirm hypotheses based on smaller sets of data.

For most purposes the same linguistic element has to be classified according to features belonging to different levels of linguistic analysis, e.g. morphological, syntactic, semantic, pragmatic. If all these features have to be taken into account, the researcher is faced with the necessity of performing analytical tasks on multivariate sets of data, for which the traditional methods of linguistics fail.

The results presented here could not have been achieved without the work of pioneers in this field. Jan Svartvik belongs to the small group of scholars who have not only provided the very basis of this work through the compilation and preparation of machine-readable corpora. He has also set important guidelines in the development and application of statistical methods, numerical taxonomy and multivariate analysis in corpus-based linguistics (Svartvik 1966, Quirk and Svartvik 1966, Svartvik 1968, Carvell and Svartvik 1969).

Notes

[1] Crystal restricts his study to adverbs, which are clearly not the only elements which determine the temporal interpretation of a verb form. There are a number of additional methodological problems in Crystal's study which do not, however, diminish its importance as a pioneering investigation into the relationship of syntax and semantics (for a discussion see Mindt 1987a: 41f).

[2] All the examples quoted in this article are taken from *The Corpus of English Conversation* (Svartvik and Quirk 1980), the LOB Corpus and from a corpus consisting of twelve contemporary plays. See Mindt (1987a: 50–5), Tesch (1990: 60–71) and Note 4.

[3] For this study only cases of the simple present in main clauses were taken into account.

[4] This corpus contains the following plays:
Ayckbourn, A., 1977, 'Table Manners', in Ayckbourn, A., 1977, *The Norman Conquests: A Trilogy of Plays*, Penguin, pp. 13–88.
Gray, S., 1971, *Butley*, Eyre Methuen.

Gray, S., 1975, 'Otherwise Engaged', in Gray, S., 1975, *Otherwise Engaged and Other Plays*, Eyre Methuen, pp. 9–60.

Griffiths, T., 1976, *Comedians*, Faber & Faber.

Hampton, C., 1976, *Treats*, Faber & Faber.

Hare, D., 1980, *Dreams of Leaving*, Faber & Faber.

Keeffe, B., 1977, *Gimme Shelter: Gem, Gotcha, Getawa*, Eyre Methuen.

Mortimer, J., 1971, *Come As You Are*, Methuen.

Nichols, P., 1980, *Born in the Gardens*, Faber & Faber.

Poliakoff, S., 1976, 'Hitting Town', in Poliakoff, S., 1976, *Hitting Town and City Sugar*, Eyre Methuen, pp. 53–134.

Wesker, A., 1963, 'Chips with Everything', in *Penguin Plays: New English Dramatists*, 7, 1963, Penguin, pp. 15–72.

[5] For the corresponding figures for *zero*, see Mindt (1987b: 52).

[6] For both variables the study started out with a more complex set of values which could later be reduced, since the more delicate distinctions played no significant role in the analysis.

[7] The non-affirmative categories 'half-negative' and 'conditional' (see Tesch 1990: 226) have been added to the negatives.

[8] In the LOB Corpus this is the most frequently used type of *any* (Tesch 1990: 224–6).

[9] Although there is no statistically significant difference between LOB_f and LOB_s for the features studied here (Tesch 1990: 224–5), LOB_f is more similar to CONV than to LOB_s.

[10] In expository texts (LOB_s) the percentage for 'declarative' is 97.

13   On having a look in a corpus

GABRIELE STEIN and RANDOLPH QUIRK

Alongside verbs such as *walk*, *look*, *scream*, there are roughly synonymous expressions in which a nominalized form (N) of these verbs is made the object of a verb (V) of more general meaning. A commonly cited canonical example is *have a look*. Thus we have alternatives like:

(1) She swam every morning.
(1b) She *had a swim* every morning.
(2) Look at this photo!
(2b) *Take a look* at this photo!
(3) The poor woman screamed.
(3b) The poor woman *gave a scream*.

While linguists have long shown considerable interest in the V + N construction that we find in these (b) sentences, we are still far from a full understanding of it. In Stein (1991) an attempt is made to examine the phenomenon in depth and to assess and describe the function of these constructions. The present chapter is concerned with the occurrence of V + N constructions (where V is a form of *have*, *take* or *give*) in a corpus of contemporary fiction amounting to around 1.6 million words. The items comprising the corpus are listed at the end of the chapter.

There were altogether 402 examples, 297 with *give*, 72 with *have*, and 33 with *take*. For example:

(4) Shirley gave a little squeak of surprise. (Lodge: 107)
(5) Matilda had another sip of whisky. . . (Wesley$_1$: 23)
(6) Jeanne took one look at her friend. (Lurie: 56)

Two limitations on the material here examined should be noted. First, as regards V we have ignored a minority of items such as *do* (as in *Mac did an expert dip*, Lurie: 218) and the much bigger minority with *make* (as in *and we all had to make a dash for it to get to the building*, Lurie: 93). Second, as regards N we ignore nominalizations which are other than (a) isomorphic with the base form of the corresponding verb, and (b) replaceable semantically and idiomatically with the verb. Thus we exclude:

(a)   She's giving it deep thought.
        (cf. She's thinking about it deeply.)
(b)   He gave no hint about his intentions.
        (cf. He did not hint about his intentions.)

We analysed the whole material in terms of broad grammatical and semantic distinctions, to investigate contrasting distributions and co-occurrences as between the *take, have* and *give* examples. Indeed, since it is clear that there can be cases where monotransitive *give* may occur but not ditransitive *give* (for example *He gave a sigh*, but **He gave his brother a sigh*), we separated for the purposes of analysis the instances with monotransitive *give* from those where *give* was ditransitive. The results of the analysis are given in Table 13.1 and we can now proceed to discuss them.

While the grammatical distinctions made in the table are doubtless self-evident, the eleven semantic distinctions deserve a word of explanation. We have set these up on the basis of the actual corpus data (but cf. also Nickel 1968, Live 1973, Müller 1978, Wierzbicka 1982, Stein 1991, Dixon 1991), and their nature will be clear from the examples that follow:

perception, as in:
    'Really!' explodes Claudia. She gives him a *look* of contempt.
    (Lively: 168)
mental activity, as in:
    I went for a walk and had a *think*. (Wesley₁: 166)
verbal activity, as in:
    On their runs, they began by having little *chats*... (Wilson: 175)
consumption, as in:
    He took a *sip* of coffee. (Lurie: 268)
bodily care, as in:
    ... she had a quick *wash* and felt much better. (Hocking: 75)

contact activity, as in:
Jeanne gave her a grateful *hug*. . . (Lurie: 74)
physical action, as in:
We screamed and spattered in the breaking waves while Mrs Brock took her real *swim*. (Keane: 50)
tentative action, as in:
It might be worth having a *try*. (Hocking: 28)
involuntary reaction, as in
Louise, who might have given the guilty *start* Alice anticipated . . . replied at once, 'The love of my life! How did he seem?' (Hocking: 117)
potentially voluntary reaction, as in:
Garrett gave a forced-sounding *laugh*. (Lurie: 99)

Table 13.1 Grammatical and semantic distinctions with *take-*, *have-* and *give-*constructions

Grammatical and semantic distinctions	*Take*	*Have*	monotrans. *Give*	ditrans. *Give*
V present	4	5	7	13
past	17	28	101	136
aux + V	2	15	2	13
imperative	3	12	—	2
non-finite	7	12	3	20
First person	2	27	—	10
Second person	—	8	—	2
Third person	21	19	108	150
N indefinite	31	69	107	177
definite	2	3	6	7
pre-modified by adj.	13	24	90	126
unpre-modified	20	48	23	58
perception	15	15	3	84
mental activity	—	2	—	—
verbal activity	—	11	—	—
consumption	12	16	—	1
bodily care	—	4	—	—
contact activity	—	—	1	17
physical action	5	9	1	7
tentative action	1	6	—	2
involuntary reaction	—	—	27	9
potentially voluntary reaction	—	9	61	53
voluntary reaction	—	—	20	11

voluntary reaction, as in:

> At the sight of his reassuring back, Rose gave a *shout* of joy.
> (Wesley$_2$: 119)

We should draw attention first to a grammatical feature of N which, as the table shows, is overwhelmingly an *indefinite* noun phrase, typically singular with the indefinite article, irrespective of the V. This has, of course, been frequently remarked (cf. Olsson 1961, Renský 1964, Nickel 1968, Prince 1972, Wierzbicka 1982, Akimoto 1989, Dixon 1991) and provides the most obvious basis for distinguishing the V + N construction as a special type.

When we look at grammatical properties of V, however, we see that *have* is very different from *take* and *give*. This shows up most notably in the category of person, with a contrast that is statistically significant.

	First and second person	Third person
have	35	19
take/give	14	279
(χ^2 : $p < .001$)		

To a somewhat lesser extent, the grammar of *have* contrasts with that of *take* and *give* also in respect of the occurrence of auxiliaries, imperative and non-finite forms.

	Simple finite	Not simple finite
have	33	39
take/give	278	52
(χ^2 : $p < .001$)		

It should be noted that the skewed distribution with *have* includes within the total of thirty-nine numerous instances of modalized finites such as:

(7)   I suppose you thought we *should have* a little talk. (Keane: 169)

Such factors are doubtless to be connected with the semantic categories of N that appear in construction with *have*, notably verbal activity, physical and tentative action, all of which are more associated with *have* than with *take* or *give*. The table also draws attention to one semantic category – consumption – where N can be combined uniquely with either *have* or *take*. It is here where the specific meanings brought into the construction by *have* (casual experience) and *take* (purpose-directed) (Stein 1991) become most manifest. Compare:

(8)   Matilda *had another sip* of whisky and looked down towards the harbour. (Wesley$_1$: 23)
(9)   She gave in, she *took a sip*, but put the glass down at once on the window-ledge in front of her. (Fowles: 213)

A grammatical feature that distinguishes sharply between *give* on the one hand and *have* or *take* on the other is the occurrence of adjective modification in the noun phrase that realizes N:

	Pre-modification	No pre-modification
give	216	81
have/take	37	68
(x^2 : $p < .001$)		

Again, there is a link between this skewed distribution and the semantic factors among the Ns that co-occur with *give* and those that co-occur with *have* and *take*. *Give* tends to be used with *realized* experience which is thus more prone to invite detailed description and evaluation. Such modification is quite frequently multiple:

(10)   She searched his face for a long moment, gave him a *still faintly doubting* smile back, then lifted her jacket to put it on. (Fowles: 607)
(11)   Polly gave a *loud, angry, uneven* sigh. (Lurie: 287)

Finally, we must look at the differences between monotransitive *give* and ditransitive *give* that relate to this grammatical difference in transitivity. We see that the monotransitive occurs much more freely where N relates to involuntary reaction and somewhat more freely where N relates to voluntary reaction. For example, respectively:

(12)   He gave a wretched sob. (Hocking: 59)
(13)   She gave a small nod. (Fowles: 664)

On the other hand, the ditransitive occurs more freely where N relates to physical activity and contact activity. For example, respectively:

(14)   Farthing gave his barrow a heave and moved on. (Wesley$_2$: 159)

(15)   Jeanne ... gave Polly a warm hug. (Lurie: 278)

But above all, the ditransitive is overwhelmingly associated with an N of perception, a semantic type that scarcely occurs with monotransitive *give* at all. For example:

(16)   Hubert gave her a pitying glance and rode on. (Keane: 57)

Ditransitive *give* with Ns of perception seems to occur predominantly in narrative texts as a means to characterize verbal and nonverbal turn-taking in dialogue. For example:

(17)   'Now you must suffer for it.' She gave his smile a doubting look. (Fowles: 578)

(18)   Papa never said an actual thank-you for all this labour. Perhaps during luncheon, if he was wearing a resuscitated old ghost of other days, he might pat himself and give her a look – a look like a ray of light from a distant star, a look that suggested warmth and pleasure. (Keane: 53)

Ns denoting potentially voluntary reaction are prominent with both mono- and ditransitive *give* and seem to fulfil the function of describing the effect and emotional basis of dialogue in narrative texts. For example:

(19)   'No salad dressing for me, please.' 'Oh, that's right.' Garrett gave a little apologetic chuckle. (Lurie: 90)

(20)   'What's the hurry, hon?' Lee gave her a wide friendly, maybe even more than friendly grin. (Lurie: 193–4)

There may well be a correlation between these occurrences in narrative and the grammatical features of *give* (past tense 237, third person 258).

It will be clear from Table 13.1 that we have by no means exhausted discussion of the differences in distribution – nor does the Table exhaust the analytic categories implicit in the material. We hope, however, to have contributed a little to the description of the English V + N construction.

The corpus

ARCHER: *Shall We Tell the President?* J. Archer, Coronet Books, London, 1980.

FOWLES: *Daniel Martin*, J. Fowles, Triad Panther, London, 1982.
GREENE: *Doctor Fischer of Geneva or the Bomb Party*, G. Greene, Penguin, Harmondsworth, 1981.
HOCKING: *Welcome Strangers*, M. Hocking, Abacus, London, 1987.
JAMES: *The Skull beneath the Skin*, P. D. James, Penguin, Harmondsworth, 1989.
KEANE: *Good Behaviour*, M. Keane, Abacus, London, 1982.
LIVELY: *Moon Tiger*, P. Lively, Penguin, Harmondsworth, 1988.
LODGE: *Nice Work*, D. Lodge, Penguin, Harmondsworth, 1989.
LURIE: *The Truth about Lorin Jones*, A. Lurie, Abacus, London, 1989.
MOORE: *The Colour of Blood*, B. Moore, Paladin, London, 1988.
THOMPSON: *The Dream Traders*, E. V. Thompson, Pan, London, 1983.
WESLEY$_1$:   *Jumping the Queue*, M. Wesley, Black Swan, London, 1984.
WESLEY$_2$:   *Not That Sort of Girl*, M. Wesley, Black Swan, London, 1988.
WESLEY$_3$:   *Second Fiddle*, M. Wesley, Black Swan, London, 1989.
WILSON: *Love Unknown*, A. N. Wilson, Penguin, Harmondsworth, 1987.

14   On the exploitation of computerized corpora in variation studies

DOUGLAS BIBER and EDWARD FINEGAN

14.1   Introduction

In an encounter between R.B. Lees and W. Nelson Francis in the early 1960s, Lees asked Francis what he was up to at the time, and Francis replied that he had a grant to compile a computerized corpus of English. When Lees asked 'Why in the world are you doing that?', Francis answered that he wanted to uncover the 'true facts of English grammar'. As Francis recalls the incident, Lees then looked at him 'in amazement' and exclaimed: 'That is a complete waste of your time and the government's money. You are a native speaker of English; in ten minutes you can produce more illustrations of any point in English grammar than you will find in many millions of words of random text' (Francis 1982: 7–8).

The kind of language database extolled by Lees in that exchange has played a prominent role in the development of grammatical theory in the years since. Indeed, the dominant source of data in the investigation of syntactic theory has been the introspective powers of individual linguists, supplemented by questions asked of native speakers concerning grammaticality judgements of 'linguistically interesting' sentences.

At the same time, Nelson Francis and Henry Kučera did assemble the corpus of written American English whose utility Lees couldn't fathom, and their foresight has been demonstrated in numerous ways since. Moreover, a companion corpus of written British English has been developed (the LOB Corpus), as well as a number of other spoken and written corpora. These corpora have proven a boon for investigating questions not previously answerable, and indeed, in some cases the corpora have inspired what might be called Mount Everest questions – questions arising because the corpora are available but otherwise practically impossible to imagine. Thus, alongside the introspective and logical models of language structure so prevalent in grammatical theory at the present time, there are impressive studies of language structure, language variation and language history that are inconceivable from the limited vantage point of introspective data.

One irony surrounding the prevalence of introspection over corpus-based analysis for syntactic theorizing is that modern linguistics has its roots in analysis of corpora – for linguistic theorizing received its modern impetus from historical linguistics, and historical linguistics is rooted in the analysis of corpus-based data concerning lexical, phonological, semantic and grammatical evolution. Wherever insight into the historical development of languages may originate, the final appeal must be to the historical record – to the corpora of extant texts.

The past few decades have seen some rivalry between corpus linguists and introspective linguists, and while it is not our purpose to evaluate the legitimacy of the claims on either side, it bears observing that both corpus linguists and introspective linguists have made impressive strides in achieving understanding of language. In light of the ways in which corpus linguistics has made possible the investigation of certain questions that cannot be tackled introspectively, it is our purpose to make some observations about the reliability and validity of the systematic analysis of language variation using the existing and envisioned corpora.

The existence of English-language corpora has opened up to investigation new approaches to artificial intelligence and to syntactic theory itself. Sampson (1987b) makes a persuasive case for the value of probabilistic models of syntax based upon analyses of corpora rather than the idealized data of introspection. He illustrates the kinds of sentences typically discussed among AI researchers by the following two: *A ticket was bought by every man* and *The man with the telescope and the umbrella kicked the ball*. And he contrasts such products of introspection with sentences chosen at random from the LOB Corpus, including these two: *Sing slightly flat* and *The libation in honour of the deceased is found as a part of the most modern customs, as when some drops are poured out before a drink is taken: the toast*. Linguists working with corpora, both those developing automatic tagging procedures (as is necessary in AI) and those using corpora as field sites in which to explore linguistic questions, are frequently confronted by the challenge of 'manually' parsing naturally occurring sentences – a challenge that only rarely confronts a linguist parsing introspectively generated sentences, which are strikingly susceptible to parsing. Indeed, students teethed on the idealized sentences generated by introspection often have considerable difficulty parsing genuine examples of natural language.

As a consequence of his experience with corpus data, Sampson (1987b: 20), like others, is persuaded that grammaticality is not always an either/or proposition, and he indicates the limitations of regarding strings as being either well formed or ill formed. He writes:

Within our approach ... the concept of a grammar which defines 'all and only' the forms of the language plays no part at all. Our algorithms deal only with relative frequencies; they recognize no absolute distinctions between 'well-formed' and 'ill-formed'.

Research such as that described by Sampson for the Lancaster/ Leeds group is, of course, possible only in a world where adequately broad, adequately reliable and adequately articulated computerized corpora of natural language are available.

Other kinds of research have been enhanced or made possible with the use of computerized corpora. These include both synchronic and diachronic analysis of continuous variation across dialects and across genres, both written and spoken. Certain questions about the linguistic relations among texts and about text typology were difficult (sometimes virtually impossible) to address systematically before computer-based corpora, and tackling them has given new life to associated questions concerning the potentially related variation across time and genres, across social groups and genres, and ultimately to the relationship between competence and performance (if indeed these constructs survive). Investigation of such questions did not begin with computerized corpora, of course, but to the extent that degrees of variation and degrees of acceptability (as distinct from absolute differences) became of interest, computerized corpora have made sophisticated analyses possible and enhanced the reliability of findings.

Still, despite impressive gains in the development and exploitation of computerized corpora, certain questions have been raised about their utility, and those questions need addressing. Challenges have arisen within the field of corpus linguistics from researchers familiar with corpus development or corpus exploitation (for example by Oostdijk 1988b); the issues include the validity of certain aspects of corpus compilation and the reliability of text samples in the existing corpora. The fact that knowledgeable and sympathetic researchers have raised these questions underscores their importance. As researchers who have relied extensively on the existing computerized corpora, we were challenged by the criticisms levelled against the corpora.

14.2 Potential and practice in the use of text corpora

There is a substantial history of corpus-based study in linguistics. Readers of this volume will be particularly familiar with the computerized corpora of written texts developed for English – for example the Brown Corpus (American English), the LOB Corpus (British English), the Helsinki Corpus (historical and dialectal English), and the Melbourne-Surrey Corpus (Australian English). However, a great deal of research has also been devoted to spoken texts. The best-known computer-based corpus of spoken English is the London-Lund Corpus, but other corpora exist, notably the Lancaster/IBM Corpus of Spoken English.

Research on social dialect variation by William Labov and his colleagues has also been based on text corpora of sociolinguistic interviews since the mid 1960s. Work by more anthropologically inclined sociolinguists has been based on text corpora for at least as long (including work by Dell Hymes, William Bright and Elinor Ochs). As is well known, linguists in the American structuralist school (including Edward Sapir, Stanley Newman, Leonard Bloomfield and Kenneth Pike) earlier in this century focused on the analysis of languages without written traditions (especially native American languages) and depended on narrative texts for their linguistic database.

All text corpora are *not* created equal, however. Most obviously there are differences in recording medium and storage medium. Early collections of stories were either written directly by a language consultant or transcribed by a linguist as they were told. In the 1960s, the ready availability of tape recorders facilitated making permanent records of spoken texts. As a result, unfortunately, some researchers apparently dispensed with transcribing texts and relied solely on audio tapes, though it is difficult to find published information on the form of these early corpora. More typically, researchers used tape-recorded versions of texts to make written transcriptions. In this case, besides the permanent taped record of the original text, a transcribed version enables a careful linguistic analysis on several levels. More recently, transcribed texts have been stored in machine-readable form, enabling types of analysis that were not previously feasible. Jan Svartvik led the way in this regard with the London-Lund Corpus (cf. Svartvik and Quirk 1980).

Text corpora have evolved in other respects also. First, researchers have become increasingly sensitive to the importance of collecting 'natural' discourse, which is typically considered to be ordinary, relaxed conversation. Earlier corpora relied on folk tales, while most of the material in the corpora for social dialect studies consists of interviews. There has been considerable concern with the issue of 'naturalness' by mainline sociolinguists. For example, Labov (1972) structured his interviews to include narratives of close calls with death in an attempt to collect more natural speech, while Wolfson (1976) argues that interviews are as 'natural' as ordinary conversation. Other studies argue for the importance of participant observation, in which researchers record discourse in which they participate as interlocutors. The hope in this approach is that, over time, recording devices will become less obtrusive. Other researchers have surreptitiously recorded speech in everyday contexts where the participants are unaware of any recording devices. This is true of most texts in the Survey of English Usage and the London-Lund Corpus, which include a large number of completely 'natural' face-to-face and telephone conversations.

Finally, text corpora differ in the range of variation that they represent. As noted above, early corpora comprised primarily folk tales. Mainline sociolinguistic corpora focus on the range of social variation among speakers, but they represent quite restricted ranges of textual variation (typically only a formal interview, word lists, and sometimes a narrative). Other corpora concentrate on conversation, under the assumption that it represents the most basic and important type of text. In contrast to all these approaches, researchers in the computerized corpora tradition have attempted to represent as many different types of text as possible. Thus the Brown and LOB corpora contain written texts from nine expository genres and six fictional genres; the London-Lund Corpus contains texts representing an extremely wide range of speaking situations in English, including face-to-face conversation, telephone conversation, public interviews, panel discussions, radio broadcasts, parliamentary debates and speeches, court cases, dinner speeches, sermons and academic lectures. In summary, corpora compiled in the tradition of the Brown, LOB and London-Lund differ in three major respects from other corpus projects: (1) they are computer-based; (2) they represent 'natural' discourse; and (3) they represent a very wide range of the types of speaking and writing in English.

Potentially, these corpora enable a range and scope of research opportunities unmatched by earlier corpus projects. In practice, though, researchers have not always fully exploited this potential. First of all, relatively few studies have exploited the machine-readable character of these corpora. In fact, many studies are based simply on printouts of the corpora, making them equivalent to any other collection of written or transcribed texts. Other studies are based on computer-generated printed concordances, in which case linguistic analysis is generally limited to partial sentential contexts. Still another type of study adopts the development of computer-based analyses as its primary research goal; these projects investigate the automated grammatical analysis of English words (grammatical 'tagging') and sentences (parsing) using the computer-based corpora (Aarts and Oostdijk 1988; Garside, Leech and Sampson 1987). In the investigation of traditional linguistic questions, however, few studies have used automated computer-based analysis as a tool.

Second, while the corpora comprise collections of texts, studies have most commonly exploited the corpora as collections of sentences, analysing particular lexical items, phrases or grammatical constructions within their sentential context. Such studies are significant, among other ways, in that they analyse particular constructions in naturally occurring discourse rather than in made-up sentences. But the research goals of most such studies could be met equally well by a corpus of isolated sentences. Reflecting the state of linguistic studies generally, few studies have exploited the corpora to analyse characteristics of texts rather than characteristics of sentences.

Finally, although the corpora represent a very wide range of the types of spoken and written texts in English, most studies have used restricted subsets of the corpora. This characteristic of corpus-based studies, understandable in light of limited computer capacity and even more limited computer literacy, is nevertheless regrettable. The original corpus compilers recognized that linguistic forms and functions vary across different kinds of text, and their corpora were designed to accommodate these considerations. But studies are frequently based on only one genre (commonly conversation) or two (e.g. conversation to represent speech and academic prose to represent writing). The importance of the differences among kinds of text, and the value of the resources provided by the computerized corpora in this respect, have not been fully exploited. With increased computer literacy among linguists (and an increasing array of sophisticated software), as well as with the dizzying explosion of power in desktop computers, appreciation for the richness of corpus linguistics is sure to grow dramatically.

In our own research we began with research goals having relatively large scope, such as the linguistic characteristics of texts, the stylistic differences among texts, and the linguistic characteristics of speech and writing in English. Subsequently we realized that the computer-based corpora provided ideal databases for research goals of this type. We thus combined our goals with the resources provided by computer-based text corpora to develop the Multi-Feature/Multi-Dimension (MF/MD) approach to the analysis of linguistic variation among texts (see Biber 1988). Some of the major characteristics of the MF/MD approach are: (1) it is corpus based, depending on analysis of a large number of naturally occurring texts; (2) it is computer based in that it depends on automated analyses of linguistic features in texts (enabling analysis of a large number of linguistic features in a large number of texts); (3) its research goal is linguistic analysis of texts and text types, and of styles or registers, rather than of individual linguistic constructions; (4) it assumes a variationist perspective; that is, it recognizes that different kinds of text differ linguistically and regards analysis of any one or two text types as an inadequate basis for conclusions concerning a discourse domain; and (5) it is multi-dimensional, acknowledging that multiple parameters of variation operate in every discourse domain.

The MF/MD approach has been used to characterize and compare varieties of use in English: spoken and written varieties (Biber 1986); British and American varieties (Biber 1987); complex and simple varieties (Finegan and Biber 1986); varieties of expository prose (Grabe 1986); styles of stance (Biber and Finegan 1988a,

1989b); stance strategies in discourse concerning nuclear war (Connor-Linton 1988); communicative strategies of Soviets and Americans in cross-cultural situations (Connor-Linton 1989). It has also served in the development of a typology of English texts (Biber and Finegan 1986; Biber 1989) and in tracing the historical evolution of three written genres (Biber and Finegan 1988b, 1989a). In addition, the MF/MD approach has been used for analyses of register variation in other languages. Besnier (1988) analyses spoken and written varieties in Tuvaluan, a Polynesian language; Biber and Hared (1989) are undertaking a diachronic analysis of spoken and written varieties in Somali; and Yong-Jin Kim is analysing spoken and written varieties of Korean in dissertation research at the University of Southern California.

In the present essay we turn to methodological questions concerning corpus-based studies generally and the MF/MD approach in particular. We first discuss several issues relating to the design of text corpora, including the nature of 'texts', the number of texts required, and optimal text length. We also discuss the characteristics of 'genres' and 'text types'. We then address linguistic features and the nature of form/function correspondences, concluding with a brief discussion of issues relating to textual dimensions. If Sampson's expectations that the probabilistic/corpus paradigm (currently the minority paradigm) is to play an increasingly important role in AI, and if the claims made by corpus linguists, about genres and text types, about the relationship between dialects and registers and about textual relationships among the diverse genres of English and other languages, are to withstand challenges to their reliability and validity, these matters must be assessed.

14.3 Methodological issues

14.3.1 Texts

There are several issues relating to the character of texts used in corpus studies of variation. The issue of optimal text length is of immediate practical concern; text samples must be long enough reliably to represent the linguistic characteristics of the full text, but not so long as to add unnecessarily to the work required to compile and use a corpus. The issue of text length presupposes answers to other questions: What constitutes a 'text'? Is it appropriate to extract 'samples' from 'texts'? Must 'texts' be homogeneous linguistically?

We do not intend to propose yet another definition of 'text'; for our purposes, texts are simply continuous segments of naturally occurring discourse. Most complete texts are complex in that they extend over numerous topics, purposes and even participants (as in the case of conversation). A typical academic article, for example, reflects a hierarchical structure of sections and paragraphs. The sections may range from description to narration to expository analysis. (An academic book would show an even wider range of variation.) Reflecting different situations and different purposes and topics, short stories and novels similarly include different kinds of textual material: description, narrative and both dialogue and inner monologue. The same holds for many spoken texts: political speeches typically include narrative, exposition and exhortation; conversations are often even more complex in that they can involve a continuous transition among sets of participants as speakers come and go from a scene.

Different sampling techniques in such cases would enable different kinds of analysis. A sampling that disregards the changing purposes and topics within a text permits overall characterizations of the text or genre. On the other hand, a sampling that extracts sections that are homogeneous with regard to purpose and topic (e.g. discussions of methodology in social science papers or descriptive settings in novels) would permit linguistic analysis of the distinctive characteristics of specific sub-genres of texts. These two approaches yield different perspectives on text variation, and both are valid.

There are few empirical investigations of variation *within* texts and of the related issue of optimal text sample length. Biber (1990) addresses this issue by analysing the distribution of linguistic features across 1000-word text samples extracted from larger texts (from 2000-word texts in the LOB Corpus and 5000-word texts in the London-Lund Corpus). With respect to the features examined, 1000-word samples reliably represent the distribution of features in a text, as indicated by very high correlations among the feature counts in the samples from each text (i.e. high reliability coefficients) and by small difference scores across samples. In most cases, reliability coefficients were greater than .80 (and many were greater than .90), while nearly all the difference scores were less than 15 per cent (and over half were less then 10 per cent). This generalization held across ten linguistic features (first and third person pronouns, contractions, past and present verb tense markers, nouns, prepositions, *wh*-relative clauses, passive constructions and conditional subordination). It held across texts taken from seven spoken and written genres (e.g. conversations, speeches, academic prose, general fiction). This study should be complemented by another analysing the linguistic differences among text portions representing specific purposes (e.g. description, narrative and dialogue in fiction). The study indicates, though, that 1000-word samples reliably represent at least certain linguistic characteristics of a text, even when considerable internal variation is anticipated.

14.3.2 Genres and text types

In previous work we distinguish between 'genres' and 'text types'. Genres are the text categories readily distinguished by mature speakers of English (e.g. novels, newspaper articles, public speeches). In our view, then, the text categories used in the standard computer-based corpora are genres. Text types, on the other hand, have a strictly linguistic basis; they are sets or groupings of texts such that the texts within each set are linguistically similar while the sets are linguistically distinct. Biber (1989) uses cluster analysis to identify the salient text types of English (cf. Biber and Finegan 1986). Overall, eight text types are identified. The types are interpreted by considering their predominant linguistic features, the general communicative characteristics of the texts grouped in each type, and micro-analyses of particular texts. Functional labels are proposed for each type, such as 'Informational Interaction', 'Learned Exposition' and 'Involved Persuasion'.

While focusing on the salient text type distinctions of English, Biber (1989) also argues for the validity of genres, claiming that genres and text types represent complementary text categorizations. Other studies, though, have questioned the usefulness of genre distinctions (e.g. Oostdijk 1988b). Two questions are relevant here: (1) To what extent are genre categories linguistically homogeneous? (2) Does linguistic heterogeneity entail that a genre category is invalid?

With regard to the first question, there is considerable evidence that genre categories are relatively homogeneous linguistically. Biber (1988) shows that the genres of English can be effectively characterized linguistically and that there are large (and statistically significant) differences among them. Biber (1990) compares the linguistic characteristics of ten-text and five-text subsamples drawn from five genres (face-to-face conversation, public speeches, press reportage, academic prose, general fiction). A comparison of frequency counts for six linguistic features (nouns, first and third person pronouns, past tense markers, prepositions, passives) showed an extremely high degree of stability across the subsamples (reliability coefficients greater than .95 for the ten-text samples; greater than .90 for the five-text samples). These results indicate that there is a high degree of internal linguistic consistency at least in these five genre categories, and that a ten-text sampling of a genre provides a good representation of the category.

Not all genres are equally homogeneous, of course, and a complete linguistic description of a genre should include both a characterization of the central tendency (i.e. of the average or typical text) as well as a characterization of the range of variation. Genres can have a relatively wide range of linguistic variation for several reasons. First of all, some genres include distinguishable sub-genres. For example, academic writing includes articles and books from a number of fields, ranging from humanities and the arts to engineering and business; newspaper texts include articles covering spot news, society news, sports news and financial news, as well as reviews and editorials. These sub-genres are often significantly different in their linguistic characteristics (Biber 1988: 180ff). Second, genres show considerable differences in the extent to which they have a focused norm, even when they lack identifiable sub-genres. General fiction has a much wider range of variation than science fiction (Biber 1988: 171ff), possibly reflecting differing degrees of latitude to experiment with styles and perspectives. A wide range of variation can also reflect a transitional period diachronically. Both fiction and essays had an extremely wide range of variation in English during the eighteenth and early nineteenth centuries, in part as a reflection of disagreement concerning the appropriate purposes and audiences for these genres (Biber and Finegan 1989a). In none of these cases does a wide range of variation invalidate the genre category; rather the ranges reflect various functional and developmental characteristics of that category, and they should be seen as a descriptive fact that requires explanation.

14.3.3 Linguistic features and form/function associations

Textual dimensions (the parameters of variation) in the MF/MD approach are based on quantitative co-occurrence patterns among linguistic features which are interpreted functionally. The individual features chosen for analysis, and their particular functional associations, are thus important prerequisite considerations.

One issue in the selection of linguistic features concerns the grouping of individual forms into feature categories. In Biber (1988) this grouping was undertaken on functional grounds, so that the forms included in a feature class were claimed to have the same discourse functions. For example, the class of private verbs (or verbs of cognition) such as *assume, believe, conclude, discover* and *doubt* all indicate some private, mental process. Conjuncts include *consequently, furthermore, hence* and *therefore*, which function to mark particular logical relations between clauses.

Despite the enormously useful classificatory resources of *A Comprehensive Grammar of the English Language* (Quirk *et al.* 1985), two difficulties arise in defining classes of linguistic features: (1) because form/function associations can be considered at different levels of generality, decisions are required concerning the most appropriate level for a given feature class; and (2) because the classes must be exclusive of one another for use in a factor analysis, decisions are required for forms having multiple functions (*viz* most forms). English pronouns exemplify the first type of difficulty. All pronouns could be considered members of a single feature class, including all persons, personal and impersonal forms and demonstrative forms; this feature class functions to mark anaphoric or deictic reference. There are, however, more specific feature classes in this grouping that also have identifiable functions. Thus, first and second person pronouns refer to the immediate participants in an interaction, while third person pronouns can refer to persons or objects not immediately present. An example of the second type of difficulty is past participial adverbial clauses. On the one hand, these might be grouped with other adverbial clauses as a subordination feature class functioning to mark structural elaboration, but they could also be grouped with other passive constructions in a general passive feature class functioning to mark a scientific style.

Our approach to these challenges has been to separate out all potentially distinct form/function classes and to rely on statistical techniques to identify the functionally salient groupings shown by strong co-occurrence associations. Thus, in the first example above, each type of pronoun is treated as a separate linguistic feature, and in the second, past participial adverbial clauses are treated as a separate class rather than grouped with either a general passive class or a general adverbial clause class.

This approach is based on the premise that formal differences reflect functional differences, a premise that can be traced back at least to Labov's (1966, 1972) argument against too freely relegating variation to 'free variation'; in the context of his research he found that many erstwhile free variants in fact reflected social differences. Extending this view, we believe that linguistic variation is generally conditioned by some combination of social, situational, discourse and processing characteristics. From this perspective, 'function' can be of three types: (1) the work that a form does in discourse; (2) the situational or processing constraints that a form reflects; and (3) a situational or social distinction that a form (arbitrarily) indexes. In the first type, linguistic forms can be said actually to perform particular tasks. Thus, first person pronouns 'function' to refer to the speaker/writer; relative clauses 'function' to elaborate and make explicit referential identities; some types of adverbial clauses 'function' to set a frame for discourse segments; passives 'function' to rearrange the information structure of a sentence. In the second type, the choice of form directly reflects the speech/writing situation in some sense. For example, generalized content words such as hedges (*kind of, sort of*) or general nouns (e.g. *thing*) reflect the difficulty of more precise lexical expression under real-time production circumstances (although they can also be used to be deliberately vague or imprecise).

Whereas the first type of 'function' is active, actually performing some task, this second type refers to a passive, but direct, reflection of the production and processing circumstances. Some features can be functional in both senses. For example, a high degree of lexical diversity (type–token ratio) increases the semantic precision and informational density of a text; at the same time it typically reflects opportunity for careful production (as in writing), as opposed to the real-time constraints characterizing speaking situations.

The third type of 'function' refers to the way that forms can index particular situations or social groups. For example, argot and jargon mark speakers as members of particular groups – fraternities, professions, gender groups. This is also true of formal and informal situations, where terms of address and various other lexical items function to index degrees of formality. 'Function' in this sense refers to an *arbitrary* or strategic association of particular forms with particular situations or social groups. Many forms, though, are functional in both of the last two senses (i.e. they index a situation and reflect its circumstances of production). For example, hedges (e.g. *kind of, sort of*) index informal, conversational discourse, while the functionally similar downtoners (e.g. *barely, mildly, partially*) index more formal, written discourse. However, the latter set is more specific than the former, indicating particular aspects or degrees of uncertainty, whereas hedges mark a more generalized uncertainty. The differential distribution of these forms reflects the greater opportunity for careful word choice in writing situations, in addition to indexing those situations.

In practice we have not considered arbitrary indexing as functional. In fact we argue elsewhere (Finegan and Biber 1989) that few features are purely indexical (i.e. arbitrary); instead, most seem to have a functional basis (reflective of either discourse task or situation), and indexical marking appears to derive from these more basic functions. In our work on register variation, this approach has meant that we have made relatively fine distinctions among feature classes (as with downtoners being kept distinct from hedges). One extreme case concerns *that* complement clauses with and without an expressed complementizer (e.g. *I think <that> he went*), which we count separately. It might be claimed that these are both complement clauses which perform the same tasks in discourse and that the only difference between them is an indexical one, with the deleted *that* arbitrarily indexing speech. We would claim, on the contrary, that this indexing is derivative; that the clauses with deleted *that* reflect more constrained production circumstances than the marked clauses and are thus functionally distinct. Of course, functional features can always be used to index particular situations for rhetorical effect. For example, the careful, edited writing of dialogue in a novel or drama requires the indexical use of spoken features.

In our analyses we have deliberately included features that are functional in that they perform discourse tasks as well as features that are functional in that they reflect the communicative situation. As a consequence, the textual dimensions identified from these features in our earlier work (Biber 1988) show how these two functional domains are intertwined in discourse. Dimensions are based on groups of linguistic features that co-occur frequently in texts, because they share discourse functions; that is, they perform the same sets of discourse tasks or reflect the same sets of situational circumstances.

In fact it appears that text types evolve so that their discourse tasks fit the production possibilities of their situation. Consider the important dimension labelled 'Informational versus Involved Production'. It combines linguistic features associated with two communicative parameters: (1) the primary purpose of the speaker/writer (informational versus interactive, affective and involved); and (2) the production circumstances (those enabling careful production and revision of a text versus those dictated by real-time constraints). The distribution of features on this dimension shows that these two parameters are intimately intertwined: discourse constrained by real-time production circumstances typically has an involved, affective purpose, and vice versa. It is not surprising that these two functions should be related if discourse purposes evolve to accord with the production possibilities of a communicative situation. Writing situations enable careful word choice and structural integration, and thus the discourse produced in these situations has developed for highly informational purposes. Conversely, although discourse produced under the constraints of real time will tend to be limited in its lexical precision and informational density, these constraints have relatively little impact on the interpersonal and affective purposes typical of unplanned conversation. Similar interrelations between these two senses of function could be given for the other textual dimensions. Our purpose here has been to justify a relatively broad use of the construct 'function' in selecting and classifying features for the study of textual variation.

14.3.4   Textual dimensions of linguistic variation

There are two main issues relating to the textual dimensions: (1) their functional interpretations, and (2) their statistical reliability and significance. The functional interpretations depend in large part on the set of linguistic features chosen for analysis and on the certainty of the functions associated with those features. As noted, we have tended to define feature sets at a low level, distinguishing among functions both as discourse tasks and as reflections of communicative situation. Under this approach we take sets of co-occurring features (as identified by factor analysis) to represent the salient discourse functions, rather than an *a priori* higher-level grouping based on intuitions concerning the relative importance of different functions.

Five major dimensions of variation have been identified to date (see Biber 1988), and the statistical significance of these dimensions has been explored in a number of places. Biber (1988) analyses the relations among spoken and written genres and finds significant differences with respect to all dimensions. Biber (1989) uses the same dimensions to identify a model of English text types (cf. Biber and Finegan 1986). Biber and Finegan (1989a) report significant differences among written genres from different historical periods with respect to three of the dimensions. Biber (1990) analyses the reliability of the dimensions based on analyses of various sub-corpora, finding that the overall factorial structure is highly stable and reliable.

14.4   Conclusion

Besides giving linguists access to certain kinds of data that are otherwise unavailable, computerized corpora of English and other languages have greatly extended the domain of linguistic inquiry. Certain questions that were not in the forefront of linguistic inquiry have been foregrounded by the existence of computerized corpora.

In the present paper we have discussed several issues relating to the use of computerized corpora for variation studies. We first discussed the issue of text length and reported that the size of the Brown, the LOB and the London-Lund corpora and the lengths of their texts are reliable samples of many types of grammatical and lexical features. We have not addressed semantic or phonological features, although semantic features (related as they are to pragmatic context) may require corpora larger than a million words, while (at least segmental) phonological features appear sufficiently often even in a relatively small corpus. Next we discussed some issues relating to genres and text types. We reviewed some previous studies addressing the statistical significance of genre and text type distinctions, and we discussed some of the theoretical implications of heterogeneity within genre classes. Third, we addressed the grouping of linguistic features into form/function classes, distinguishing among three notions of 'function'. Finally we briefly summarized findings relating to the interpretation and reliability of textual dimensions.

We have also offered some observations on the exploitation of existing corpora, especially in the exploration of textual variation. Because of relatively limited skills at manipulating computerized corpora, many researchers who could benefit from the data available in the LOB, London-Lund and Brown corpora are not yet exploiting these impressive (and now highly articulated) resources. But the situation is likely to change as desktop computers become simultaneously more powerful and more economical and as the corpora are transferred into formats that can be manipulated on these machines. Computer literacy among linguists is on the increase, and with it will doubtless come a dramatic increase in the exploitation of computerized corpora. It is our hope that as the use of computerized corpora increases, the reliance on introspection and intuition so characteristic of much linguistic theorizing in the second half of the twentieth century will be balanced by more empirically grounded theorizing based on the facts of usage in English and every other language.

In conclusion, we expect that as computerized corpora extend the range of possible research questions, and provide a more adequate database upon which to address existing questions, the field of linguistics will be enriched by the foresight of the pioneer compilers of computerized corpora.

15   Stylistic profiling

DAVID CRYSTAL

15.1   Background

Fruitful analytic concepts have unpredictable futures. This paper reports on the possibilities and problems encountered in extending one such concept from its original domain, clinical linguistics, into an area of inquiry for which it was never intended, stylistics.

The early 1970s saw the development at Reading University of an approach to the study of language disability which came to be called grammatical *profiling*. This was simply an extension of the everyday use of the term. In the same way that one can identify people by singling out their distinguishing features, and presenting them in a coherent manner, so it was thought possible to identify the most salient features of emerging grammatical structure in a language-handicapped person, and to present these also in a systematic and clinically illuminating way. The LARSP profile (Language Assessment, Remediation and Screening Procedure; Crystal, Fletcher and Garman 1976), as it eventually transpired, was a single A4 chart on which were located four main kinds of information.

(1) Developmental information was given about the order of emergence of grammatical structures, presented vertically as a series of seven 'stages'.

(2) Structural information was given about the range of connectivity, clause, phrase and word constructions thought to be relevant to diagnosis as well as to the other clinical tasks of screening, assessment and remediation; this was presented horizontally, using the notational conventions and analytical approach – with slight modifications – of Quirk *et al.* (1972).

(3) Discourse information was given about the nature of the grammatical interaction between T (the teacher or therapist) and P (the

patient or pupil), such as the types of response to a question stimulus; this was presented in a separate section towards the top of the chart.

(4) Various kinds of procedural and clerical information were given, relating to the patient and the sample, presented at the top and bottom of the chart.

The approach proved to be fruitful in that it was successfully applied to a wide range of patients in speech therapy clinics and in a variety of educational settings (e.g. language units, schools for the deaf), and was quickly extended to other domains of clinical linguistic inquiry. Profiles were devised for segmental phonology, prosody, grammatical semantics and lexical semantics (Crystal 1982). At the same time, other scholars were making use of the profile concept in independent ways, such as in phonology (e.g. Grunwell 1985) and pragmatics (e.g. Dewart and Summers 1988). It also continued to be widely used in the field of psychological and clinical testing, where an analogous concept has a long history as a way of presenting sets of test results. In the 1980s the term *profile* came to be encountered in a prodigious number of linguistic contexts, especially in foreign language teaching and the first language curriculum. For example, in the new approach to English studies advocated as part of the British National Curriculum (Department of Education and Science 1989), the three main areas of language teaching (speaking/listening, reading, writing) are dubbed *profile components*, and the concept of profile emerges as central to the whole teaching and assessment task.

Why do linguistic profiles help? They are, firstly, conveniences: their design enables the user to bring together into a single place a great deal of relevant data which would otherwise be fragmented on cards, notes or the like. Secondly, the data are organized in such a way that significant patterns emerge quickly. Thirdly, when information from a sample is plotted on a profile chart, it is immediately apparent (in terms of the categories represented on the chart) not only what *is* in the sample but also what is not – in clinical terms, often a more significant factor. Fourthly, the fact that an attempt has been made to choose and grade only the most important features makes the task of learning to use a profile relatively easy – some training schools, in fact, eventually used the procedure as a way of introducing students to English grammar.[1] And fifthly, profiles have a clear numerical dimension, which makes them good sources of input to statistical or computational procedures. In a subject where numerical precision is rated highly, profiles have a natural place.

When a concept becomes so fruitful, it makes sense for any field which has not hitherto made use of it to probe its potential also. Stylistics is one such field. I have come across the term *profile* used in an ad hoc way from time to time in stylistic discussion, and the concept seems to inform, implicitly, a great deal of analysis; but I have not found its use as part of an explicit, principled approach to the study of style. Yet there is an immediate, intuitive plausibility about the idea of a 'stylistic profile', and the possibility of devising a single procedure for explicating the notion of stylistic identity ought to be explored.

But, it might be argued, is such an exploration necessary? If the primary focus of stylistics is linguistic distinctiveness, is not the whole subject, almost by definition, an exercise in profiling – whether it be the style of an individual or of a social group? To answer this objection, a distinction needs to be drawn between means and ends. It is indeed the case that the goal of stylistics is the explication of linguistic distinctiveness, but this leaves open the question of how this goal might be achieved. To arrive at statements of linguistic identity (profiles), a profiling procedure must be adopted, and it is this which has so far been lacking.

I should rephrase this: it is rather that we have too many procedures. Each stylistics article develops its own approach, which is often as idiosyncratic as the characteristics of the style it investigates. As a result, it proves extremely difficult to make comparisons between different analyses. Article A might provide a fascinating insight into the use of noun phrases in Dylan Thomas's poetry; Article B also provides a fascinating insight into the use of noun phrases in T. S. Eliot's poetry. It *ought* to be possible to carry out a comparative analysis – how similar, how different, are the two authors in this respect? But it has *never* been possible to do this. The only meaningful comparative studies I know are those where an individual scholar has set up a specific framework of comparison for a single study. Inter-study comparisons, even of studies by the same author, are conspicuous by their absence. Stylistics is a world of single-subject (author, variety) case studies, with as yet little progress made towards the goal of increasing the descriptive generality of the subject. There is no stylistic typology of authors, or of varieties (though the use of multivariate analysis to provide a description of the variation between speech and writing is an extremely promising development – see, for example, Biber 1988, Biber and Finegan, this volume).

But again, it might be argued, is not your own stylistic work, notably Crystal and Davy (1969), such a typology? Not a bit. The aim of that work was to devise a single procedure which could be used for the investigation of all varieties. It took samples and identified the linguistic features of these samples, enabling us to develop our awareness of how a particular text 'worked'. But it was no typology. It was too selective (in terms of the varieties chosen) and too comprehensive (in terms of the linguistic features described) to be a typology. And even though a single linguistic procedure was used for all the varieties examined, the distance between the individual descriptive accounts and the demands of an illuminating typology remained very great. For example, there are chapters on journalese, legal language and religious language, and in each chapter information is given about the types of noun phrase and verb phrase which are used. But what if you were to ask such questions as: What are the differences in noun phrase use between legal and religious English? Are legal and religious English closer together, in terms of verb phrase complexity, than either of these to journalese? Or (to broaden the point), are the spoken varieties analysed in this book distinguishable from the written varieties in terms of noun or verb phrase complexity? Does variation in formality correlate at all with verb phrase type? Many such questions can be formulated, and none of them can be answered, using Crystal and Davy (1969) as it stands.

There is a second kind of limitation in this work. Very few judgements are in fact made about the relative significance of the linguistic features described. For instance, of all the features that one might identify as 'belonging' to a particular variety, which are the most important? Which have the greatest variety identifying capability? Native speakers can and do make judgements of this kind, such as rating -*eth* verb endings as a major characteristic of religious English. Crystal and Davy (1969) made few such judgements, and those they did make were ad hoc and impressionistic. These matters need to be made more precise, and the judgements extended to incorporate a comparative dimension. In the legal English samples, for example, it is pointed out that the style is graphologically distinctive (e.g. the reduced use of punctuation), has a distinctive use of noun phrase cross-reference instead of pronouns (e.g. repeating *the Life insured* instead of using *he* or *she* for second mention), and has distinctive legal vocabulary (e.g. *hereinbefore, whereof*). But no attempt is made to evaluate these features. Looking at legal English from the viewpoint of English *as a whole*, which of these features is more and which less distinctive? Is legal English unique in its avoidance of punctuation (thus giving this feature a high rating, in any typology)? How distinctive *is* legal vocabulary, in fact? Is it more distinctive than, say, the specialized vocabulary of religion or science? What does this question mean, anyway? How does one evaluate 'distinctiveness'? Is it an important goal of stylistic inquiry?

I do not know the answer to any of these questions except the last, where my response is an emphatic 'yes'. A major aim of any theory of style *must* be to explicate the notion of distinctiveness – and not only within a single language, but across languages. Is legal French more or less distinctive than legal English? Does it make use of the same devices and principles? Several illuminating studies in comparative stylistics have shown the kind of personal insight which can be obtained (notably Ullman 1964). Can we move, from such foundations, towards a general stylistic theory? How can we begin to make really powerful comparative descriptions? This is where a profiling procedure may be of value – in bridging the gap between detailed description and typology. To see this, it is necessary to spell out the essential features of any such procedure and discuss how they would be adapted for stylistic inquiry.

15.2   Principles of profiling

Profiling procedures are in principle *comprehensive* – that is, on the chart (or other display, such as a spreadsheet) there needs to be a place for *any* feature claimed to be stylistically significant in a given variety (i.e. in the first instance, in a sample of that variety).[2] This principle does not mean that all linguistic features need separate labelling. To require this would make any procedure too large to be assimilated by anyone/thing other than a computer, and to begin with one would like to be able to demonstrate intuitive immediacy. Rather, the principle means that there must be a place to assign any feature, even if this place is a catch-all category such as 'Other' or

'Miscellaneous'. (This was the procedure adopted in LARSP: about 120 grammatical features were 'named' and located on the chart, the remainder being assigned to the category of 'Other', at different stages of development.)

How does one decide, then, which features are to be given separate identity and which are not? There is obviously an important evaluative judgement being made here. It should be stressed that the question cannot be answered *a priori*. Rather, one uses a mixture of criteria to develop a working model of a profile, and then refines this model as a result of its systematic use. Let us look at how the decision was made for LARSP. We used three criteria. A feature was named separately if: (1) we knew from our clinical experience that it was likely to be an important diagnostic or assessment feature; (2) it was frequently used as a remedial target in the teaching situation; and (3) it was cited as an important developmental feature in the literature on child language (here, grammar) acquisition. On this basis, for example, PrN (= Preposition + Noun, as in *on house, in there*) was given a separate label; it is widely encountered in the abnormal language of language-delayed children, aphasic adults and others; simple prepositional phrases are a widely accepted teaching goal (as evidenced by many teaching packs); and PrN is given separate listing in several studies of emerging syntax as an important developmental step.

It was not possible to be sure that we had identified the right features, in all cases. Child language studies have not been carried out on all structures, and there is sometimes disagreement about the developmental significance of a structure. Also, our clinical experience was inevitably limited and there were several instances where we were unsure just how important a particular feature was. Only by making decisions (hypotheses, really), compiling a profile chart and trying it out on a wide range of patients was it possible to see whether our first judgements had been correct. The *second* edition of any profile chart is, in a sense, the interesting one. In the event, when it came to the second edition of LARSP (1981) we in fact found only a few cases where our initial published judgement had been wrong.[3] An example was AdjAdjN (i.e. a sequence of two adjectives, as in *big red car*). We originally felt that this construction was likely to be an important clinical problem; but it turned out not to be so. Hence in the second edition, this feature lost its named status on the chart and became part of the anonymous 'Other'.

This is the paradox of profiling: one needs to devise a profiling procedure in order to discover whether a profiling procedure is possible. Profiling procedures grow as they are used. They thrive on experience and application.

It is also essential, in any procedure, to impose some order on the many descriptive features considered to be potentially significant: the features need to be *graded*. In the clinical field, this order usually comes from a developmental paradigm. On the grammatical chart the features are organized in terms of their order of emergence in speech, as observed in normal child development. Alternative ordering principles could have been tried – such as grouping features in terms of their memory load, perceptual ease or psycholinguistic complexity – but these alternatives could not provide as precise and discriminating an approach as that derived from child language acquisition research. Even so, because some periods of child grammar have received very little study (notably, from age 4½), the profile classification in places (e.g. Stage VII on the chart) lacks detail. In segmental phonology the ordering principle used was essentially the standard classification of vowels and consonants as developed by the IPA (in terms of place and manner of articulation, voicing, etc.). We felt it premature, given the limited research in phonology acquisition and the demonstration there that individual differences loom large, to impose a developmental ordering on the data.[4]

Other kinds of information and principles of organization can be incorporated into the design of a profile chart. For example, it seemed important to recognize a sociolinguistic principle in the clinical profiles; because language disability is essentially an interactive phenomenon – a disorder does not manifest itself unless T attempts to communicate with P – it is desirable to include information about the properties of T's language (both stimulus and reaction) into any analysis. This kind of information, of course, would not be immediately relevant to a stylistics profile (unless one wished to capture the interaction between author and reader in some way).

15.3   Towards a stylistic profile?

What problems arise when we try to extend this clinical experience into the field of stylistics? Is a stylistics profile possible?

An immediate problem is the increased number of variables likely to be relevant to stylistic analysis. This point was early encountered even in the clinical context; when normal children or adults were profiled, to provide a normative perspective, the totals under the different descriptive headings became very large, and in particular the totals under the various 'Other' headings inflated dramatically. No clear grammatical profile of an author would emerge if we were to use LARSP, for example, precisely because many of the named structures on that chart, being 'core' structures, are those likely to be least illuminating stylistically, and many of the stylistically relevant structures would remain indistinguishable, grouped under 'Other'. Obviously, careful consideration needs to be given to the selection of headings, and to the cut-off point between named headings and 'Other'.

What grading principle might be implemented? How might we rank features which an analyst would claim to be stylistically distinctive? Three evaluative criteria come to mind. First, we can rate the feature for its frequency of occurrence in the variety (or sample). To begin with, impressionistic judgements would suffice, but these could be replaced by precise statistics in due course. Having experimented with various types of frequency information, I would propose six stylistically significant categories, three referring to 'positive' features and three to 'negative' ones:

– the feature is used *only* in variety X
– the feature is used with *very high* frequency in variety X, compared with other varieties
– the feature is used with *above average* frequency in variety X, compared with other varieties
– the feature is used with *below average* frequency in variety X, compared with other varieties
– the feature is used with *very low* frequency in variety X, compared with other varieties
– the feature is *never* used in variety X

Secondly, we need to rate the feature for its overall distinctiveness, in its own right, regardless of frequency. Some distinctive features of a variety are used only once in a text but are criterial (a good example is the headline in a newspaper article). Here, too, a positive and a negative classification can be made:

– the feature is *very* distinctive
– the feature has *some* distinctiveness
– the absence of the feature has *some* distinctiveness

– the absence of the feature is *very* distinctive

Thirdly, we need to rate the feature in terms of the level of precision with which it can be defined and identified. Some features are highly determinate (e.g. 'use of post-modifying noun phrase'), others are less determinate (e.g. 'complex noun phrase') and some are extremely vague (e.g. 'long clauses'). At least these three levels of precision need to be recognized in grading the discriminating power of putative stylistic features.

Table 15.1 summarizes these feature-grading possibilities, assigning numerical values to each decision: the higher the value, the greater the stylistic distinctiveness of the feature. In this way, a score of 7 represents a maximal level of distinctiveness. Anything below 4 would hardly seem to be a serious contender for stylistic status. The interesting discriminations will be between 4 and 7. Any stylistic profile would need to be able to handle features rated 7, in the first instance, and it may be that these would be enough to capture the identity of the variety. If not, we would proceed to those rated 6, and so on. In this way, some degree of control might be exercised on the potentially vast numbers of features which manifest themselves in any sample.

Table 15.1 Evaluative criteria and arbitrary values for calculating the stylistic distinctiveness of a variety or sample

Frequency of occurrence					
	Feature present		Feature absent		
Only	Very frequent	Above average	Below average	Very low	Never used
3	2	1	1	2	3
Overall distinctiveness					
	Feature present		Feature absent		
High	Medium	Unclear	Medium	High	
2	1	0	1	2	
Precision					
Very precise	Some indefiniteness	Vague			
2	1	0			

Where do the lists of features come from? As with the clinical domain, they derive from a mixture of published descriptions and relevant analytical experience. There has to be an inductive approach in which previous stylistic descriptions are trawled for data, and the profile is based on the features considered to be relevant in those descriptions. For the present chapter, I shall illustrate the next step from the data provided by Crystal and Davy (1969).

Immediately, two broad approaches to stylistic profile construction suggest themselves, corresponding to the widely recognized distinction between language *structure* and language *use*. In the former approach, the main dimensions of the profile correspond to the structural 'levels' of the linguistic model used, namely phonetics, phonology, graphetics, graphology, grammar and semantics. Within each of these levels, formal features would be classified and their stylistic role interpreted in relation to the functional categories recognized in the 'use' component of the theory (e.g. formal, occupational, regional). In the latter approach, the profile's main dimensions correspond to these functional categories, and the structural features are classified with reference to each category. In the

Table 15.2 Structural stylistic profile chart: schematic

Variety:	Sample:
Phonetics	*Phonology*
Graphetics	*Graphology*
Grammar Sentence connectivity Sentence structure Clause structure Nominal group Verbal group	
Semantics	
General	*Problems*

Table 15.3 Stylistic features in a sample of legal writing (after Crystal and Davy 1969): evaluation

	F	D	P	Total
Graphetics				
Unbroken format, 197−8	3	2	2	7
Gothic type, 198	2	2	2	6
Graphology				
Words in capitals, 199−200	1	2	2	5
Initial capitals, 199−200	1	1	2	4
Little punctuation, 200−1	3	2	2	7

(Table 15.3 continued)

	F	D	P	Total
Grammar				
Sentence connectivity				
Very long sentences, 201	3	2	1	6
No sentence linkage, 201–2	2	2	2	6
Sentence structure				
Only complete major type, 203	3	1	2	6
Mainly statements, 203	2	1	2	5
Adverbial clauses (especially				
conditional/concessive), 203	2	1	2	5
Sentence-initial clauses, 204	2	2	2	6
Clause structure				
Long clauses, 204	2	2	0	4
Adverbials, 204	2	1	2	5
Adverbial place varied, 204	2	2	2	6
Unusual adverbial place, 204	1	2	2	5
Adverb + participle, 204	2	2	2	6
Adverbs coordinated, 204	2	2	2	6
Frequent coordination, 204–5	2	2	2	6
Nominal group structure				
Complex NPs, 205	2	2	1	5
Complex postmodification, 205	2	2	2	6
Non-finite clauses in NP, 205	1	1	2	4
Unusual place for				
postmodification, 205–6	1	2	2	5
Limited premodification, 206	2	1	1	4
Determiner present, 206	2	0	2	4
such as determiner, 206	1	2	2	5
said as premodifier, 206	1	2	2	5
Mainly abstract nouns, 206	2	1	2	5
Verbal group structure				
Few types of verbal group, 205	2	2	1	5
Non-finite groups, 206	2	1	2	5
Modal + *be*, 206–7	2	1	2	5
Separation of aux + verb, 207	1	2	1	4
Semantics				
Lexical repetition, 201–2	2	2	2	6
Few lexical verbs, 207	2	2	0	4
Wide range of vocabulary, 207	1	1	0	2
Archaisms, 207	2	2	2	6
witnesseth formula, 207	2	2	2	6
Adverb + preposition words				
(*hereon*, etc.), 207–8	2	2	2	6
Formal vocabulary, 208	2	1	1	4
Synonym coordination, 208	2	2	2	6
Original French words, 208–9	2	2	2	6
Other French vocabulary, 209	1	1	1	3
Latinate vocabulary, 209	2	2	1	5
Original Latin words, 209	2	2	2	6
Technical vocabulary, 209	2	2	2	6
Terms of art, 210–11	2	2	2	6

Key: F = frequency; D = distinctiveness; P = precision

Table 15.4 Stylistic features in a sample of newspaper writing (after Crystal and Davy 1969): evaluation

	F	D	P	Total
Graphetics				
Range of type sizes, 174	2	2	2	6
Headline type, 178	3	2	2	7
Short paragraphs, 178	3	2	0	5
Subheadings, 178	2	2	2	6
Large initial letter, 178	2	2	2	6
Graphology				
Comma omission, 178	1	1	1	3
Inverted commas, 179	2	1	2	5
Dashes, 179–80	2	1	2	5
Phonology				
Alliteration, 180	1	2	1	4
Grammar				
Sentence connectivity				
Short paragraphs, 180–1	3	2	1	6
Complex sentence position, 184	2	1	1	4
Strong sentence linkage, 184	2	2	2	6
Initial conjunctions, 184	2	2	2	6
Anaphora, 185	2	1	2	5
No antecedents, 185	2	2	2	6
Sentence structure				
Telegrammatic headline, 180	3	2	2	7
Restricted sentence types in headline, 180	2	1	1	4
Mainly statements, 181	2	1	2	5
Rhetorical questions, 181	2	1	2	5
Imperatives, 181	2	1	2	5
Minor sentences, 181	1	1	2	4
Clause structure				
Verb–subject order, 181	1	2	2	5
Adverbials frequent, 182	2	1	2	5
Initial adverbials, 183	2	2	1	5
Coordination rare, 183	2	1	2	5
Lists rare, 183	2	1	1	4
Subordination rare, 183	2	2	2	6
Parenthesis rare, 183	2	1	2	5
Nominal group structure				
Complex NPs, 186	2	1	0	3
Adjectives, 186	2	2	2	6
Adjective sequence, 186	1	2	2	5
Concrete nouns, 186–7	2	1	1	4

(Table 15.4 continued)

	F	D	P	Total
(Grammar continued)				
Premodifying genitive, 187	1	2	2	5
Whole titles, 187	1	2	2	5
Verbal group structure				
Mainly simple past tense, 187	2	1	2	5
Frequent modals, 187	2	1	2	5
Active voice, 187	2	1	2	5
Contracted forms, 187	1	2	2	5
Semantics				
Unusual word formation, 187	2	2	2	6
Simple vocabulary, 187	2	1	0	3
No technical vocabulary, 187	3	2	1	6
Emphatic vocabulary, 187	2	2	1	5
Informal vocabulary, 188	2	2	1	5
Jocular vocabulary, 188	2	2	2	6
Colloquial speech, 188	2	2	1	5
Word-play, 188	2	2	2	6

Key: F = frequency; D = distinctiveness; P = precision

structural approach we are asking such questions as 'What range of stylistic effects does formal structure X convey?' or 'In what range of stylistic contexts (varieties, authors) is formal structure X used?' In the use approach such questions include 'What are the formal ways of conveying stylistic effect X?' or 'What range of formal linguistic features characterize author or variety X?' Both approaches have their value, but in the present state of the art the former is altogether more promising. Theories of language use are more inchoate, less well defined and far less coherent in the classifications they generate than are theories of linguistic structure.[5] The primary organization of a structural stylistic profile is represented schematically in Table 15.2. No principle underlies the horizontal/vertical ordering, which is simply one of many possible layouts. Within each of these levels there is, in principle, a complete model of linguistic description, which for the present chapter is the one outlined in Crystal and Davy (1969: Ch. 2).

Tables 15.3 and 15.4 list the stylistic features identified in the chapters of Crystal and Davy on legal English (Table 15.3) and

newspaper English (Table 15.4). Only the features related to one of
the newspaper samples (taken from the *Daily Express*) are considered in the tables. No attempt is made to explain the terminology
or status of the features in these lists; for further information,
reference must be made to the original book, using the page
references given in the tables. Each feature is assigned a numerical
value, using the evaluative criteria listed above. These are impressionistic values using the intuition of the author, but also taken
into account are the relevant observations made in the book concerning the degree of importance of particular features. In any
development of the approach, this stage would have to be investigated more objectively.

Of course, as soon as we commence an exercise of this kind, various
problems arise. There is, to begin with, an element of redundancy
between certain features, which ought to be eliminated – for
example, if long sentences are identified in a text, there will inevitably be less sentence linkage. While this overlap might not be
noticed in a discursive stylistic account, it cannot be hidden in a
profile approach. There is also some terminological redundancy
which could be eliminated – such as referring to abstract nouns in
Table 15.3 and concrete nouns in Table 15.4. But generally this
exercise is helpful in that it makes possible a point-for-point comparison which previously could not have been carried out using the
discursive approach, and suggests further questions which might be
asked of either variety. It also immediately highlights the distance
we have to travel before we arrive at a stylistic model capable of
making comprehensive descriptions. While most of the differences
between Tables 15.3 and 15.4 are trivial (e.g. the absence of jocular
vocabulary in the legal sample), some are intriguing and need to be
followed up (e.g. are imperatives never used in legal writing?).

Assuming that there is at least some reliability in these numerical
values, Table 15.5 summarizes the number of features at each value
level for the two samples (it is purely a coincidence that a total of
forty-five was found in each sample).

Several hypotheses can be generated from the data in this table
(using N for newspaper style and L for legal style), such as:

– L uses more distinctive features than N – nearly half the features
  of L are rated 7 or 6, whereas only a third of N's are so rated;
– N is graphetically more distinctive than L, but less so graphologically;

Table 15.5 Rated stylistic features of legal and newspaper style: summary

	7	6	5	4−	Total
Legal style					
Phonetics					
Phonology					
Graphetics	1	1			2
Graphology	1		1	1	3
Grammar					
Sentence connectivity		2			2
Sentence structure		2	2		4
Clause structure		4	2	1	7
Nominal group structure		1	5	3	9
Verbal group structure			3	1	4
Semantics		9	1	4	14
Total	2	19	14	10	45

	7	6	5	4−	Total
Newspaper style					
Phonetics					
Phonology				1	1
Graphetics	1	3	1		5
Graphology			2	1	3
Grammar					
Sentence connectivity		4	1	1	6
Sentence structure	1		3	2	6
Clause structure		1	5	1	7
Nominal group structure		1	3	2	6
Verbal group structure			4		4
Semantics		4	3	1	7
Total	2	13	22	9	45

– L is semantically more distinctive than N;
– L's grammatical distinctiveness is primarily at the levels of nominal group and clause structure, while N's is at the levels of sentence structure and connectivity;
– neither style makes much use of verbal group features.

Several other comparative observations could be extracted from the tables, and these observations would become progressively more interesting as sample size and range of varieties increased. The application of a statistical analysis to developed tables of this kind would be particularly insightful.

At this point it would be possible to begin experimenting with various kinds of visual display, on which the main distinguishing features could be located. One such display is shown in Figure 15.1.

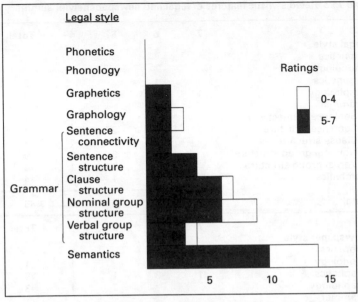

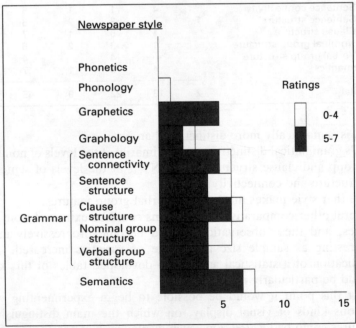

Figure 15.1 Histographic profile of stylistic features: legal and newspaper style

Even at this level of generality, it is possible to make out main areas of similarity and contrast between legal and newspaper style. An extension of this approach would be to take any one level and 'blow it up' so that the substructure of the level could be seen. Such *micro-profiles* could be at varying levels of detail. For example, for an area of grammar, successive statements might be made at the following levels:

Nominal group structure
1st order approximation: premodification – head – postmodification
Example of 2nd order approximation: *premodification structure* predeterminer – determiner – postdeterminer
Example of 3rd order approximation: *postdeterminer structure* ordinal – cardinal – adjective – etc.

In phonology, successive statements might be as follows:

Phonological structure
1st order approximation: segmental – non-segmental
Example of 2nd order approximation: *segmental structure* place – manner – voicing
Example of 3rd order approximation: *place of articulation* use of labials – fronting – etc.

In a full profile, various other kinds of information would have to be added (see Table 15.2). There is a need, as ever, for 'clerical' data, which would provide details of the sample (date, size, type, etc.) and the theoretical approaches used at the different descriptive levels. There would be a 'Problems' section, in which points of analytical difficulty would be listed. And there would be a 'General Observations' section, in which general statements could be made about the style of the sample as a whole. Examples here would include the conservatism and concern for precision found in legal language, and the focus on clarity, interest and compression of information found in newspaper language.

Will such approaches prove to be fruitful? Stylistic profiling is largely uncharted territory. Or, to steal a metaphor from an earlier exercise in profiling, it is a 'relatively uncultivated field' (Svartvik 1968). The present paper has done little more than find a tractor to help plough over some old ground. My feeling now is that it will be worth driving it around some other fields, to see what might grow.

Certainly, when Jan Svartvik was driving such a tractor a generation ago, the ground yielded a valuable crop in the form of the analysis of the Timothy Evans papers – now a classic study in forensic linguistics. That paper provided a fertile furrow for stylistic plough-men to follow. My metaphor is almost dead from nervous exhaustion, but I none the less plant the present offering firmly in this furrow; and if it grows even half as well as its illustrious predecessor did, I shall be well satisfied.

Notes

[1] Not a path I would recommend. The LARSP chart is a distillation of a great deal of grammatical reasoning, much of which can come only from a proper course on English grammar. For example, the question of whether certain constructions should be analysed as SVOO or as SVOA would be debated in such a course. On LARSP, this distinction is arbitrarily made. An aware LARSP user would recognize this arbitrariness and make allowances for it. But this awareness could come only from a theoretically grounded course in English grammar.

[2] This is not the place to investigate the role of discovery procedures in arriving at stylistic judgements. There are important problems here also (cf. Crystal 1972). For the present, I assume that the selection of features to be represented in any typology can be justified, whether with reference to intuition, statistical survey or experimental procedure.

[3] I say 'published' because the LARSP chart had previously gone through many unpublished draft stages in the course of development, and been quite, widely trialled. Doubtless this is what gave the published result its permanence.

[4] Not everyone agrees on this point. Grunwell (1985), for example, has a developmental phonology chart (keyed into the LARSP grammatical stages).

[5] For an amplification of this view, see Crystal (1985: Ch. 3).

16 Expletives in the London-Lund Corpus

ANNA-BRITA STENSTRÖM

16.1 Introduction

Surprisingly little has been said about expletives in the linguistic literature, despite their frequent use in the spoken language. One reason is likely to be the lack of spoken corpora, where the use of expletives can be studied. As far as English is concerned, the only extensive spoken corpus that is available so far is the London-Lund Corpus of Spoken English (described in Greenbaum and Svartvik 1990).

This article describes the expletive repertoire of some of the 'adult educated native speakers of British English' in the London-Lund Corpus with special emphasis on expletives used as interactive devices.[1]

The study is based on the thirty-four face-to-face conversations reproduced in *A Corpus of English Conversation* (Svartvik and Quirk 1980) and five telephone conversations (7.2, 7.3, 8.2, 8.3, 9.1).

16.2 Defining expletives

I shall use the term 'expletive' for a set of words and expressions that are sometimes referred to as 'swearwords'.[2] Words of this type, which are totally or partly prohibited in social intercourse, are often referred to as 'taboo words' (cf. e.g. *The Oxford English Dictionary*), in particular concepts related to religion, sex and excretion (Ljung 1986: 28–9). If such words are used figuratively, signalling the speaker's emotions and attitudes, they are used for swearing,

239

according to Ljung (1986: 28). Swearwords are usually also taken to include fairly innocent exclamations that are no longer considered taboo, such as *blimey, crikey, cor* and *gosh*.

Stankiewicz (1964: 242) argues that practically 'every word can be endowed with emotive connotations if it is placed in an appropriate social situation or verbal context' and points to the conventionalizing of certain lexical items 'as metaphorically expressive terms par excellence', e.g. names of animals (*pig, rat*). A number of American conventionalized swearing expressions, e.g. *Up yours!, Kiss my eye!*, and *Hop on it!* are listed in Ljung (1984: 117–20).

We can conclude with Stankiewicz that the scope of swearing is not limited to taboo words. For the present purposes, however, I shall adopt the following general definition of expletives:

Expletives are realized by taboo words related to religion, sex and the human body, which are used figuratively and express the speaker's (genuine or pretended) emotions and attitudes.

16.3   Uses of expletives

Expletives are either interactive or non-interactive. As interactive devices they are used, for instance, as 'reaction signals' which show the addressee's reaction to a message, and 'go-on signals' which encourage the current speaker to continue. As non-interactive devices they are used mainly as emotional amplifiers (*bloody bastard*; cf. Quirk *et al.* 1985: 1418), as intensifiers (*damned good reasons*), as emotionally coloured substitutes (*what devil took over*?), and as markers of emphasis (*what the fucking hell are you doing*?; cf. Ljung 1986: 36). But regardless of whether they have an interactive or a non-interactive role, they always mirror the speaker's emotional involvement to some extent.

In addition, expletives can also have the subsidiary function of 'covert prestige signals', reflecting the speaker's secret wish to be looked upon as vigorous and unsophisticated (cf. Ljung 1986: 19), and as 'intimacy signals', aimed at building up an informal, chummy atmosphere. In this case, the emotional involvement may be almost non-existent.

Of course, the expletive repertoire is tied to personality, and for some individuals the use of expletives is just a reflection of routine behaviour.

16.4   Inventory of forms

Semantically, the expletives in the corpus can be divided into three broad categories, as outlined in Figure 16.1.

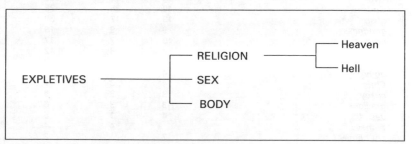

Figure 16.1 Classification of expletives

An inventory of the items is presented in Table 16.1 (for the origin of certain corruptions and euphemisms, such as *cor, crumbs, golly,* etc., see e.g. Partridge 1984). The items are listed in order of frequency within each category and divided into male and female utterances.

Table 16.2, which sums up the frequency of expletives by category and sex, shows that the British speakers in the London-Lund Corpus preferred expletives originating in religion to other types. This should be compared with Ljung's (1986) American data, where sex was the most important source. However, Ljung addressed a somewhat different category of speakers, university students.

Table 16.2 also shows the distribution per category between male and female speakers. Interestingly, the female academics used expletives more often than their male colleagues, although the figures, 146 (male) and 129 (female), seem to indicate the opposite. The fact that 47 (60 per cent) of the speakers were male and only 33 (40 per cent) female means that the average number of expletives per female speaker was seven and that of the male speakers only five. By and large, most of the talk in the material was produced by men.

Men and women did not use the same types of expletive. The female speakers were, for instance, more inclined than the male to use expletives related to 'heaven' and corrupted and euphemistic forms, while the male speakers were more inclined to use expletives ˉelated to 'hell' and 'sex'. Moreover, male and female speakers diˉ

Table 16.1 Expletives in the London-Lund Corpus

Types	Male	Female	Total
Heaven	103	103	206
God	40	35	75
gosh	13	17	30
goodness	9	9	18
Lord	10	7	17
heaven	4	8	12
cor	6	3	9
golly	4	3	7
Christ	4	3	7
crikey	3	3	6
gracious	3	3	6
Jesus	4	1	5
blimey		4	4
cor blimey	2		2
gawd		1	1
gad		1	1
crumbs	1		1
lummy		1	1
cor lummy		1	1
oh God God God		1	1
oh my God goodness		1	1
ooh good Lord wow good heavens		1	1
Hell	27	16	43
bloody	11	10	21
hell	5	4	9
damn/damned/dammit	4		4
devil	3		3
what the fucking hell	3		3
bloody hell	1	1	2
dash		1	1
Sex	10	5	15
fucking	7	2	9
bastard	2		2
cow		2	2
sod		1	1
buggered	1		1
Body	3	4	7
ass	1	1	2
shit	1	1	2
arse		1	1
fathead		1	1
snooks	1		1
Heaven & hell	3		3
God dammit	1		1
God damnation	1		1
good Lord hell	1		1
Hell & sex			
that bloody old cow		1	1
Total	146	129	275

Table 16.2 Frequency of expletives by category and sex

Categories	Men	%	Women	%	Total	%
Heaven	103	71	103	80	206	75
Hell	27	18	16	12	43	16
Sex	10	7	5	4	15	5
Body	3	2	4	3	7	3
Heaven & Hell	3	2	0	0	3	1
Hell & Sex	0	0	1	1	1	0
Total	146	100	129	100	275	100

not use expletives in exactly the same way. Examples (1) and (2) illustrate both the difference in choice of item and the difference in purpose.

(1) A: I mean this . the {CH\AP that} G\/OT it# . I M=EAN# has W\/ORKED# . CONS\/ISTENTLY# \/ALL the way through the C\/OURSE# \/YOU know# almost every N\IGHT# – – and he knows a L\OT# . *a H\ELL of* a lot# (2.9:408–16).

(2) B: so he might go and live with his P\ARENTS for a while# A: ooh – *good L/ \ORD#* . W\OW# (7.3:879–81).

The male speaker in (1) uses *a hell of* to lend extra weight to his words; the female speaker in (2) uses *good Lord* to stress her surprise at what the previous speaker said. In other words, the expletive in the former case is 'self-oriented', in the latter 'other-oriented'. This is not to show that men are more selfish than women, rather that women typically use expletives to give feedback.

16.5 Expletive force

Using some of the expletives listed in Table 16.1 is not really regarded as swearing. I asked nine British colleagues to grade the expressions on a scale from 'strong' to 'weak' and also to indicate whether they found that some of them did not qualify as expletives. The result (which agrees entirely with that of Quirk *et al.* 1985: 852) is shown in Figure 16.2. Only *snooks* (occurring in *snooks to* Y\OU) was not considered an expletive but an insult accompanied by non-verbal action (thumb to nose and fingers splayed).

```
STRONG
  ↑   fucking
      shit
      bugger, bastard, sod
      cow, Jesus, Christ
      bloody
      damn, God, hell
      fathead, Lord
      ass, golly, heavens
      blimey, cor, crikey, crumbs, goodness,
  ↓   gosh, gracious, lummy
WEAK
```

Figure 16.2 Expletive force

16.6 Position and function

In all analysis of discourse the situational context in its widest sense plays a crucial role, i.e. who the speakers are, their common ground and mutual relationship, what they are talking about, what the conversational atmosphere is like, and so on. However, the immediate function of expletives in a dialogue, interactive as well as non-interactive, cannot be identified without considering the position of the item in the discourse.

My analysis of function in relation to position is based on the hierarchical model outlined in Figures 16.3 and 16.4, which is inspired by Sinclair and Coulthard (1975). In this model the ex-

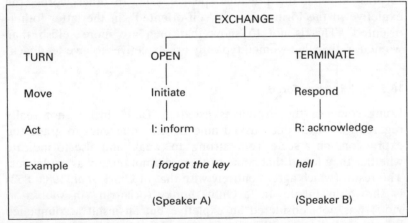

Figure 16.3 Exchange structure (informing exchange)

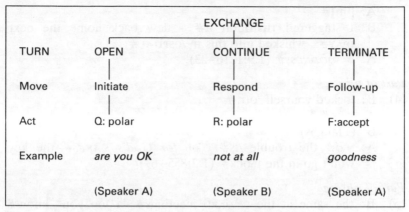

Figure 16.4 Exchange structure (questioning exchange)

change is the minimal unit of interaction. In my version, the exchange is described as consisting of at least two turns produced by different speakers. Each turn consists of one or more moves and each move of one or more acts.

An 'informing exchange' is generally made up of two turns, as illustrated in Figure 16.3. In the first, opening, turn speaker A initiates the exchange by an act with the function 'inform'; in the second, terminating, turn speaker B responds with an 'acknowledge'.

'Questioning exchanges' often consist of three turns, as illustrated in Figure 16.4. The opening turn consists of an initiating polar question and turn two of a continuing polar response, which is followed by a terminating third turn consisting of an accepting follow-up.

My point is that what decides what a particular expletive does, from both an interactive and a non-interactive point of view, is ultimately its position in the discourse. In the following discussion I shall proceed stepwise, going from purely interactive functions in the exchange structure to non-interactive functions in the syntactic structure of the turn, as illustrated in examples (3) to (5).

Separate turn
(3)   B: I couldn't keep ST/ILL# and I – I didn't want him to
          T\/ELL them# and I didn't had no /\APPETITE# for
          F\/OOD#

A: [\m]#
B: I staggered THR/OUGH it# – flew back home the next
   D\AY# . whisked into this H\ /OSPITAL#
A: G/ \OODNESS# (1.9:1216–23)

Part of turn
(4) B: locked yourself /OUT#
    A: Y\ES#
    B: (. laughs)
    A: N\O# the trouble /IS# . oh *for God's* S\AKES# the key
       won't go in the L\OCK# (1.2:855–61)

Part of phrase
(5) B: the same at the B/\OARD meetings# *T/\OO you* kNOW#
    I mean he takes over
    A: *Y\ES#*
    B: the whole *bloody* TH=ING# (1.1:803–5)

Goodness in (3) in a separate turn is speaker A's reaction to what
speaker B just said, thus an interactive device; *for God's sakes* in
(4), which is part of A's turn and apparently serving as an appealer
for sympathy, is also interactive; *bloody* in (5), which is not only
part of a turn but also of a noun phrase in the turn, is a syntactic
element (premodifier of *thing*) reflecting the speaker's attitude to
what he is talking about.

Roughly one third of the expletives in the corpus constituted a
turn of their own; the other two-thirds were part of longer turns. On
this basis the expletives in the corpus can be classified as in Figure
16.5. The first cut separates expletives that make up the speaker's
entire turn, 'independent', from expletives that are part of a longer
turn, 'dependent'. The second cut indicates that independent expletives serve only interactive functions, while dependent expletives
can be interactive or non-interactive. The distinction is a matter of
integration; the more integrated they are in the turn, the more likely
it is that they are part of the syntactic structure and non-interactive;
the less integrated they are, the more likely it is that they serve
interactive functions.

16.7   Expletives as separate turns

Opening turns do not generally consist of only an expletive; many

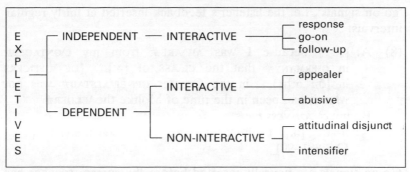

Figure 16.5 Classification of expletives

second and third turns do. In informing exchanges, for instance, the second turn was often realized by an expletive expressing B's reaction to what A said in the first turn:

(6) Initiate: inform   A: I was in there for an H\OUR#
     Terminate: response   B: G\OSH# (2.5:31–2)

All the items listed under 'heaven' in Table 16.1 occurred as responses (in a wide sense) in this position, e.g. *God, heavens, goodness, crikey*. They were generally pronounced with a falling or rising–falling tone, indicating 'information received' and 'end of exchange', besides reflecting what the speaker felt.

Unlike informing exchanges (6), questioning exchanges (7) often consist of three turns. The third, terminating turn was frequently realized by an expletive reflecting the questioner's reaction to the answer.

(7) Initiate: question   A: did you use to do English
                                    for foreign ST\/UDENTS#
     Continue: response   B: I did a silly C\OURSE thing#
     Terminate: follow-up   A: G\OSH# (2.11:1250–1)

Gosh, crumbs and *goodness* with a falling or rising–falling tone were found in this position.

More than half of the independent expletives (58 per cent) were used as exchange terminators, mostly serving as response moves in two-turn exchanges but also as follow-up moves in three-turn exchanges. The remaining 42 per cent (except (9) below) served as 'go-on signals', i.e. the listener's feedback inserted at fairly regular intervals:

(8)   A: [. . .] because I was AW\ARE# from my C\ONTACTS#
      in G\ERMANY# that the CL\ASS of [ə:] . {OF \OFFICERS
      in [ði: ə:]#} – in the Grosser GENER/ALSTAB# was not
      what it had been in the time of Moltke the \ELDER#
      B: *my G\OODNESS me#*
      A: B=UT [ə:] I think it was very IMPR\ESSIVE# [. . .]
      (2.3:381–90)

Go-on signals are typically inserted before the current speaker has finished talking. In (8), however, A's utterance can be described as syntactically, semantically and prosodically complete before the go-on is inserted; in other cases go-on signals cause syntactic and semantic clashes, but even then they are usually not interruptive, and the current speaker continues as if nothing had happened. Typical go-on signals were *good gracious, cor blimey, oh God* and *oh Lord*, often with an encouraging rising tone.

All the independent expletives quoted so far have been directed towards what was said in the immediately preceding turn. In (9), by contrast, the reference is extra-linguistic:

(9)   A: have a glass of SH/ERRY#.
      B: /\OH# that's N/ICE of you# as I'm not DR/IVING#
      TH\ANK you#
      A: *bloody H\ELL#* – – – (1.2:844–9)

Speaker A (male) apparently does something foolish when offering B a glass of sherry; maybe he spills sherry on his guest or knocks over a glass. *Bloody hell* serves both as a forceful self-reproach and as an apology, as it were.

16.8   Expletives as part of a turn

The dependent expletives were either turn-initial, turn-medial or turn-final. They occurred more often within (45 per cent) and at the beginning of the turn (43 per cent) than at the end (12 per cent). Only one in five could be analysed in syntactic (non-interactive) terms.

16.8.1   Beginning the turn

Expletives in turn-initial position were usually purely interactive, uttered as a reaction to what the previous speaker had just said. They would have constituted a perfect turn of their own had the speaker not chosen to continue, e.g. by showing excitement, as in (10), or by initiating a new exchange, as in (11).

(10)   Initiate   B: [. . .] I'm also attempting to shift all my children out of the state school s\YSTEM# s/o#
       Terminate A: G\OLLY#   .   what   an   UPH\EAVAL# (7.2:1047–9)

Golly expresses A's reaction to what B said and is further emphasized by *what an upheaval*.

(11)   Initiate   B: [. . .] I got {\ULCERS} in my \EYES you see# which was B\EASTLY# * – the same T\IME#*
       Terminate A: *\OH# G/\OODNESS#* – have they sort of
       /Initiate   settled D\OWN N/OW# (1.9:1232–7)

Oh goodness is A's response to what B said and terminates the first (informing) exchange, while *have they sort of settled down now* in the same turn initiates a new (questioning) exchange. This means that the expletive is used interactively despite its dependent (part-of-turn) position.

Other expletives used as reaction signals at turn beginnings were *God damnation, oh God, cor, oh heavens, oh Lord, oh Christ, gracious, oh gosh, oh golly* and *goodness*, in other words the same items as occurred with the same function as a separate turn. Like those, they generally carried a falling or rising–falling tone. One in three of the turn-initial expletives was preceded by *oh*.

In the following extract, where the parties discuss a job interview, *God* (preceded by *oh* and a long pause) seems to reflect both A's reaction to speaker B's request and her attitude towards what had happened at the interview.

(12)   B: – – how did you get on at your \INTERVIEW# . do T\ELL us#
       A: . oh – – G\OD# what an EXP\ERIENCE# – – – I don't

know where to ST\ART# you KN\OW# it was just such
a N\IGHTMARE# (1.3:215–22)

16.8.2   *Within the turn*

Slightly more than one third of the expletives uttered within the
turn, i.e. after the first word (except *oh*) and before the last, were
more or less closely integrated in the syntactic structure of the turn:

(13)   B: we could have gone by PL/ANE# if we hadn't got this .
        bloody great amount of L\UGGAGE . {to carry
        AR=OUND#}# (2.1:1180–1)
(14)   B: [...] hidden among in [?] the R\/ACE# are all these
        odd P/\EOPLE# who have these strange QU/\IRKS#
        you see
        A: *it's* a pity it takes a war to bring them \/OUT
        though#
        B: [/m] well Y\ES# MAYB/E# but *thank G/OODNESS* they
        they come /OUT# when the [tə:] when the occasion
        AR\ISES# (2.3:611–21)

Bloody is always a dependent part of an utterance and closely
integrated in the syntactic structure. It serves as a premodifier
intensifying an adjective, as in (13), or emphasizing a noun, as in
(5), but it cannot serve (interactively) as a reaction signal on its own
(cf. (9)). *Thank goodness* (14), on the other hand, can be either
independent (and interactive) or dependent (and non-interactive).
As a turn of its own, it would serve as a reaction to what was said in
the previous turn. As part of the turn, it is loosely integrated in the
syntactic structure; in (14), for instance, it is used as a disjunct (cf.
Quirk *et al.* 1985: 612ff) possible to paraphrase by *fortunately*.

A third function met with in turn-medial (and also turn-final)
position was that of 'abusive' vocative.

(15)   B: oh you take the G\OOD one# and leave M\E the old
        one# F/ATHEAD# you might have to T\AKE her
        {S\OMEWHERE#}#
        A: oh Y\ES# ALL R/IGHT# (7.2:443–8)

The excerpt is from a telephone call where speaker B uses a fairly
mild expletive (cf. Figure 16.2) to reproach her husband for not
using the good car to take a friend for a ride.

16.8.3 Ending the turn

Turn-final expletives were generally not integrated in the syntactic structure of the turn.

(16) B: no you were terribly POL\ITE# on the way H/OME# you said G\OSH D/EB# you are frightfully F\/UNNY you know# you really are quite {T\ERRIBLY} W\/ITTY at times# it {[?] \IS going to be} AM\/USING# sharing my L/IFE with you# ha H/A# .

A: I never said TH\AT# . not on the way H/OME# *good H\EAVENS#* (– – laughs) (2.10:1092–1102)

Good heavens is apparently used to emphasize A's own statement. Other expletives found in the same position and with a similar function were *God, oh God* and *oh Lord*, also with a falling (or rising–falling) tone. Complex expletives in turn-final position were also used as a kind of deprecatory appealers, e.g. *in God's name, for God's sake* and *for heaven's sake*.

Expletives used as emotive substitutes for a noun were relatively rare. In (17) *the bastard* replaces 'him':

(17) A: he he he is really God ALM\IGHTY# he knows \EVERY-THING#

B: ((if)) I don't CR\OWN *((the))* B/ASTARD# (1.1:807–9)

Summing up, what expletives do in the discourse does not always depend on whether they occur as separate turns or as part of a turn. In the former case the expletive is purely interactive, but in the latter case what it does is a matter of integration. If the expletive is not at all or marginally integrated in the syntactic structure of the turn, what it does can only be described in terms of interaction; if it is fully integrated, it is best described in non-interactive (syntactic) terms.

Exactly what the expletive does from the interactive point of view is related to what was done in the immediately preceding turn. For instance, *gosh* in the second turn in (6) was identified as a terminating response due to its position after the initiating 'inform'; *gosh* in (7), which does not appear until turn three, after the response, was identified as a terminating follow-up; *my goodness me* in (8) was identified as a go-on, since the current speaker does not stop speaking, which means that the exchange goes on.

Exactly what the expletive does from a non-interactive (syntactic) point of view is connected with its place or function in the clause. For instance, *bloody* in *the whole bloody thing* in (5) was identified as an emphasizer, while *bloody* in *a bloody great amount of luggage* in (13) was identified as an intensifier.

16.9   Conclusion

Expletives referred to the category 'heaven' were used in roughly three-quarters of the cases (Table 16.1). A direct comparison between male and female speakers showed that, although the female speakers used expletives more often than the male speakers, their expletives can be characterized as 'weak', judging by the British informants' evaluation. Only the male speakers used words like *bastard, damn* and *devil*, while most of the female expletives were realized by words related to 'heaven'. It was also the female speakers who used most of the corruptions and euphemisms (e.g. *blimey, gad, dash* and *lummy*).

The male and the female speakers did not only use a partly different expletive vocabulary, they also used expletives for partly different purposes. The male speakers used 'strong' expletives for emphasis and as intensifiers. The female speakers used 'weak' expletives to give feedback in the form of responses and go-ons.

The majority of the expletives investigated (Table 16.1) involved a noun phrase (*God, Lord, heavens, hell, devil*); a second category involved an adjective phrase (*bloody, gracious*) and a third category an adverb phrase (*bloody, damn, fucking*; for a different analysis of *fucking*, see Ljung 1980: 116–28).

All the expletives under 'heaven' and 'body' and most of the complex expletives were used interactively as responses, go-ons, follow-ups and appealers, but only *dash* under 'hell', and none of the items under 'sex'. *Bastard* and *cow* ('sex') were used as substituting abusives; *fucking* ('sex'), like *bloody, damned* and *a hell of* ('hell'), served as premodifying emphasizer or intensifier. *Arse* in the combination *my arse*, *buggered* in the combination *I'm buggered if*, and *sod* served to give more emphasis to an utterance (e.g. s\OD they'll be L/IVID#.

Many of the dialogues on which this study is based date back in time to the 1950s and 1960s. It would therefore be interesting to find out to what extent the expletive repertoire of these speakers differs not only from that of present-day adult educated British speakers but also from that of other categories of speakers, e.g. young teenagers. This in turn points to the urgent need for new and more comprehensive spoken corpora, representing not only Britain but the entire English-speaking world. Without such corpora extensive discourse studies will be impossible.

Notes

[1] I wish to thank Magnus Ljung and Michael Knight for reading and commenting on an earlier version of this article, and colleagues at the Survey of English Usage, University College London, and the English Department, Stockholm University, for acting as informants.

[2] *The Oxford English Dictionary* uses the term 'expletive' about words and phrases that fill up a sentence, eke out a metrical line, etc. 'without adding anything to the sense', with the addition that it is often 'applied to a profane oath or other meaningless exclamation'. *Collins COBUILD English Language Dictionary* (1987) emphasizes the pragmatic aspect by simply stating that an 'expletive is a rude word or expression such as *Damn!* which you say loudly and suddenly when you are annoyed, excited, or in pain'.

17 Conversational style in British and American English: The case of backchannels

GUNNEL TOTTIE

They were strolling along the high road easily... the Toad and the Water Rat walking behind the cart talking together – at least Toad was talking, and Rat was saying at intervals, 'Yes, precisely; and what did *you* say to *him*?' – and thinking all the time of something very different...
(Kenneth Grahame, *The Wind in the Willows*)

17.1 Introduction[1]

British and American English differ at several levels: lexis, phonology, orthography and, to some extent, syntax. These differences are fairly well known, at least in principle, even if much work remains to be done on details. One area which has been much less studied but where the differences are obvious to any speaker of British or American English faced with the 'other' variety, or to foreign learners having to negotiate both types of English, is that of pragmatics, taken in a wide sense. The realization of speech acts such as greetings, offers, requests, etc. differs a great deal on opposite sides of the Atlantic, and so does conversational style.

Tannen (1984: 1) discusses conversational style as follows:

...conversational style... refers to aspects of talk that have been observed by scholars but are also apparent to many nonscholars who are people watchers by nature... [M]any of the basic elements of how people talk, which seem self-evidently appropriate, in fact differ from one person to the next and from one group to the next. Ways of showing that you're interested, glad, or angry... when to start talking and when to stop; when (or whether) it's okay to talk at the same time as someone else or to interrupt... what intonation to use – these and many other features of language... can be very different, depending on a speaker's individual

254

habits as well as such differences as gender, ethnicity, class, and regional background.

One largely uncharted area of conversational style has to do with the use of what Tannen refers to as 'ways of showing that you're interested', often called 'backchannels'. Backchannels are the sounds (and gestures) made in conversation by the current non-speaker, which grease the wheels of conversation but constitute no claim to take over the turn. On the basis of informal observations, it seemed to me that these were among the features of language that differ according to regional background, in this case between British and American English, but I could find no corroboration of this in the literature.

One reason why the use of backchannels has attracted little previous attention among linguists is certainly that they occur only in spoken language, long a stepchild of descriptive linguistics. Furthermore, they are mostly realized by what Du Bois *et al.* (forthcoming) call 'marginal words', i.e. vocalizations that are usually rendered as *m, mhm, uh-(h)uh*, and the like in writing. These items are only rarely captured by writers of fiction or drama and are badly represented or left out by most dictionaries (cf. Tottie 1989, Altenberg 1990a). As Svartvik points out (1980: 167), the 'lexicographer still has a tendency to consider the occurrence of a word in print the chief or sole criterion for its inclusion in the dictionary' – yet, as shown by Svartvik *et al.* (1982), *m*, with various intonation patterns, is one of the most frequent 'words' in British English conversation; thus *m*, with falling intonation, ranked 31 and was one of the most common lexical items in the London-Lund Corpus of Spoken English. Similarly, *m* is one of the most common items in spoken Swedish (cf. Nordenstam 1987, Allwood 1988) but is missing from all dictionaries of Swedish.

There is thus a vicious circle: because words of this kind have been regarded as marginal words, they have attracted little research, in spite of the fact that they are used for a large number of functions in spoken communication – as hesitation signals, feedback signals in question–answer sequences (cf. Stenström 1982), affirmative and negative responses, etc. (cf. Tottie 1989). My purpose here is to examine their use as realizations of backchannels in British and American English, along with *bona fide* words and phrases, in casual everyday conversation between educated speakers, and to demonstrate how they differ in the two varieties.

Such comparative work is now possible thanks to the creation of the new Corpus of Spoken American English, which is currently under way at the University of California at Santa Barbara. For decades, the London-Lund Corpus of Spoken English and its precursor, the Survey of English Usage at University College, London, have made possible research on spoken British English, but the lack of publicly available parallel material for American English has impeded comparative studies. Although the Santa Barbara Corpus is compiled from a different theoretical stance and makes use of a different transcription system from the London-Lund Corpus of Spoken English, the two corpora are sufficiently parallel to permit inter-variety research, and it is on material from these two corpora that I base the present study.

17.2   Backchannels: function and form

The term 'backchannel' was coined by Yngve in his pioneering 1970 study (p. 568).

When two people are engaged in conversation, they generally take turns.... In fact, both the person who has the turn and his partner are simultaneously engaged in both speaking and listening. This is because of the existence of what I call the back channel, over which the person who has the turn receives short messages such as *yes* and *uh-huh* without relinquishing the turn.

The term backchannel has since been extended to designate 'backchannel message', and that is the practice I shall follow here. When it is necessary to speak of a particular linguistic form functioning either as a backchannel or as part of one, I shall use the term 'backchannel item'.[2]

Backchannels have several functions, which normally occur simultaneously. They signal understanding and agreement – what can be termed the 'supportive function' – and/or encourage the speaker to continue his/her turn, and thus have a 'regulative function'. Different researchers have emphasized either function; thus Yngve (1970), Fries (1952) and Oreström (1983) emphasize the supportive function, while Schegloff (1982) takes a more mechanistic view and regards the regulatory function as more important. This is emphasized by the fact that he uses the term 'continuer' as a label for backchannels. Nordenstam (1987) considers backchannels capable of having both functions at the same time. She stresses the regulatory function; it is possible to signal to the speaker to continue without having heard or agreed with what the speaker has said. The epigraph to this article is a case in point; however, it seems to me that some basic component of agreement is normally present, or the non-speaker would not refrain from claiming the turn for any length of time.

What can be a backchannel? Duncan (1974) includes five types: (1) 'readily identified, verbalized signals... such... as *m-hm, yeah, right*, and the like', (2) sentence completions, (3) requests for clarification, (4) brief restatements, and (5) head nods and shakes. However, many of the items included under (1) can also function as turns, in response to overt or implied questions, and so can (3). Moreover, what starts as a backchannel may end up as a turn, if the previous speaker shows no willingness to continue speaking. Some of the difficulties involved in delimiting backchannels will be discussed in Section 4.

The relation between the function and form of backchannels is an interesting problem which seems to have received little attention in the literature, but limitations of space preclude the treatment of that problem here (see, however, Kendon 1967). I shall instead concentrate on the form of backchannels, with special attention given to differences between British and American English. As there are no videotapes for either the London-Lund Corpus or the Corpus of Spoken American English, I will be able to deal only with audible backchannels, leaving head nods and shakes aside.

17.3   Previous work

I know of no earlier study devoted to qualitative differences between backchannels in British and American English. Duncan, Fries, Yngve and Schegloff are all Americans and assume that backchannels normally take the forms *uh-(h)uh, mhm, yeah*. Duncan also includes backchannels quoted by the British scholar Kendon, viz *yes quite, surely, I see* and *that's true*, but does not comment on the possible existence of differences between varieties. *Yes* is mentioned by Yngve and Fries; none of the Americans includes *m*, however. Moreover, none of these scholars makes any quantitative observations regarding backchannels. Fries gives the most extensive catalogue of backchannels, occurring in descending order of frequency in the telephone conversations he studied (1952: 49).

Yes (most frequently with rising intonation)
Unh/hunh (with rising intonation)
Yeah (most frequently with rising intonation)
I see
Good
Oh (usually with rising intonation)
That's right (often with rising intonation)
Yes I know
Oh\oh (with falling intonation)
Fine
So (with rising intonation)
Oh my goodness
Oh dear

The most detailed studies of backchannels in British and American English that I have been able to find are Oreström (1983) and White (1989). In his study of turn-taking Oreström studied the use of short backchannels ('simple, brief supports') in ten conversations from the London-Lund Corpus, a total of 50,000 words, with the purpose of describing their loudness and overlap with the other speaker's output. The most important items were, in descending order of frequency, *m* (50 per cent), *yes* (34 per cent), *yeah* (4 per cent), *mhm* (4 per cent), *no* (3 per cent), with a smattering of *quite, aha, good*, etc., totalling 702 instances. (For a survey of the prosodic features of backchannels, see Oreström 1983: 122.)

White (1989) is a study of cross-cultural communication between Americans and Japanese, undertaken with the purpose of establishing the role of backchannelling in the conversation of native speakers of American English as compared with Japanese speakers of American English as a second language. Only the five most frequent backchannels were included in White's statistics, together accounting for 74 per cent of the total. The distribution of backchannels used by the Americans in these intra-cultural conversations (White 1989: 63) was: *yeah* (42 per cent), *mmhm* (sic) (35 per cent), *uh-uh* (10 per cent), *oh!* (9 per cent), *hmm* (4 per cent), thus a very different set from the ones recorded by Oreström. The items that are most common in British English, the one-syllable nasal *m* and the lexical item *yes*, do not even appear among the top three-quarters in American English.

Even if this juxtaposition of results would seem to be pretty conclusive, there are problems inherent in the comparison of Oreström's and White's findings, due to the different ways in which the data were gathered and differences between speakers and situations. What Oreström and White have in common is that they are both based on dyadic conversations. Moreover, both Oreström and White concentrated on short and frequent backchannels, excluding longer and more complex ones. However, White's subjects were all female and the recordings were non-surreptitious, whereas the material from the London-Lund Corpus used by Oreström was partly surreptitious, partly non-surreptitious, and the dyads were of three different kinds, male, female and mixed. Furthermore, Oreström excluded supports following utterances containing *you know* or *you see*. It also seemed necessary that the same scholar should listen to the original recordings of both American and British material to ensure that differences in written renderings – e.g. *m* and *mhm* – were not artifacts of the transcriptions but reflections of real phonetic differences.

In order to achieve the greatest possible comparability, I therefore decided to carry out a detailed investigation of some American spoken material from the Santa Barbara Corpus of Spoken American English (CSAE) and compare it with a detailed re-examination of part of the material from the London-Lund Corpus of Spoken English (LLC) previously used by Oreström, applying the same criteria of definition and inclusion of backchannels for material from both corpora and restricting the investigation to dyadic conversations.

17.4   British and American backchannels compared

So far, there is only one transcription available in the Santa Barbara Corpus of a dyadic conversation. This is a fairly long conversation (nineteen minutes), appropriately labelled 'Aesthetics and Advertising'. The participants are two academics who know each other well, one a woman in her forties and the other a man about ten years younger. The subject matter is entirely intellectual, dealing for the most part with the use and abuse of aesthetic principles in advertising, and there is a great deal of consensus between the speakers. Like the rest of the Santa Barbara Corpus, it was non-surreptitiously recorded.

For comparison, I examined two conversations from the London-

Lund Corpus, both of them also dyadic and non-surreptitiously recorded, S.5.9 and S.5.10. Neither of them is a perfect match against 'Aesthetics and Advertising'. In S.5.9 there is also one male and one female speaker, but they are younger than the participants in 'Aesthetics and Advertising', aged twenty-two and twenty-three respectively, and the topics under discussion are less abstract, dealing with reminiscences of the university that both speakers attended and experiences of temporary jobs and vocational training. S.5.10 is a better match from the point of view of subject matter: the participants, both teachers of English, discuss topics such as the requirements for a happy marriage, sex education and racial bias in schools. However, in S.5.10 both speakers are male and aged about thirty. A perfect match of all parameters is probably impossible to achieve; in what follows, I shall keep track of differences between participants and topics when accounting for results.

I will quote transcriptions from the two corpora as they have been available to me in computerized format. Some caution will therefore be necessary on the part of the reader not accustomed to the transcription systems. LLC and CSAE use different conventions and to some extent focus on different prosodic characteristics of the texts. Thus, the LLC transcription records tone (rising, falling, etc.) in detail but does not account for lengthening, which is shown in the CSAE transcription. In a few cases the same symbols are used for different purposes in the two transcription systems; the most import-ant ones are '@', which indicates laughter in CSAE and the schwa sound in LLC, and '=', which marks lengthening in the CSAE transcription but level tone in the computer version of LLC which I used. By contrast, different symbols are often used to indicate the same phenomenon in the two corpora; thus in LLC asterisks indicate simultaneous speech, but in CSAE numbered brackets are used (for full details see Svartvik and Quirk 1980, Du Bois et al. forthcoming, and Chafe et al., this volume).[3] I have added italics in the extracts below to highlight backchannels.

The difficulties involved in determining what is to be regarded as a backchannel and what constitutes a turn were mentioned above in Section 2 (see also e.g. White 1989: 62). Most problems arose with longer backchannels. A couple of them are illustrated in examples (1) and (2). The most important principle is that backchannel status can be determined only on the basis of the following utterance. Thus in (1), A's utterance *oh God yes that's the worst one* might have been a backchannel, but as it provoked a response from B, *yeah it's really awful*, it came to serve as a turn.

(1) B: we ˆcame 'back 'by · from ˆWindlebury \East#
        ˆthat's the one that ":st\ops at# ·
        ˆevery !st\ation#
     A: *ˆoh G\od 'yes*#
        ˆthat's the :w\orst 'one#
     B: **ˆy\eah#
        ((it's)) ˆreally** !\awful# (S.5.9:1221–7)

Similarly, in (2) B's *yes quite* could have been regarded as a backchannel, but as it is then followed up by *well if you will ask leading questions*, to which A responds by uttering *that was a bit of a swine that*, I regarded it as part of a turn rather than as a backchannel.

(2) A: · you ˆwant to be [g]\areful# ·
        *ˆhow much you !m\ention (('here#)) ·
        (– · laughs)*
     B: *ˆyes qu\ite#
        (– laughs)* · well if you ˆ{w\ill 'ask} :leading :qu\ /estions#
        (– – laughs)
     A: **(– – laughs)** ˆy\es#
        ˆthat was a 'bit of a sw/ine 'that# – · (S.5.9: 180–7)

Sentences such as these present problems for the analyst, and it is probably the case that no two researchers will arrive at exactly the same solutions. The best one can do is to state one's criteria for inclusion of backchannels as explicitly as possible.

As appears from the above, I included not only the shorter backchannels described by Oreström and White but longer and more complex ones as well. I also decided to make a further subclassification into backchannels and backchannel items, where the former could consist of one or more of the latter; thus the sequence *yeah · sure · right* can function as one backchannel but consists of three backchannel items. I did this to get a more accurate idea of the frequency and complexity of backchannels; simply counting backchannel items as backchannels might lead to misleading results.

Obviously, then, decisions had to be made as to when two or several backchannel items occurring close to each other in the discourse made up one or several backchannels. My principle was to regard two or several backchannel items as one backchannel if they were adjacent in time, even if they occurred in different tone units, but to regard them as separate backchannels if they were separated by several words or by a long pause. Both transcriptions were extremely helpful in this respect, as they indicate simultaneity with the turnholder's speech. By way of example, see extract (3) from 'Aesthetics and Advertising'. In it all backchannels are italicized; the problematic ones are marked I and II.

(3)   B: (H) ... (1.0) poets "and ad me=n ,
         .. are ... (H) doing the same "thi=ng ,
         at [1 a 1] ... very different "le=vel .
I   A: [1 *hm* 1] .
         m=hm ,
      B: ... It's "[1 no=t 1] the ques- – –
      A: [1 *mhm* 1],
      B: .. It's [2 not that% 2] .. that%
         ... (.8) "a=ds become "ar=t .
      A: [2 *unhhunh* 2],
      B: .. It's that%
         ... (.8) the= "mechanisms of "intera=ction ,
         that an "artist u=se ,
         .. "uses ,
         ... (1.2) a=re the [1 o=nes 1] ,
      A: [1 *Hm* 1].
      B: that a- "a=d people= | .. "disco=ver= ,
         and% – –
      A: ... (HX)
      B: an=d [2 attempt 2] to put to the=ir "purposes .
II   A: [2 *Hm* 2] .
         . *Hm* .
         ... (1.1) *Hm* .

Number I was regarded as two backchannels; the first *hm* was simultaneous with part of B's previous utterance, as indicated by the numbered square brackets, and separated from *mhm* by several words. Similarly the three items at II were regarded as three backchannels because of the simultaneity of the first *hm* with the previous speaker's utterance and because of the pause of 1.1 seconds between the second and third instances of *hm*. A good transcription is obviously of great help for a first analysis; however, all back-channels were also checked against the actual recordings.

In (4), however, also from 'Aesthetics and Advertising', A's sequence *m=hm mhm* was regarded as one backchannel, as it is clear from the numbered brackets that they occurred in close sequence, overlapping with B's turn and separated only by a two-dot pause.

(4)   B: .. (H) can= – –
      .. Something that's "grea=t ,
     A: .. m=hm ,
     B: ... (TSK) in "one area is – –
      .. is – –
      ... (1.0) i=s ba=d in [1 "another 1] .
     A: [1 *m=hm* 1] ,
      [2 *mhm* 2] ,
     B: .. [2 And may- 2] .. <@ whether that's "cha=nged @> ,
      no=w .

In order to achieve a workable classification system of back-channels, I decided to follow Nordenstam (1987) and categorize long backchannels as instances of the most frequent backchannel item constituting one of their parts, thus establishing an 'emic' level of description. I shall use small capitals to designate this level. For cxample, *yea–h . . . right* and *that's true, yea=h*, were both classified as instances of YEAH, the most frequently occurring backchannel item in the American text.

Backchannels were further subclassified as either 'simple', as e.g. *yeah*, 'double' (including multiple repetitions of the same item), as e.g. *mhm mhm (mhm)*, or 'complex', consisting of one or several items from different backchannel categories and/or one or several open-class lexical items, as in *yeah . . . right* or *yeah I know*. Classifying complex backchannels as instances of their most frequent constituent will to some extent obscure the incidence of minor categories, such as RIGHT; however, other solutions that I contemplated, such as using the first item as a basis for categorizing, would also have had drawbacks. As can be seen from Tables 17.1 and 17.2 below, this is a minor problem because of the low frequency of long or complex backchannels, and it can be counteracted by scrupulous accounting for the complex forms as in Tables 17.4 and 17.5.

Table 17.1 Major types of backchannels in 'Aesthetics and Advertising'

Types	Simple	Double	Complex	Total	%
YEAH	94	18	16	127	40
MHM	93	12	4	109	34
HM	32	3	1	36	11
RIGHT	10	2	2	14	4
UNHHUNH, UHUH	9	1	2	12	4
SURE	1	1	2	4	1
YES	1	2	—	3	1
HUNH	1	2	—	3	1
VARIOUS (incl. laughs)	3	—	6	10	3
Total	244	41	33	318	100

Table 17.2 Major types of backchannels in LLC texts S.5.9 and S.5.10

Types	Simple	Double	Complex	Total	%
YES	59	17	42	118	44
M	90	1	7	98	36
NO	12	—	3	15	6
YEAH	8	1	1	10	4
REALLY	4	—	—	4	1
OH	2	—	2	4	1
MHM	3	—	—	3	1
HM	2	—	—	2	1
VARIOUS (incl. laughs)	10	—	6	16	6
Total	190	19	61	270	100

The results of my examination of 'Aesthetics and Advertising' from CSAE and texts S.5.9 and S.5.10 from LLC are accounted for in Tables 17.1 and 17.2. Table 17.1 confirms White's observations concerning the nature of backchannels in American English: the leading items in the American conversation are YEAH (40 per cent), MHM (34 per cent), HM (11 per cent), RIGHT (4 per cent), and UNHHUNH/UHUH (4 per cent). Table 17.2, for obvious reasons, confirms Oreström's observations: the most important British English backchannel types are YES (44 per cent) and M (36 per cent), with NO (6 per cent) and YEAH (4 per cent) following far behind. Higher frequencies of YEAH occur in other texts from LLC, but it is used by only a small number of speakers and is not characteristic of the sample as a whole. The fact that YES ranks higher than M in my subset of LLC texts than in the larger set studied by Oreström is probably due to our different ways of identifying backchannels; Oreström concentrated on short, simple backchannels, whereas I also included longer, complex ones, frequently headed by *yes*.

Furthermore, listening to the tapes proved that the difference between the largely American MHM and the British favourite M is not an artifact of the transcriptions. M, mostly pronounced with falling intonation, is a short monosyllabic consonantal nasal, whereas MHM is disyllabic, with [h] pronounced between the nasals, and in American English it is often lengthened – see Table 17.3, which shows lengthening in 62 of 109 cases (57 per cent). When MHM occurs in British English, it seems to be a personal idiosyncrasy of a few speakers and is usually short. UNHHUNH and UHUH can perhaps be considered to be vocalic variants of MHM, with and without nasalization.

Table 17.3 Variants of MHM in 'Aesthetics and Advertising'

Speaker	A	B	A+B	Lengthened
Simple				
mhm	20	22	42	—
m=hm	31	6	37	37
m=hm=	8	1	9	9
mhm=	5	—	5	5
Double				
m=hm mhm	5	—	5	5
mhm mhm	3	—	3	—
mhm= mhm	2	—	2	2
mhm mhm=	1	—	1	1
mhm mhm mhm	1	—	1	—
Complex				
mhm hm=	1	—	1	—
m=hm . u=nhhunh	1	—	1	1
m=hm mhm yea=h	1	—	1	1
m=hm .. mhm, gee	1	—	1	1
Total	80	29	109	62

The fact that NO occurs only in the British texts examined is probably due more to chance than anything else. It is worth noting that it occurs as a support signal only after a negative utterance by the speaker, as in (5), never as an exclamation of surprise, in the present material (cf. Bald 1980: 184f).

(5)   B: I ^find that it's !no good 'giving 'people ad:vice at *\all#*
          I ^mean they !don't !listen to adv/ice#
      A: *^n\o#*
          ^n\o#   (S.5.10:213–16)

REALLY as a backchannel item has been treated by Stenström
(1986), who remarks that Schegloff (1982) does not include it among
'continuers' and adds that her material, derived from LLC, 'shows
that *really* often has the same effect as *uh huh*' (1986: 161). This
probably reflects a real difference between British and American
English, if not in absolute terms at least in terms of frequency of
occurrence.

In the present material there were very few instances of the
backchannel types listed by Duncan (1974) as sentence completions,
requests for clarification or brief restatements. One instance of
sentence completion is illustrated in (6):

(6)   A: it's ^happened* a !l\ot at 'school#.
          ^parents who have been !very
      B: **^[\m]#**
      A: !w\orried a'bout their 'son's 'going to univ/ersity#
          you *^kn/ow#*
          they ^don't "!w\ant it# –
          ^they don't
      B: *^[\m]#*
      A: "!want to im'agine their s\on sort of# –
          ^leaping into 'bed with 'every other :g\irl and#
      B: *or ^taking dr\ugs *or {^something like th\at#}#*
          ^y\es#*
      A: *or ^taking dr\ugs 'or#*
          or . [m] ^sitting :\in and#
          ^staging
      B: **^[\m]#**
      A: this 'that and *the :\other#
          you ^kn/ow#*   (S.5.10:763–77)

Otherwise, the backchannel items listed under the label VARIOUS
were either laughs or short items like *of course* or *that's true*.

The British and American conversations were similar in that

simple backchannels were in the majority in both, 244/318 (77 per cent) in 'Aesthetics and Advertising' and 190/270 (70 per cent) in the British conversations. In either material, it is one major backchannel type that tends to be expanded into complex realizations, but in the American material it is YEAH, and in the British it is YES. Tables 17.4 and 17.5 show the occurrence of expansions of YEAH and YES in 'Aesthetics and Advertising' and, by way of example, in S.5.9. (Other expansions – even more numerous – occur in S.5.10.) Notice that in both cases the majority of the complex backchannels tend to start with the prototypical item; only rarely is it added at the end.

Table 17.4 Variants of YEAH as backchannels in 'Aesthetics and Advertising'

Variants	A Fem	B Male	A+B
Simple			
yeah	26	32	58
yea=h	18	8	26
y=ea=h	2	1	3
y=eah	3	—	3
yeah @@	1	1	2
yea=h @@	1	—	1
yeah=	1	—	1
Double			
yeah (...) yeah	5	6	11
yea=h yea=h	5	1	6
yeah yeah @	1	—	1
Complex			
y=eah ... right	1	2	3
yea=h right yeah	—	1	1
yeah, you did something	1	—	1
yeah, not very many	1	—	1
yeah, I know	—	1	1
yeah. sure. right	—	1	1
yeah you just have to	—	1	1
yeah, right, that's @@@ true, yeah @, they have to	—	1	1
I see, yea=h	1	—	1
it's a nice insight, yeah	1	—	1
that's true, yea=h	1	—	1
that's right, yea=h yea=h	1	—	1
o=h yea=h o=h y=eah	1	—	1
Total	71	56	127

Table 17.5 Variants of YES as backchannels in LLC S.5.9

Variants	A Male	B Fem	A+B
Simple			
y/ \es	1	—	1
y\es	13	5	18
y=es	1	—	1
Double			
y\es # y\es	4	—	4
y\es # y\es # y\es	4	—	4
Complex			
y\es # qu\ite	—	5	5
y\es qu/\ite	—	2	2
y\es # ex\actly	—	3	3
y\es # \m	—	2	2
y\es # that's the trouble	—	1	1
y\es # that's true	—	1	1
oh y\es	2	—	2
oh I see # y\es	—	1	1
that's right # y\es	—	1	1
ex/actly # y\es	—	1	1
\m # y\es	2	—	2
oh y\es of course	—	2	2
oh yes they have	—	1	1
\oh yes # y\es	1	—	1
Total	28	25	53

Tables 17.4 and 17.5 also give information about the sex of the speakers who produced the extended backchannels. It will be noticed that in both conversations it is the female partner who produces both the largest number of backchannels and also the greatest variety. This may reflect a truly gender-related difference. Fishman (1978) and Nordenstam (1987) both found more backchannelling in female speakers, and Coates (1986: 102) quotes several other studies with similar results. However, in S.5.10 one of the male speakers is an extremely prolific backchanneller, in addition to being the greatest contributor to the conversation, and other studies have also failed to show a higher proportion of backchannels by women than by men. Because of great individual variation, much more work is required to clarify this question.

One interesting difference between 'Aesthetics and Advertising' and the LLC texts is that backchannels are much more common in the American conversation. In nineteen minutes of conversation there are 318 backchannels, whereas in the LLC texts, which are much longer, fifty-three and a half minutes in all, there are only 270 backchannels altogether. This means that there are more than sixteen backchannels per minute in 'Aesthetics and Advertising', compared with just over five per minute in the LLC texts. Whether more frequent backchannelling is indeed a characteristic feature of American English is impossible to determine on the basis of the scant data of the present investigation. It is a fact that the other CSAE conversations currently available have much fewer backchannels, but this should probably be related to the greater number of participants in those conversations (cf. Tottie 1990). That there is great variation between the British conversations is clear from Table 17.6, which shows that S.5.10 has almost twice as many backchannels as S.5.9 (178 versus 92) in spite of the fact that it is somewhat shorter.

It is tempting to speculate on the reason for the difference between S.5.9 and S.5.10; one feature that S.5.10 has in common with 'Aesthetics and Advertising' is that it is an intellectual discussion, something which might be conducive to more frequent backchannelling. However, there are also individual differences between the

Table 17.6 Backchannels in texts S.5.9 and S.5.10 in the London-Lund Corpus

	Types	Simple	Double	Complex	Total
	YES	20	8	25	53
	M	15	1	—	16
	YFAH	4	—	1	5
S.5.9	OH	2	—	2	4
	NO	1	—	3	4
	REALLY	3	—	—	3
	VARIOUS (incl. laughs)	1	—	6	7
	Total	46	9	37	92
	M	75	—	7	82
	YES	39	9	17	65
	NO	11	—	—	11
S.5.10	YEAH	4	1	—	5
	MHM	3	—	—	3
	HM	2	—	—	2
	VARIOUS (incl. laughs)	10	—	—	10
	Total	144	10	24	178

speakers in the two conversations; in both cases, one speaker is a much more active backchanneller than the other.

17.5   Concluding remarks

Assuming that CSAE and LLC are representative of standard British and American English, it seems clear that the use of back-channels differs between the two varieties. Why this should be the case is probably a question that will never be answered, as we have no access to spoken material from earlier centuries. It has been suggested (by Peter Trudgill, personal communication) that the peculiarly American signals UHUH, UNHHUNH, etc. might have their origins in African languages, certainly an interesting hypothesis.

Other questions brought up in this study – whether Americans backchannel more than British speakers and whether subject matter, sex and number of participants determine the use of backchannelling – must await further research to be answered. Further important questions are, for example, whether backchannels are elicited by particular types of utterances by the current speaker, how their prosodic realization is linked to discourse function, and what function backchannels have in the production of spoken discourse. As Sinclair and Coulthard have put it (1975: 2), conversations 'are everyday examples of the fact that several participants can jointly produce coherent texts', and it would be surprising indeed if backchannels did not play a crucial part in this process. All of these questions are now likely eventually to find answers, thanks to the availability of reliable corpora of spoken English.

Notes

[1] I thank Sidney Greenbaum for giving me access to recordings of the London-Lund Corpus at the Survey of English Usage at University College, London and René Quinault for locating the ones I needed. I am deeply grateful to Wallace Chafe and Jack Du Bois for permission to use existing parts of the Corpus of Spoken American English, to Charles Fillmore and Jane Edwards for access to and help with the facilities of the Institute for Cognitive Studies at Berkeley, to Christer Geisler for computational help and to Ingegerd Bäcklund for valuable comments on an earlier version of this article.

² Several other terms have been used in the literature. Fries (1952) speaks of 'signals of attention', Kendon (1967) calls them 'accompaniment signals', and Sinclair and Coulthard (1975) use the term 'acknowledge'. Oreström (1983) uses the term 'supports' for a subset of short backchannels, excluding exclamations and 'non-linguistic vocalizations', and so does Stenström (1982), who includes them as a subset of 'feedback signals'. Stenström (1986) follows Schegloff (1982) in using the term 'continuer'. Another term frequently used in British literature is 'minimal responses' (cf. e.g. Coates 1986: 99ff).

³ For the transcription symbols used in the Corpus of Spoken American English, see Chafe et al. (this volume), and Du Bois et al. (forthcoming).

The use of transcription symbols in the computer version of the London-Lund Corpus of Spoken English which I have used is consistent with the Survey slip version as described in Svartvik and Quirk (1980: 21ff) except in the following cases:

#	End of tone unit
^	Onset
{yes}	Subordinate TU
y\es	Fall
y/es	Rise
=m	Level
y\ /es	Fall–rise
y/ \es	Rise–fall
[@]	Schwa

18 On the history of *that*/zero as object clause links in English

MATTI RISSANEN

18.1 Introduction

The main purpose of this chapter is to illustrate the new openings that a large computerized corpus can offer to the study of the history of English syntax. As an example, I will discuss the question of the variation between *that* and asyndeton as object clause links. For the sake of brevity, asyndetic linking is called 'zero' in the following discussion. It will be shown how the zero link, scantily attested in Old and Early Middle English, gains ground in late Middle English writings and becomes very common in the seventeenth century. The most obvious factors supporting the growing popularity of zero can easily be pinpointed, and a quantitative analysis reveals how the change spreads from zero-favouring structural and textual environments to others.

18.2 The corpus

The corpus used as the basis of the study is the Helsinki Corpus of English Texts: Diachronic and Dialectal (henceforth 'the Helsinki Corpus'), compiled at the English Department of the University of Helsinki. The corpus project was begun in the mid 1980s and completed by the end of the decade. Most of the pre- and post-doctoral research staff of the department participated in the project work.[1] Our work was encouraged and inspired by the existence of the standard text corpora of present-day English, written and spoken, and by the pioneering work of the ICAME group, with which we became associated as early as 1984.

272

As its full name indicates, the Helsinki Corpus consists of two parts, the diachronic and the dialectal.[2] The diachronic part contains around 400 samples of continuous text covering the time span from Early Old English (*c.* AD 750) to the beginning of the eighteenth century. The size of the basic corpus[3] is about 1.5 million words, and the length of the samples extracted from longer texts normally varies between 2500 and 10,000 words.

In selecting the samples, particular attention was paid to the chronological spread. Ideally, each century should be represented by roughly the same amout of text, comparable in regard to text types, registers and genres. In practice, however, this is an impossible ideal to reach, particularly for the earliest periods of the language. In Old and Middle English, dialectal coverage was an important factor in selecting the samples; in Early Modern English, attention was paid to certain sociolinguistic features of the authors, such as social status, age and sex.

A description of the text in the form of parameter coding is appended to each sample. These codings make it possible to collect sets of examples either from the whole corpus or from parts of it. The most natural division of the corpus is chronological; we use the WordCruncher program, developed at Brigham Young University, for searches of words, their parts or combinations, in texts dating from different centuries. With the Oxford Concordance Program, on the other hand, the retrieval can be restricted to sets of instances that fulfil a certain combination of parameter constraints (private letters written by female authors from 1570 to 1640; religious treatises representing the South-West Midland dialect from 1150 to 1250; tenth-century charters with Mercian influence, etc.). For the survey of the object clauses discussed in the present chapter, the time and text type parameters have been particularly useful.

18.3   Object clause links

A large computer corpus can be effectively used in studies of variation and, in diachrony, in studies describing the actuation of change through variation. The history of the noun clause link variants *that* and zero is a typical instance of a topic in which a corpus-based variational study may give interesting results. For one thing, these two variant structures represent a high degree of synonymy – a question which poses constant problems for the student of variation (cf. e.g. Romaine 1982; Rydén 1987).

To highlight the essential characteristics of development, the present chapter concentrates on the two most common links of the object clause, zero and *that*; for the same reason, the variation of these links in complement clauses is omitted (*It is sad/a pity [that] he couldn't come*). Zero is impossible when the object clause precedes the main clause (*That he could not come she knew well*), and *that* is practically impossible when the subject of the main clause begins with a 'push-down element' of the object clause, as in *Who did she hope was the winner* (Quirk *et al.* 1985: 15.4); both these constructions are left outside the present discussion.

With verbs indicating verbal expression, the variation between *that* and zero is possible only when the clause following the verb contains indirect speech (or thought). At the earlier stages of English, particularly in Old English writings, the conjunction *that* could, however, be placed before utterances which unquestionably represent direct speech, as in the following instance quoted from a New Testament translation (Mitchell 1985: §1940–1).

(1) þa cwæð se Hælend þæt ðu segst. (West Saxon Gospels, Matt. 27:11; cf. Auth. Version, *And Jesus said unto him, Thou sayest.*)

Furthermore, the structure of the object clause does not always reveal whether it represents direct or indirect speech or thought; sometimes it contains characteristics of both. In the present discussion I have included such instances in which the general context or the character of the text speaks in favour of the indirect speech alternative; in actual practice, the choice is in most cases fairly obvious.

(2) but dost thou conceive that Saints can play with each other? nay, for I say unto thee, *if thou dost not thou art not a Sanctified Sister* (*Penny Merriments*: 148)
(3) and as for thy Dame, I say *she is departed*; therefore Mary, again I say unto thee, that the Spirit within does move me to refresh thee; (*ibid.*: 148)

Both the rhythm of the prose and the direct or indirect presentation in neighbouring sentences indicate that in the former instance we are dealing with direct speech, in the latter with indirect.

The fundamental question in the variation between *that* and zero in noun clauses is which of the two should be regarded as the 'original' object clause link. On the one hand, in less technical contexts, we often speak about 'the omission of *that*', as if the expressed link would be the original one. On the other hand, the generally accepted theory that the conjunction *that* developed from the deictic pronoun, anaphoric or cataphoric, would imply that the asyndetic link was at least as old as *that* (cf. e.g. *OED* s.v. *that* conj.; Ellinger 1933: 78).

Jespersen (1967: 76–7) suggests that the zero link was due to Scandinavian influence. His theory is questioned by Kirch (1959), who points out that there are fairly early Old English instances of zero in unambiguously subordinating contexts, and that the evidence of the existence of this structure in runic Old Norse prose is inconclusive. As shown below, the evidence from the Helsinki Corpus points to a fairly late Middle English popularization of zero; even this fact fails to support Jespersen's idea of early Scandinavian influence. All in all, it is plausible to assume that both zero and *that*, which are attested from Old English onwards, represent very old ways of linking object clauses to superordinate clauses.

18.4   Collecting evidence from the corpus

While a study of the variation between *that* and zero illustrates the new openings for text-based research provided by a computerized corpus, it should also give a realistic picture of the restrictions of corpus study. As the diachronic part of the Helsinki Corpus is not provided with grammatical tagging, collecting the object clause subordinators from among the other conjunctive and pronominal uses of *that* means toil and trouble. Furthermore, even in the existing tagged corpora, such as the Brown Corpus and LOB, there is no direct way of picking out the instances with the zero link. The problem of tracing zeros must, in this case, be solved in an indirect way, by checking all occurrences of all verbs which take an object clause with *that*, in order to find the possible instances of zero. In this way, collecting a 'complete' set of instances of *that* and zero from the entire Helsinki Corpus and printing it into workable text files is a matter of a few days' hard work.

Theoretically speaking, the method suggested above could be

regarded as invalid as it does not guarantee the finding of all zeros, but as a heuristic device it seems adequate. It is unlikely that there would be any verbs with which only the zero link occurs and which therefore remain outside the search. It may also be beneficial to be constantly reminded that the evidence extracted from a corpus is necessarily limited; certain aspects of linguistic reality are bound to be left outside the scope of the corpus (cf. Rissanen 1989: 17).

The above discussion of the problems of finding the zero links can also serve as a reminder of the importance of adequate grammatical tagging, including the marking of closed-class structural zero elements. This kind of tagging will, I hope, ultimately be attached to the Helsinki Corpus, although at present it is beyond our resources.[4]

18.5   *That* and zero in the Helsinki Corpus

In the present survey I discuss the variation between zero and *that* mainly in reference to their use with four high-frequency verbs: *know, think, say* and *tell*. *Say* and *tell* indicate verbal expression, *know* and *think* non-verbal mental activity or state. Although these lexical items do not represent all semantic types of verbs with clausal objects, they will adequately illustrate the changing trends in the distribution of the two links.

The diachrony of the zero/*that* variation in noun clauses has not been discussed in detail in earlier literature. Mitchell (1985: §1976ff) gives a good overall survey of earlier Old English studies; he confirms that zero existed in Old English, although the number of instances is low in comparison with the instances with *that* (§1983; cf. Ogura 1978, 1979). Warner (1982: 169–77) succinctly outlines the variation in Wyclif's sermons. In these texts the highest frequency of zero is with *say* (*c.* 9 per cent); many common verbs, such as *bid, seem, will* and *wite* ('know'), take object clauses only with *that*. Warner (pp. 171–3) also refers to two structural features which influence the choice of the link (cf. also McDavid 1964: 108–9; Elsness 1984: 523–7). One is the pronominal subject of the object clause, which favours zero, as in *He said he had been ill*, as against *He said that his old grandmother had been ill*. The other quite obvious feature is the occurrence of inserted elements between the verb and the object clause, as in *He said to his old grandmother that he had been ill*. The influence of these two features on Late Middle and Early Modern English usage will be discussed in some detail below.

The most detailed text-based surveys of zero/*that* variation in present-day English are McDavid (1964) and Elsness (1982, 1984). In McDavid's texts ('well-edited American non-fiction dating from the 1950s') the frequency of zero-introduced object clauses is surprisingly low, only around 13 per cent, but it must be taken into account that the style and register basis of her selection is narrow. Elsness's Syntax Data Corpus, which is extracted from the Brown Corpus, is more varied in content, and consequently the proportion of zero is as high as 39 per cent. Elsness's data also show that zero is more common in press reportage and adventure fiction than in belles letters and biography or scientific texts. The influence of stylistic factors on the distribution of the two variants has been pointed out by other scholars as well, most eloquently by Storms (1966). He combines zero with the 'amount of subjectivity the speaker puts into his words'. This sense of subjectivity is 'responsible for the distinction between colloquial, spoken English and so-called formal, written or elevated speech'. *That* is typical of expressions which tend to be 'less personal, less familiar, less warm, less friendly, less emotive. It is objective, factual, formal, official, sometimes tending to hostility' (1966: 262). Storms' definitions sound somewhat too categorical, but later in his article he softens this impression by referring to the large number of borderline cases.

Storms' statements imply that zero is typical of the oral mode of expression, while *that* is more characteristic of the literate mode. In view of the evidence given below, it seems possible that this dichotomy has prevailed throughout the history of English, from Old English onwards.

In Old and Early Middle English writings, the occurrence of zero is very low. Ogura (1979: 28) gives only a few instances of zero after *secgan* and *cweðan* 'say' in Old English prose texts, and the number of instances in verse is low, too (Ogura 1978: Mitchell 1985: §1982–5). My own random listings show the same tendency: there are no unambiguous prose instances of *secgan* with zero in the 950–1050 section of the Helsinki Corpus (*c.* 100 000 words). Old English examples:

(4) sægde him þæs leanes þanc,/ *cwæð, he þone quðwine* godne
     tealde (*Beowulf*: 1810)
     ('said he considered the sword good')

(5) *sægde he, he hit gehyrde* from þæm seolfan Uttan mæssepreoste
(*Bede's Ecclesiastical History*: 200)
('he said he had heard it from ... Utta')

In Early Middle English, the situation is roughly the same. A survey of the occurrences of *seien* 'say', *witen* 'know' and *wenen* 'think' in the 1150–1250 section of the Helsinki Corpus gives only isolated instances of zero, while object clauses introduced by *that* are very common.

(6) & loki nede ase stan hire wlite him liki; þe naueð nawt hire leor forbearnd i þe sunne. & *seið ha mei* baldeliche iseon hali men. (*Ancrene Wisse*: 33)
('and says she may fearlessly look at holy men')

(7) Me hwet is mare meadschipe þen forte leuen on him ant *seggen he is* godes sune þe þe giws demden & heaðene a-hongeden. *ant þt he wes* akennet of marie a meiden buten monnes man & iboren of hire bute bruche of hire bodi. (*Katherine*: 23)
('and say he is God's Son ... and that he was born of Mary')

Notice the use of *þt* ('that') in the second object clause in the *Katherine* example above.

(8) hwen tu forcwedest forþi crist ure undeðliche godes ant *seist ha beoð* idele & empti of gode. (*Katherine*: 24)
('and you say they are idle')

(9) and eft *wite crist heo is* ful biter to betene (*Lambeth Homilies*: 29)
('Christ may know it is very bitter to repent')

(10) *Wat crist þis is* a sari sahe (*Ancrene Wisse*: 48)
('Christ knows this is a grievous saying')

(11) we *witen ha beoð iwrahte* to stihen to þt stude.
(*Margarete*: 82)
('We know they are created to ascend to that place')

In (9) and (10), 'Christ knows' is probably idiomatic.

The relative frequency of zero increases rapidly in Late Middle English, as can be seen in Table 18.1.[5]

In Early Modern English, the same development continues steadily (Table 18.2).

Table 18.1 Zero and *that* as object clause links in Late Middle English

	1350–1420		1420–1500	
	zero	that	zero	that
say	35	187	52	107
tell	2	23	8	21
know	1	30	15	24
think	5	30	12	14
Total	43 (14%)	270	87 (34%)	166

Table 18.2 Zero and *that* as object clause links in Early Modern English

	Mod1 (1500–70)		Mod2 (1570–1640)		Mod3 (1640–1710)	
	zero	that	zero	that	zero	that
say	44	80	90	69	102	30
tell	8	20	34	44	56	50
know	23	17	31	27	29	17
think	22	13	86	25	67	11
Total	97 (43%)	130	241 (59%)	165	254 (70%)	108

The most dramatic overall increase takes place in the second half of the sixteenth and in the early seventeenth century, when the frequency of zero jumps from around 40 per cent to around 60 per cent. This development continues in the seventeenth century: by 1700, around 70 per cent of the instances are zero linked.

It can easily be seen that the spread of zero in the written texts advances through the linguistic and textual environments mentioned above, i.e. object clauses with a pronominal subject, combinations in which the object clause follows the verb without inserted elements, and texts which have a fairly close relationship to speech. A systematic study of these environments is rather difficult in Middle English as the textual selection is more restricted than in later periods. It is worth noting, however, that out of the forty-three instances of zero in texts dating from 1350 to 1420, twenty-eight display one or other of the 'zero-favouring' structural environments mentioned above. There are only ten instances of zero with a noun subject in the object clause (eight of them with *say*, with which zero is most common), and four in which the verb and the object clause are separated:

(12)   bi which *I knew the latitude* of my mone was – .1. ga 22 ma fro the Ecliptil (*Equatorie of Planets*: 44)

(13)   For *I telle þee trewly, it may not be* comen to by trauaile in þeim; (*Cloud of Unknowing*: 23)

In one instance only, both 'zero-resisting' features are combined. The object clause allows both direct and indirect readings:

(14)   ȝee! *I say to ȝow Iohn was* moore þan a prophete (*Wyclif's Sermons*, I: 337)

As to the textual distribution of zero at this early stage of development, the most obvious feature is its very high frequency in verse. Out of the thirty-five zero instances of *say* in the texts dating from 1350 to 1420, nineteen occur in verse; this figure is even more revealing if we note that these verse extracts (sampled from *The Northern Homily Cycle*, Mannyng's *Handlyng Synne*, *Prick of Conscience*, *Cursor Mundi*, Chaucer's *Canterbury Tales* and Gower's *Confessio Amantis*) contain only eleven instances of *that*. It may be added that in the samples from *Canterbury Tales* zero occurs seven times as against two occurrences of *that*, while in the extracts taken from the prose tales (*Tale of Melibee* and *Parson's Tale*) there are fifty-six instances of *that* and not a single one of zero. The possibility to choose between *that* and zero obviously offered the poet a handy metrical device; it does not, of course, tell us anything about the frequency of zero in spoken expression beyond the fact that it must have been an acceptable structure.

The number and variety of existing texts allow a more systematic survey of diachronic developments in Early Modern English than in Middle English. The Early Modern English section of the Helsinki Corpus is divided into three sub-periods, as seen in Table 18.2. For the sake of brevity, the period 1500–70 is referred to as Mod1, 1570–1640 as Mod2, and 1640–1710 as Mod3. In the following discussion, only the figures for Mod1 (1500–70) and Mod3 (1640–1710) are compared in detail.

In Mod1 the differences in distribution between the verbs can be clearly seen. *Know* and *think*, which show a rapid increase of zero even in the fifteenth century (see Table 18.1), have zero in more than half the instances, while with *say* and *tell* the development is slower; the proportion of zero is only about one third of the instances. Examples:

Zero

(15) Thys good kyng hering their conclusion would not assent there vnto, *but sayde, he had rather be sycke* euen vnto death then he wold breake his espousals (Latimer: 36)

(16) and *tell me it were* none of mine (Roper: 84)

(17) *you know well ynough, the Law doth adjudge* the Procurer there, a Felon or a Murtherer (*Trial of Throckmorton* 73, col. 2)

(18) since I shall not speake, *thinking you all know* what you haue to doe (*Trial of Throckmorton* 64, col. 1)

That

(19) The king *would say that he had* .iii. concubines (More, *Richard III*: 56)

(20) he cam to the King, *telling him that the French king wold see that* ... (Edward VI, *Diary*: 265)

(21) it is *openly knowen that of wines they ought to be chosen that* are yelow in color (Turner, *Wines*, f. C7r)

(22) And *me thinketh in good faith, that so were it* good reason that ... (More, *Corresp*.: 507)

As can be seen in Tables 18.3 and 18.4, even in Early Modern English zero extends its domain first in the 'zero-favouring' environments.[6] In Mod1, zero and *that* are equally common with pronominal subjects and in structures without insertion (77/79 and 77/83). With other subjects and with insertions, *that* predominates (20/51

Table 18.3 Zero and *that* in Early Modern English: subject types

	Mod1 (1500–70)				Mod3 (1640–1710)			
	pron.		other		pron.		other	
	zero	*that*	zero	*that*	zero	*that*	zero	*that*
say	37	47	7	33	80	8	22	22
tell	6	13	2	7	47	25	9	25
know	18	12	5	5	22	13	7	4
think	16	7	6	6	48	2	19	9
Total	77	79	20	51	197	48	57	60

Table 18.4 Zero and *that* in Early Modern English: insertions between main clause verb and object clause

	Mod1 (1500–70)				Mod3 (1640–1710)			
	no insert.		insert.		no insert.		insert.	
say	42	60	2	20	94	18	8	12
tell	—	2	8	18	1	2	55	48
know	16	11	7	6	28	15	1	2
think	19	10	3	3	64	9	3	2
Total	77	83	20	47	187	44	67	64

and 20/47 respectively).[7] In Mod3, zero has become by far the more common variant in contexts in which the environment does not support the use of *that*: 197 instances as against 48 with a pronominal subject and 187 as against 44 when the object clause immediately follows the verb. Even in other contexts zero is as common as *that* (57/60 and 67/64). The spread of zero seems neatly to follow the principle of Bailey's (1973) wave model.

Although the development follows the same overall pattern with all the four verbs, there are differences in the speed of the change. With *say* and *tell*, zero spreads more slowly than with the verbs indicating mental activity and state (*think, know*). The high frequency of *that* after *tell* with a non-pronominal subject is particularly revealing. The resistance of this verb to zero may be due partly to the fact that an indirect object is in most instances placed between the verb and the object clause.

Table 18.5 Zero and *that* in object clauses governed by finite and non-finite verb forms in Early Modern English

	Mod1 (1500–70)				Mod3 (1640–1710)			
	finite		non-finite		finite		non-finite	
	zero	*that*	zero	*that*	zero	*that*	zero	*that*
say	32	52	12	28	87	13	15	17
tell	4	14	5	6	37	29	19	21
know	23	10	0	7	20	6	9	11
think	19	9	2	4	48	2	19	9
Total	78	85	19	45	192	50	62	58

Table 18.6 Zero and *that* in various text types in Mod1 (1500–70)

	Trials		Sermons		Fiction		Comedies		Letters		Other	
	zero	that	zero	that	zero	that	zero	that	zero	that	zero	that
say	12	15	3	1	14	15	6	2	1	11	8	36
tell	1	5	—	1	2	3	3	1	—	—	2	10
know	6	—	1	1	3	1	8	1	2	3	3	11
think	5	—	6	1	1	—	5	1	3	5	2	6
Total	24	20	10	4	20	19	22	5	6	19	15	63

A structural feature which has an easily recognizable influence on the variation between zero and *that* is the form of the verb of the main clause (cf. McDavid 1964: 110–11). If the verb is in a non-finite form (examples 18, 20–21 above), particularly in the present or past participle, *that* is almost as common as zero even in Mod3. As can be seen in Table 18.5, this feature becomes particularly noticeable with the growing frequency of zero – in Mod1 with *know* and *think* and in Mod3 with *say*. The complete absence of zero after the non-finite form of *know* in Mod1 is noteworthy.

A survey of the distribution of the links in relation to text type clearly implies that zero was closely related to spoken expression; it may have been the unmarked link in speech throughout the Old and Early Middle English period. Tables 18.6 and 18.7 give the distribution of the two variants in text types which are related to speech or the oral mode of expression: in the Helsinki Corpus, most typically trial records, sermons, fiction and comedies. The category 'others', given as a contrast to the aforementioned types of text, contains laws, handbooks, scientific and educational treatises, historical writing, travelogues, diaries, biographies and official correspondence. Private correspondence is given as a separate category, as this text type often shows characteristics of the oral mode of expression.

In Mod1 the proportion between zero and *that* in speech-related text types (excluding private letters) is 76/48, i.e. a clear prevalence of zero, while in private letters and other text types it is 21/82, i.e. only 20 per cent of zero. In Mod3 the frequency of zero increases in all types of text, but it is still significantly more common in the speech-related categories (113/35 or 76 per cent), while the percentage is 66 (141/73) with the other text types. The proportion of zero in trials

Table 18.7 Zero and *that* in various text types in Mod3 (1640–1710)

	Trials		Sermons		Fiction		Comedies		Letters		Other	
	zero	*that*	zero	*that*	zero	*that*	zero	*that*	zero	*that*	zero	*that*
say	25	3	1	—	6	5	1	1	11	6	58	15
tell	11	4	1	5	7	4	4	3	3	4	22	23
know	9	2	—	1	8	3	6	1	2	2	4	8
think	11	1	1	—	6	2	16	—	9	—	24	8
Total	56	10	3	6	27	14	27	5	25	12	108	54

and comedies is particularly striking. The sermons do not have the same proportion of zero as the other text types, but this may be due to the low number of instances.

There are also differences in the distribution of the two variants in regard to individual verbs. In Mod1 zero is slightly more common than *that* with *say* in the 'oral' text types (35/33), while *that* predominates with *tell*. With both *know* and *think*, zero is the dominant variant (18/3 and 23/2). The differences are less significant in Mod3: *say* 33/9; *tell* 23/16; *know* 23/7; *think* 34/3.

The figures in Table 18.7 also show that, while in general private letters do not differ from the other texts representing the literate mode, in Mod3 the verb *think* is followed only by zero. Although the figures are here, as with the sermons, too low for definite conclusions, a stylistic shift towards the oral mode of expression is not unlikely.

For the sake of brevity and clarity, the present discussion has concentrated on object clauses linked with four high-frequency verbs only. By and large, other verbs show the same patterns of distribution as these four. As to verbs of perception, *see* is closer to *say* than to *know* in Mod1: the distribution is zero 14/*that* 29. In Mod2 and Mod3 the same rapid increase of zero as with *say* is shown: the figures for Mod2 are zero 35/*that* 18; and for Mod3 zero 21/*that* 9. *Hope*, a verb of 'modal' mental activity, has too few instances of object clauses in Mod1 to allow quantitative statements; in Mod2 and Mod3 it very distinctly favours zero: the figures for Mod2 are zero 32/*that* 3; and for Mod3, zero 43/*that* 2. This implies that even those verbs with which object clauses become common fairly late can easily adopt either of the two links. It seems, however, that verbs with low frequency (with object clauses), or with a more specific meaning, favour *that*. The figures for *answer* in Mod1 are zero 3/*that* 15; in Mod2, zero 4/*that* 11; in Mod3 zero 3/*that* 5. *Advise* and *complain* have no instances of zero in the Early Modern section of the corpus; the figures for *that* are also low: 5 and 7 respectively. On the other hand, *confess*, which is a central (and first person oriented) verb in the Trials, shows a fair proportion of zero: Mod1 zero 3/*that* 8; Mod2 zero 10/*that* 11; Mod3 zero 7/*that* 2. Examples:

Zero:
(23) The king mused at it; but, to grace the jest better, *he answered, he knew not.* (Armin: 45)
(24) the party that had stollen it should come thither, *and confesse he had it;* (Gifford, f. E3v)

That:
(25) *I answered him that I was* there also. (Taylor, John f. B1, col. 2)
(26) *I would advise that all children might be put* to the Grammar-School (Hoole: 25)
(27) *they complain that the brats are* untoward (Locke: 50)
(28) before whom Geffrye was whipped, *until he confessed that Jesus Christ was* in heaven. (Hayward: 87)

The existence of computerized corpora, particularly the Brown Corpus, the Lancaster-Oslo/Bergen Corpus and the London-Lund Corpus, makes it possible to correlate historical corpus studies with structural variation in present-day English. A quick survey of parts of LOB[8] shows that the rapid increase of zero in Early Modern English came to a halt some time in later Modern English: with *say*, the figures are zero 40/*that* 72; and with *think*, zero 79/*that* 21. It is significant that with *say* the later seventeenth-century predominance of zero has, once again, been replaced by a predominance of *that*. In part, however, this impression may be due to the different textual structures of LOB and the Helsinki Corpus; the first-mentioned corpus does not contain, for instance, drama, trials or private correspondence. That zero is acceptable even in less colloquial styles in present-day English is shown by the 35 instances of *say* + zero in newspaper text and by the ten instances of *think* + zero in scientific texts.

A sampling of parts of the London-Lund Corpus (texts 3.1–6 for *say*; 3.1–3 for *think*) confirms the impression given by LOB. With *say, that* is as common as zero (zero 21/*that* 23); the proportion clearly differs from the LOB figures. With *think* the predominance of zero is highly significant: zero 46/*that* 4. It is worth pointing out that all the instances in the sample had either first person (50 instances) or second person (2 instances) subjects.

What, then, are the primary factors behind the variation between zero and *that* in object clauses and the changes in the relative frequency of these two structural variants? Although a conclusive answer is impossible to give, it is obvious that structural simplicity and clarity are a prerequisite for the use of zero; as Warner puts it, *that* 'helps to mark a clause boundary, and it tends to be deleted more as this function is less useful' (1982: 174; cf. Quirk *et al.* 1985: 15.4b). A pronominal subject beginning the object clause also tends to mark the clause boundary; furthermore, a personal pronoun in subject position, as opposed to a noun, increases the cohesion of the sentence. Thus, it is no wonder that this feature favours zero. A non-finite form of the main-clause verb and elements inserted between the verb and the object clause increase the complexity of the structure and consequently favour the use of *that*. It is also obvious that zero is a feature which is typical of spoken expression, both in its present-day usage and, as the present survey suggests, in centuries past. This is not unexpected: formal clause boundaries are less relevant in speech than in writing; there is also a greater variety of ways of keeping the meaning of the expression sufficiently unambiguous. Furthermore, spoken language is less concerned with a formal, clear-cut distinction between the direct and indirect representation of speech and thought.

The diachronic development towards a greater popularity of zero is no doubt due to a variety of factors. Stylistic shift towards less formal ways of writing is perhaps one factor working in this direction, although the evidence presented above shows that zero was never systematically rejected even in formal writing. It would also be tempting to suggest that the development of the language towards a stricter ordering of the elements supported the increasing use of zero by diminishing the risk of ambiguity. Some support for this hypothesis is given by the relative frequency of cases in which the verb and the object clause are separated by lighter or heavier insertions (Table 18.4). If we discount *tell*, with which the insertion of the indirect object is more or less a rule, the percentage of insertions is 21 (41 out of the total of 199 instances) in Mod1, while it sinks to 11 per cent (28 out of 256 instances) in Mod3. With *know* and *think*, the number of insertions is particularly low in the later seventeenth century.

We should also ask why the proportion of the two links varies with different verbs. It is obvious that the occurrence of the linguistic features supporting one or the other variant link may be more likely with some verbs than with others. Yet, as shown by Table 18.4, such bias is clearly visible only in the case of *tell*. There are no doubt other factors, semantic and structural, which affect the closeness of the link between the verb and the clausal object and thus have an influence on the simplicity and clarity of the sentence. Furthermore, the meaning of the verb probably determines the likelihood of its occurrence in different modes of discourse. An indication of this can be found in a simple survey of the person of the subject of the verbs under discussion. As can be seen in Table 18.8, with *know* and *think* first and second person subjects very clearly predominate; with *say* and *tell*, third person subjects predominate. This indicates a close connection of the two former verbs with the oral mode of expression, in contrast to the other two (cf. Chafe 1982: 46).

Table 18.8 The person of the subject of the verb governing the object clause: Mod1 + Mod3

	1st	2nd	3rd	Total
say	44 (17%)	18 (7%)	194 (76%)	256 (100%)
tell	31 (26%)	8 (7%)	80 (67%)	119 (100%)
know	38 (44%)	23 (27%)	25 (20%)	86 (100%)
think	66 (58%)	18 (16%)	29 (26%)	113 (100%)

18.6   Concluding remarks

The present survey can perhaps shed new light on the old question of whether or not we can speak about 'omission' of *that* (admitting that the whole question as such is mainly semantic and terminological). Unquestionably, both zero and *that* existed from the time of our earliest written texts, and intuitively it seems unlikely that zero linking would simply be the result of dropping a conjunctive element. At the level of spoken expression zero may well have been the unmarked object clause link throughout the history of English.

Thus the term 'omission' is certainly inaccurate. But the changing distribution of the two variant links indicates that in written English *that* was originally the unmarked link, and the growing popularity of zero may well have been regarded as an innovation interpretable as 'omission' of the expressed conjunction. After the heyday of zero in the late seventeenth century, this feeling may have resulted in a reversal of the tide in the norm-loving eighteenth century, a time when grammarians were keen on sorting out and evaluating variant expressions. As a result, *that* is once again favoured, e.g. with *say*, particularly in more formal styles of writing.[9]

In a discussion of this kind, the differences between individual verbs are of major importance. As early as the fifteenth century, *think* has favoured zero and very distinctly does so even today, while there has been much more variation in linking with *say*. Newly borrowed verbs probably favour the explicit link and adopt the variation pattern only when they are well established in the language; this is natural as they mostly represent 'change from above' (cf. e.g. Traugott and Romaine 1985) and typically appear in literate modes of expression.

Text-based surveys of variation and change are very much simplified and speeded up by the use of computerized corpora. Nevertheless, intensive research work and development are still needed in computer linguistics, in the areas of storing, retrieving, classifying and combining linguistic information. The solution of tagging problems would seem to be the most important short-term goal in the field of historical corpus development.

Finally, whatever the advantages of computerized corpora, the ultimate analysis, synthesis and interpretation of the results remain the responsibility of the scholar – at least in the foreseeable future. And so it should be!

Notes

[1] As in all contexts in which I refer to the Helsinki Corpus, I here wish to thank all the members of the Corpus project team. Our thanks are also due, among others, to the editors of the *Dictionary of Old English* for kind permission to use their computerized text tapes, and to the Oxford Text Archive and the Norwegian Computing Centre for the Humanities for expert advice.

[2] For a description of the dialectal part of the corpus, see Ihalainen in this

volume. For a detailed description of the contents of the diachronic corpus, see the *Manual*, Vol. 1 (Kytö 1990). See also Kytö and Rissanen (1988), Nevalainen and Raumolin–Brunberg (1989) and Rissanen (forthcoming in *ESEL* 2).

The abbreviated titles of the corpus texts quoted in the present article refer to the alphabetical bibliography in Kytö (1990).

[3] The basic corpus is formed of texts written in England. There are, at present, two supplementary corpora under preparation: early Scots (by Anneli Meurman–Solin) and early American English (by Merja Kytö).

[4] We have had fruitful cooperation with Edward Finegan and Douglas Biber of the University of Southern California in developing an automatic tagging program for a historical corpus. This work is, however, still in its initial stages.

[5] In the Helsinki Corpus, the division between the last two Middle English sub-periods is made at 1420 instead of 1450, as the first-mentioned date seems more natural from the point of view of the study of the developing standard.

[6] In Table 18.3, simple personal and demonstrative pronouns have been taken as pronominal subjects. In addition, existential *there* is included in this category as it seems to have the same effect on the choice of the link as the pronominal subjects proper. Indefinite and reflexive pronouns have not been included, nor are the cases in which the subject pronoun is the head of a long postmodifying element.

[7] In these figures, all insertions, even light-weight pronouns, have been included. If only heavier insertions are included, the predominance of *that* is even more obvious.

[8] Sections A1–10, B1–10, J1–20, K1–20, and L1–20 were checked for *say*, and all of Categories A, B and J, and sections 1–10 of K, for *think*.

[9] Another factor which may have affected the diachrony of the distributions in modern English is the development of non-finite structures of complementation. Unfortunately, this question must be left outside the present discussion.

19 A point of verb syntax in south-western British English: An analysis of a dialect continuum

OSSI IHALAINEN

In their admirable study of the voicing of initial fricatives in the south of England, Jan Svartvik and his colleagues argue that computers are particularly suitable for dialectology (Francis, Svartvik and Rubin 1969). One might be tempted to go even further and suggest that there are some crucial aspects of dialectology that are extremely difficult, perhaps even impossible, to handle without the help of a computer. What I hope will emerge from the discussion below is that grammatical continua and mixed lects are precisely such areas.

19.1 The problem

The problem that I would like to introduce here is an instance of variation in the syntax of the verb in south-western British English. In some parts of the South-west tense is expressed periphrastically, as in *They do make paths*, whereas in others an inflection is used, as in *They makes paths*.

The interesting thing is that while these forms have their favourite areas and while for many south-western speakers they are mutually exclusive, there are speakers who have both of them. However, it turns out that in these mixed lects one form clearly dominates to the extent that the secondary form strikes one as being exceptional. Whether this is true of mixed grammatical systems in general or simply an idiosyncrasy of the feature concerned (or possibly the material being analysed), I am not in a position to answer now. However, I hope to be able to show that a transitory belt lies between a prototypical *do*-area and an *s*-area, so that one can

290

actually plot the thinning out of the feature concerned. The 'development' outlined here is the change of periphrastic tense formation into inflectional marking.

The distribution of the periphrastic form in the South-west is far more restricted than the distribution of the *s*-form. One are where periphrasis is relatively frequent is East Somerset. On the other hand, there are areas in the South-west where it does not seem to occur at all. One of the most striking *do*-less areas in the South-west is Devon. What I hope to be able to show here is that the change from one type to another is gradual, with a transitional area in which the two systems overlap even in the speech of individual speakers. This study differs from most earlier studies of dialectal grammar in that the data are frequencies rather than statements of the absence or presence of some feature in a particular area.

In fact, in dialect studies one often comes across features that the writer described as 'frequent' or 'rare'; but usually no evidence, besides the writer's intuition, is given for these judgements. Large machine-readable transcriptions of spontaneous speech can provide such evidence quite easily.

19.2   The South-west

Although scholars have been somewhat vague on the particulars, they seem to agree that there is a linguistic area in England called the South-west. This is typically an area where people say *I ben't sure* instead or *I'm not sure*, *vinger* (with a prominent retroflex *r*) for *finger*, *Where be em to?* (*Where be mun to?*) for *Where are they?* and *What's do that for?* for *Why did you do that?* In his book *The South-west of England* (1986), Martyn Wakelin includes in the South-west, 'with its several sub-varieties', Cornwall, Devon, Somerset, Dorset, Wiltshire and South Avon. Avon north of Bristol and the western extremities of Gloucestershire, Berkshire and Hampshire are regarded as forming a marginal area. This seems to be a conservative estimate in that some scholars might extend the South-west slightly further east and north, but the differences are not great (cf. Viereck 1980, Wells 1982).

It is interesting to note in passing here that, although phonological, lexical, morphological and syntactic features seldom co-occur to form clear-cut dialect boundaries, it appears that the *vinger-*

pronouncing area is more or less identical with the area where people say *What's do that for?* for *Why did you do that?*

19.3   Two sub-areas in the South-west: East and West Somerset

Dialectologists also agree that the South-west is not linguistically unified. For example, Elworthy in his *The Dialect of West Somerset* (1875) calls attention to the fact that Somerset is linguistically split into eastern and western varieties. He sets the boundary between East and West Somerset at the Quantocks. He also points out that West Somerset shares many features with the Devon dialect, but that there are differences:

In many respects the dialect of North Devon is the same as ours, and it much more nearly resembles it than the East Somerset does, but there are however many marked differences. One of the most striking is that in Devon they use *us* as a nominative, while in Somerset we do not. Again they use the old inflexion *th* more than we do; they would say, *u goo°ŭth, u tau°keth*, 'he goes', 'he talks'; we should say, *ai du goo, ai du tau°kĕe*, 'he do go', 'he do talk'. (Elworthy 1875: 7)[1]

Although Elworthy makes the point that 'In many respects the dialect of North Devon is the same as ours, and it much more nearly resembles it than the East Somerset does', he does not elaborate on this point. However, one gathers from his discussion that one critical sound was *oo* (i.e. /u:/, which in some parts of the West, including West Somerset, was fronted to /ʏ:/ in words like *food*. This situation obtains even today, as anyone travelling in the West Country can tell.

More recent studies, too, have recognized the split of Somerset into eastern and western varieties (e.g. Wakelin 1975, 1977, 1986; Fischer 1976; Viereck 1980, 1985; Ihalainen 1987). Again scholars may not agree where the precise boundary is. This seems to depend on whether one chooses to emphasize phonological, grammatical or lexical evidence. On the strength of phonological evidence, the eastern boundary of West Somerset would seem to be Stogumber, as suggested by Wakelin (1975: 138). However, although dialectologists may disagree about the details, they nevertheless agree that West Somerset goes linguistically with Devon and the eastern part of Cornwall.[2]

It is the division of Somerset and its neighbourhood into an eastern and a western variety that will be explored here in some detail. I shall try to show that computerized texts can be profitably and conveniently used for this type of exploratory work. Also, I shall refer to evidence that, to my knowledge, has not been used in discussions of this particular point.

19.4   Periphrastic *do*

One of the features Elworthy discusses in relation to the Devon–Somerset linguistic border is the use of periphrastic *do* versus the inflected form (*They do like it* vs *They likes it*). His position on the distribution of these forms in the Somerset–Devon area changes slightly over the years. The point he makes in *The Dialect of West Somerset* (1875: 7) is that Somerset uses periphrastic *do* (*They do talky*) where Devon would use an inflection (*They talketh*). Later in his *Somerset Word-Book* (1886: xlvi) he modifies his position and points out that *do* is being replaced by the infected form:

Another advance apparently connected with increasing instruction is the more common use of the inflection *us* in the intransitive and frequentative form of verbs instead of the periphrastic *do* with the inflected pres. inf. 'I workus to factory' is now the usual form, whereas up to a recent period the same person would have said, 'I do worky to factory'. An old under-gardener, speaking of different qualities of fuel for his use, said, 'The stone coal *lee·ustus* (lasts) zo much longer, and gees out morey it too', i.e. does not burn so quickly – Feb. 2, 1888. He certainly would have said a few years ago – 'The stone coal du·lee ustee (do lasty) zo much longer.' This form is also superseding the old form *eth*, which latter is now becoming rare in the Vale of West Somerset.

West Somerset, then, was becoming more like Devon in that the periphrastic form was being replaced by the inflected form.

My impression from the tape-recorded material that I have been working on (reflecting the situation among elderly speakers of Somerset English in the 1970s and early 1980s) is that, although periphrastic *do* does occur in the speech of West Somerset speakers, it is indeed rare compared with the inflected form (*They makes paths*). The trend, whose beginning Elworthy had obviously spotted, has almost reached completion. In East Somerset, on the other hand, the periphrastic form clearly dominates. Compare the two samples from my material given below, the former recorded in Wedmore, the latter in Fitzhead:

(1) Didn't us get that? Well, you . . . got this rod with the worms
     tied on to the end and . . . you could always tell when a eel is
     biting because he did shake . . . you do feel the rod shake, and
     then you pull up the rod and put un over the top and just
     shake like that and the eel would let go and he is down in the
     tub. You caught un, you see. (L.V.)
(2) (Q: What did they do?)
     Oh, goes up on their horses – hounds – and they single out the
     stag they wants, you see, and chases un. Sometimes they
     catches un, sometimes they don't. (J.M. T19, p. 29)

In (1) the speaker uses periphrastic forms (*did shake, do feel*) or
standard verb forms. This contrasts sharply with the speech of a
West Somerset informant like J.M. in sample (2), where *s*-forms
occur instead.[3] (Notice incidentally how both speakers have similar
pronominal forms: the masculine third person singular pronoun *un*
'him' is used instead of the neuter pronoun.)

   In addition to the forms discussed so far, there is an uninflected
singular form (*He live by the pub*) that occurs sporadically in
Somerset. However, since its regional and linguistic distribution are
not yet known, I shall not deal with it here.

19.5   The primary data

To study the assumption that there is a tendency for West Somerset
speakers to use less periphrasis than East Somerset speakers, a
sample of 6400 words was drawn from the Somerset transcripts of
the Helsinki Dialect Corpus.[4] The speakers are elderly working-
class people from rural Somerset. Four of the speakers represent
areas west of the Quantocks and four east. The East Somerset and
West Somerset samples are of equal length.[5]

   The informants share features such as the voicing of initial
fricatives, the use of *he* and *him/'m/'n* for *it* (as in *Where's the knife?*
He's on the desk. Where you left'n), the use of the enclitic *er* for *he*,
she and *it* (as in *He's nice, in' er?*), the use of nominative objects (as
in *Mr Difford, you know he?*), the use of *to* in the sense 'in' (as in
Where do er live to? 'Where does she/he live?'), and the use of
second person singular forms (as in *How't thee getting on? 'How art
thou getting on?'*).

   They differ with respect to such features as the fronting of /u:/ or the use of *were* with singular subjects. Like Devon speakers, West Somerset speakers typically have a fronted vowel in words like *move* and they use *was* rather than *were* with all grammatical subjects.

Although the samples were selected at random, they are comparable in terms of formality, speakers and topic. What variation there is, then, must be mainly regional. There is evidence that periphrastic *do* tends to occur in general rather than specific statements, so that speakers who have periphrasis say *They did go to Taunton every Saturday*, but usually not *They did go to Taunton last Saturday*. The latter idea would be expressed by *They went to Taunton last Saturday* (Ihalainen 1976; however, see Weltens 1983). To put this somewhat differently, periphrasis is used to express habitual aspect.

The texts allowed ample chance for the use of habitual aspect, mainly with past time reference. The following list shows the various explicitly marked habitual past tense forms in the texts.

	Did	*Used to*	*Would*	Totals
East	20	36	16	72
West	2	48	33	83

The difference between the totals here (72 habitual aspect verbs in the East Somerset sample versus 83 in the West Somerset sample) is not statistically significant (chi-square = .762, d.f. = 1), which suggests that the samples represent basically the same kind of text. However, the difference between the frequencies of *did* (20 vs 2) is so striking that no statistical testing is necessary to convince one of its significance.

The present tense form *do* was much rarer in the recordings (people seem to be more interested in the past than in the present), but its regional distribution was that which might be expected on the basis of *did*: 6 instances in the East Somerset samples and none in the West Somerset samples.

These figures confirm one's impression that *do* is rare in West Somerset as compared with East Somerset. Although it is true that even those western speakers whose samples showed no traces of the periphrastic formation here may occasionally use them, I feel that the figures presented above square rather well with one's general impression of the frequency of periphrasis across Somerset. As for sample size, the high West Somerset figure for *used to* shows that there was ample chance for *do* (which is a habitual aspect marker) to occur.

19.6   The inflected form: *They makes paths*

Although there were fewer present tense than past tense forms in the samples, there were nevertheless 199 present tense contexts, which provided enough material to show, among other things, that (in addition to regional verb forms) both East and West Somerset speakers also have standard present tense forms like *They bite a lot better in thundery weather*; or perhaps I should say 'standard-looking' rather than 'standard', considering that Somerset speakers also say *He live by the pub*. However, the inclusion of these forms would complicate the basic question here: the distribution of the traditional vernacular tense formations.

What interests us in particular is the inflected non third person singular -*s* (*They bites*), because in sentences like *He lives down to Latcham*, one does not really know whether this is a standard form or an instance of the unified present tense marker -*s* – unless one makes the rather unrealistic assumption that the informants speak a 'pure' dialect.

Only fifteen instances of non-standard present tense marking were found (*I says*, eight instances; *I still dos* /duːz/ *a bit of gardening; some says; they uses; women uses; we lives; they gets*). The interesting thing is that all fifteen instances occurred in the speech of West Somerset speakers, who have *do* only rarely (as was shown above, only two instances of *do* were found in the West Somerset sample). Therefore, what is clear is that West Somerset speakers use the inflected form regularly and have *do* as a marginal form. But what of non-standard *s* in East Somerset? A look at some additional transcripts shows that at least L.V. has this form occasionally, but that it is by no means a favourite even with him. Clearly, it is marginal in the East in precisely the way that *do* is marginal in the West. What the figures suggest, then, is that there is a loose kind of complementarity: if one uses inflection, one does not need the auxiliary, and vice versa. However, I would like to emphasize the word 'loose' here; as was seen above, in some lects the two constructions are not mutually exclusive.

19.7   The advantage of a restricted sample

Paradoxically, in some cases a relatively small sample may help us see trends that a much larger sample might obscure. Thus, the evidence provided by the samples suggests that we have two basic types of speaker: speakers who say *They do make paths/They did make paths* and speakers who say *They makes paths/They did make paths/They made paths*. The interesting thing is that the obvious combination *They do make paths/They makes paths* does not occur in the 6400-word sample. However, additional material outside this sample shows that there are speakers who say *They do make paths/They makes paths* (for instance, one of the eastern speakers represented here). But this type of lect is somehow exceptional, not at all on a par with the other types, and one is under the obligation to find some kind of explanation for it (either linguistic or non-linguistic). It seems to me that here a relatively small sample helped identify a pattern and an exception that a very large sample might have made it difficult to spot. The difficulty, of course, is in not making one's sample so small that not even the characteristic patterns stand out clearly. However, if one has computerized texts it is easy to find a convenient size simply by experimenting with different sample sizes.[6]

19.8   No *do* in Devon?

As was shown above, there is a thinning out of periphrastic *do* when one moves west from the Quantocks. In the following I shall try to look at what happens when one actually goes into Devon.

It has been generally assumed that periphrastic *do* does not occur in Devon at all. For example, Wakelin (1977: 120; 1984: 83) and Rogers (1979: 39), on the strength of evidence provided by the *Survey of English Dialects* (SED), leave Devon out of their list of *do* areas. (However, Rogers points out that the survey questionnaire did not necessarily always manage to elicit the obvious vernacular form.)

Older studies of Devon English (Chope 1891, Hewett 1892, Wiegert 1921) do not mention periphrastic forms. Ellis's dialect test, whose items 2 and 6 were particularly designed to elicit periphrastic *do* (Ellis 1889: 8–16), has no evidence for it in Devon, although several instances were attested in Somerset, including West Somerset (Wedmore, Montacute, Wellington).

My own explorations of the SED material have again not revealed any instances of periphrastic *do* in Devon. In addition to the evidence provided by the actual responses published in the SED volumes, I listened to the eleven recordings made in the Devon localities. These recordings represent about three and a half hours of spontaneous speech. No instances of periphrastic *do* occurred in any of the recorded samples.

However, it should be noted that the SED does not cover the Somerset–Devon border area very well. Fortunately, the Helsinki Dialect Corpus includes 74,000 words of Devon English collected from the border area between Tiverton and the Somerset boundary. These recordings were made and transcribed by Ossi Stigell in the mid 1970s. A search of these texts revealed eleven instances of *do* in affirmative statements, but careful listening to the tape recordings showed that they were all emphatic, as in *One thing we do grow is teddies* (as opposed to the many things that we do not grow any more).

Although it seems to me almost impossible to accept that one can find *do* periphrasis in and around Brompton Ralph but not around Tiverton, which is only about fifteen miles away, this is what the evidence suggests. There is, then, a radical thinning out of the use of *do* periphrasis when one crosses the Quantocks, and a total disappearance when one goes into Devon. However, the large number of emphatic *do* forms in the Devon sample (eleven instances per 74,000 words) may suggest that there is a readiness to use this construction. But they were emphatic forms nevertheless, quite distinct from the sixteen instances found in the 6400-word Somerset sample (which also had two sentences with emphatic *do*).

Furthermore, the Stigell recordings show that, as in West Somerset, non-standard agreement of the type *They likes it* is common in Devon and is quite obviously the preferred form in the area covered by those texts.

Periphrastic *do* reappears in western Cornwall, so that Devon forms a *do* less island in the west. For the time being I have no convincing explanation for this interesting gap in an area that is in many other respects quite uniform linguistically. It will not do to say that Devon is innovative, because it can be shown that in many ways, for example as regards the use of invariant *be*, Devon is far more conservative than Somerset.

19.9   Marginal *do*: the problem of rare forms

As was pointed out above, the West Somerset texts (four samples of

800 words each) had only two instances of periphrastic *do*. These came from two speakers (J.M and W.W.). An additional 12,000-word sample of the speech of J.Cr., whose 800-word sample did not have a single instance of periphrastic *do*, showed that he has this feature but it must be very rare (three instances of periphrasis were found). It is easy to see that one has reached the limits of one's inquiry here. It is likely that there are definite constraints on the distribution of *do* in the language of speakers like J.Cr. However, it is not possible to create a corpus large enough to enable one to formulate testable hypotheses about the nature of these constraints. And without hunches as to what might be going on, it is difficult to set up a successful elicitation experiment.

To give an idea of the amount of material needed to study the above problem, it is instructive to look at one possible conditioning factor that would in theory be easy to study. For instance, it might be the case that in varieties having a marginal *do*, periphrasis is favoured in subordinate clauses with a pronominal subject, as in *They wanted to see how long that did take*. However, in order for any kind of convincing pattern to emerge, one would need ten to fifteen instances of *do* of this type. This means some 60,000 words, given speakers like J.M. and J.Cr.

Another problem is that, even if one had a hunch about what was going on, it might be very difficult to elicit information on that point. For example, the available evidence suggests that those who have *do* marginally have it just before a hesitation pause which is followed by either a new start or a completion of the original thought, as in *She did...uh...she used to salt it in* and *She did...uh...salt it in*. I do not see how one could possibly set up experiments to study structures like these.

19.10   A methodological postscript

Although the use of computerized transcriptions makes linguistic analysis much easier than it would be otherwise, there are at least two ways in which the situation could be made even better. For example, a computer will be able to locate all the instances of *do* in no time and list them in a nicely arranged concordance that is easy to study. But the problem is that it lists all kinds of unrelated structures. If we are working on *do* in affirmatives, like *They do like it*, we do not want cases like *Do they like it?*, or *What we did was open the gate*, or *Yes, they do*. That is, the pattern concerned is *do* followed by a verb (either immediately or possibly separated by, say an adverb, as in *We did always salt it in*). However, with word-tagged texts, one could simply search for the pattern *do* + VB and eliminate the unwanted *do* contexts. One program that adds word tags to running texts is the CLAWS package developed at the University of Lancaster (Garside, Leech and Sampson 1987). Here is a sample analysis of the sentence *They do call it scrumpy* (after the word *scrumpy* was added to the CLAWS wordlist).

A01	0 001	
A01	0 010 they	02 PP3AS
A01	0 020 do	02 DO
A01	0 030 call	02 VB NN
A01	0 040 it	02 PP3
A01	0 050 scrumpy	54 NN
A01	0 051 .	01 .

Given a tagged text like the short sample above, it would be easy to write a simple search program that would look for patterns of tags, say DO + VB (*do call*), and thus eliminate much unwanted material from the listing.

Another problem I encountered in this study was that I wanted to check the actual pronunciation of some of the forms found by the computer. For instance, in the case of periphrastic *do* the pronunciation is extremely important because *do* is also used emphatically, as in *I never DID find him*, and this form must be kept separate from the actual periphrastic form. Also, it was important to determine which speakers had /u/ fronting and to what extent that coincided with the distribution of *do*. Possible test words for /u/ fronting (i.e. words like *move*, *school*, *food* or *you*) are easy to locate in a machine-readable text, but finding the corresponding place on tape is often far from easy. However, if one had a direct link between text and sound so that one could simply locate a passage in the transcript and then listen to it by clicking the mouse, a lot of time would be saved for doing the actual analysis. Building such an interface is, of course, no problem if one works with short stretches of speech, but whether it is practicable to do this with large amounts of sound and text material is an open question. However, given the rate of progress in technology, it seems to me we are not talking about science fiction here.

19.11   Conclusion

The data for this paper were gathered by computer from running texts. The advantage of using running texts as opposed to a questionnaire is that one gets a far more realistic picture of the nature and amount of linguistic variation involved in the phenomenon one is looking at. One sees clearly where grammatical systems overlap and how one system gradually shades into another. As in phonology, grammatical isoglosses would appear to be gradual rather than abrupt. The nicely drawn lines that we are used to seeing on dialectologists' maps turn out to be rather complex and messy constructs that probably require complex explanations. This is the price we have to pay for gaining access to unidealized data.

Notes

[1] Elworthy's point about *us* not being used as a nominative in Somerset applies only to declaratives. Sentences like *Didn's get it*? 'Didn't us get it?' are common in Somerset English today and probably were also common in Elworthy's day. However, unlike in Devon English, sentences like *Us grows barley* do not occur in Somerset. In fact, the use of *us* as a subject was singled out, even by speakers who say things like *We bought it, didn's?*, as a characteristic Devon feature (the other typical feature being /næ:f/ instead of /naif/).

[2] Wakelin (1975: 138) gives Stogumber, just west of the Quantocks, as the eastern boundary of the /ʏ:/ pronouncing area including East Cornwall, Devon and West Somerset (that is, the south-western corner of Somerset, to be quite accurate). This squared with Elworthy's definition of West Somerset.

Fischer (1976), who uses lexical evidence only, includes the whole of Somerset in a wide transitional area (labelled '2/3') between central and eastern South-west. However, he also sees reasons for including West Somerset 'to a certain extent' in the central South-west with West Cornwall and most of Devon. For Wakelin, the decisive factor seems to be the fronting of /u:/ to /ʏ:/, a feature that is found in the south-western part of Somerset, Devon and East Cornwall.

Viereck (1985: 94–112) has carried out a dialectometric analysis of 'Survey of English Dialects' data on sixty lexical and eighty morphological features in the south of England, and concludes that 'Devon, West Somerset and parts of Cornwall form an independent area'.

In my article 'Towards a grammar of the Somerset dialect: A case study of the language of J.M.' (1987), I present some syntactic evidence which supports the east–west division of Somerset, with the Quantocks as an approximate boundary.

There seems to be ample evidence, then, for recognizing a distinction between West Somerset and the rest of the county.

3 It should be pointed out that periphrastic *do* has been attested in the speech of J.M. but it is very rare. Only two instances occurred in several hours of his speech. The dominant form with J.M. is quite clearly the *s* form.

4 When completed, the dialect corpus will have a minimum of half a million words of orthographically transcribed spontaneous speech from the main dialect areas of England. The material was collected in the 1970s. The informants were elderly speakers of the local vernacular. The recordings were originally made to supplement the Survey of English Dialects material in the area of syntax. However, it has turned out (perhaps not surprisingly) that they can be used to study many other aspects of linguistic structure, including morphophonemic processes and prosody.

The dialect corpus can be used independently or in connection with the historical section of the Helsinki Corpus of English Texts to provide information about the possible continuation and further development of earlier features which may have disappeared from the standard language. For further information about the dialect corpus, see Ihalainen 1988a, 1988b, 1990.

5 The Somerset samples were taken from 'free conversation' interviews with the following informants.

East Somerset (villages east of the river Parrett):
   J. S. Age 71. Peat-merchant. Westhay, Somerset. 1975.
   L. V. Age 70. Farmer. Wedmore, Somerset. 1976.
   C. F. Age 74. Farm-worker. Wedmore, Somerset. 1974.
   L. N. Age 70. Caretaker. Hambridge, Somerset. 1975.
West Somerset (villages west of the Quantocks):
   J. Cr. Age 77. Farm-worker. Stogumber, Somerset. 1975.
   S. J. Age 68. Farm-worker. Wooton Courtenay. 1971.
   J. M. Age 80. Farm-worker. Fitzhead (b. Brompton Ralph). 1972.
   W. W. Age 77. Forestry foreman. Luxborough. 1971.

According to Wakelin (1975: 138), the eastern border of West Somerset is Stogumber. Bonaparte (1875–6) regards the Parrett–Quantocks area as transitional, nearer to East Somerset than Devon. The above speakers, then, should be good representatives of what are traditionally regarded as the two main varieties of Somerset English.

6 For an example of 'sample-size checking', see Ihalainen (1991).

Part 4

Prospects for the future

20　Times change, and so do corpora

STIG JOHANSSON

20.1　Corpora of the future will be machine-readable

When Randolph Quirk initated his Survey of English Usage project in 1959, there was no thought of computerization.[1] Just a few years later W. Nelson Francis and Henry Kučera compiled the Brown Corpus, which was to set the pattern for many computer corpus projects. Such has been the success of the computer corpus that it seems safe to predict that linguists will no longer start compiling a large corpus without planning to make it machine-readable.

20.2　Quantity of text

In the close to thirty years since the Brown Corpus was compiled, the number of machine-readable texts has grown enormously. While the Brown Corpus was converted from print in a laborious and time-consuming manner, most of the publicly available machine-readable texts today are a by-product of the printing process, for example the vast archives maintained by major newspapers. Some texts are published both in printed and in electronic form. Many others exist primarily in machine-readable form and were never intended to be distributed in a printed version, for example electronic journals or computer network messages.

We may expect continued growth of the number of machine-readable texts. In the process, the Brown Corpus model is giving way to dynamic monitor corpora (Sinclair 1982: 4), that is, gigantic, slowly changing stores of text. In the future, linguists will select their own material from the vast data sources available. Something may still be said, however, for smaller, carefully constructed sample corpora which can be analysed exhaustively in a variety of ways. These will be needed in any case for types of texts which are not readily available in machine-readable form (e.g. letters, diaries, and all types of spoken material). Such texts will have to be keyboarded in the foreseeable future.

The explosive development has left some important tasks undone. We lack systematic archiving and cataloguing of machine-readable texts, in spite of important beginnings such as the Oxford Text Archive and the recent survey by Taylor and Leech.[2] Ideally, we would like to have public-service institutions which provide records on and give access to machine-readable texts, in much the same way as libraries do for printed material. This is a (perhaps vain) hope for the future.[3]

20.3   Variety of text

Variety study is probably the area where corpus workers can make their most significant contribution. Differences between varieties are rarely absolute but a question of degree. Such matters are hard to study by introspection, which is fallible once we go beyond clear cases in our own dialect, or by elicitation experiments, which always become more or less artificial. The solution is to examine natural discourse, as evidenced in corpora.[4]

In planning the Survey of English Usage, Randolph Quirk outlined an impressive scheme to represent a wide variety of types of spoken and written English. Jan Svartvik and his research team at Lund University have done pioneering work in making spoken Survey material available as the machine-readable London-Lund Corpus, allowing new and sophisticated studies of spoken discourse.[5]

Recent studies by Douglas Biber and Edward Finegan (see their contribution to this volume) are of special importance in throwing new light on dimensions of variation in texts. Together with the International Corpus of English project (see Schmied 1989; Greenbaum, this volume), this work may be the start of an era of comprehensive multi-dimensional approaches to variety study, perhaps even leading to a general theory of text typology.

Future corpus workers must take care not to restrict themselves to types of texts which are easily available. There are encouraging signs that compilers of new corpora are aware of this, as shown for example in the International Corpus of English project. Special opportunities are provided by new technological advances. Future spoken corpora may be stored on disks in versions linking transcription and sound (cf. Chafe *et al.*, this volume) and perhaps video. In written corpora it will no longer be necessary to omit illustrations and diagrams, as was done in the Brown Corpus; the text could be accompanied by digitized images. The latter is especially important in types of texts where illustrations form an integral part, for example in instructional and scientific discourse and in advertising.

The computer revolution has brought with it new forms of discourse which also deserve systematic study. One of these is electronic mail, recently a topic of debate in the *Humanist* electronic discussion group (founder and original editor: Willard McCarty, University of Toronto; current editors: Elaine Brennan and Allen Renear, Brown University). Electronic mail uses the conventions of writing but has something of the immediacy of speech. The addressee is not actually present, but can be expected to receive the message very rapidly. The writer has little thought of revision. Hence, electronic mail is more prone to error than other types of writing. More important, it seems more playful and creative, less bound by conventions. Here are a couple of examples (reproduced by permission of the authors) showing lexical innovation, non-standard syntax and expressive punctuation.

(1) I enjoyed RZ's recent reference to Ventura's output as 'something really sleak'. This wonderful neographism brought powerfully to mind something at once sleazy and sneaky.
     Yours, ever a TeXnophile,
     Dominik

                    (Dominik Wujastyk, *Humanist*, October 1989)

(2) The thing about the Mac, which I have had since 1984, nemmine the three lemons I bought, chile! is its simplicity of use and friendliness to people who want to get on with it, apart from fonts and layouts and better-looking MSS and ease of selection of what one wishes to do. And none of all that long engineering, retrofitted stuff for word people. Now with the large portrait screen before me in black and white and crystal clear, one can write one's pages and swiftly. It is a matter of ease. My son, who uses Suns and Irises, and was an Apple kid from the start, regards this as a mere toy today, but it is not

something one has to fight or feel vain about having learned, as with the IBM things, which my colleagues curse and sweat and weep over. Just make the interface easy, and easier and easiest, is all one asks. Point and use, as with e-mail, and Yale's tincan modem program for getting through to all you folks out there swiftest, or as Beckett says, 'Instanter!'
Kessler

(Jascha Kessler, *Humanist*, October 1989)

Electronic mail reveals features of both speech and writing. Like other forms of discourse, new as well as old, it deserves the attention of future corpus workers.

20.4   Quality of text

Although a lot can be done with raw texts, more sophisticated analyses of syntax and style require texts with grammatical tagging. There are very few tagged corpora available, and most of the texts which *do* exist include only part-of-speech tags. Producing a tagged corpus is very costly and time-consuming, in spite of great advances recently made in the development of computational techniques for tagging, especially by Geoffrey Leech and his team at Lancaster (Garside *et al.* 1987). Important tasks for the future are to develop such techniques further, to build up comprehensive corpora of analysed text, and to produce software for the use of such material (like the Linguistic Database developed at the University of Nijmegen; see van Halteren and van den Heuvel 1990).

20.5   Encoding guidelines

If a machine-readable text is to be efficiently used, its features must be properly coded. In the first instance, it is necessary to provide representations for characters and special symbols. It is essential to find ways of representing significant textual features manifested by typographical conventions: headings, paragraphs, sentences, notes, lists, etc. Where there are no established conventions, it is necessary to devise new encoding schemes, for example with speech and texts containing grammatical or other extra markers to be used in the analysis of the texts.

The electronic medium offers far greater possibilities of discrimination than print, but problems arise through the large number of different encoding schemes. This causes difficulties in the interchange of texts and gives little guidance for new corpus compilers. We are now at a stage where it is highly desirable to develop general guidelines for text encoding. This task has been undertaken by the Text Encoding Initiative, a major international project sponsored by the Association for Computing in the Humanities, the Association for Computational Linguistics, and the Association for Literary and Linguistic Computing.[6]

The Text Encoding Initiative has decided to adopt the framework of the Standard Generalized Markup Language (ISO 8879), which provides a syntax for descriptive markup of texts; for a good introduction, see Bryan (1988). If successful, the project will develop a manual for electronic texts comparable with style manuals for printed texts.

20.6   Types of access

The first computer corpora were distributed on magnetic tape. With the rapid development of powerful personal computers, more and more users have gone over to diskettes. We may expect this development to continue. Other media which will be coming into wider use are various types of compact disks.

On-line access to textual databases may be expected to increase, although cost is a limiting factor for the use of commercial databases. In my work on English influence on Norwegian I have had access to the electronic archives of *Aftenposten*, the biggest Norwegian newspaper, which holds all articles printed in the morning and evening editions since April 1984. A search for forms beginning with *snack* gave an initial result as shown in Table 20.1 (the individual examples can then be inspected in context and printed out). This material gives a very good idea of the use of the English word *snack* in Norwegian (with the odd example of the Swedish verb *snacka*), showing inflectional patterns, compounds and the derivation *snacksy*, which has no counterpart in English. Details of usage, including the semantics of the words, can of course be revealed only by a closer textual study.

On-line databases provide opportunities for searching in a truly vast collection of material, in the case of *Aftenposten* some 350,000 articles/documents with a yearly growth of about 75,000 articles.

Table 20.1 Occurrences of snack-forms in Aftenposten

	Occurrences	Documents
snack	11	10
snacka	1	1
snackbar	32	29
snackbareiere	2	2
snackbaren	9	7
snackbarene	3	3
snackbarens	1	1
snackbarer	15	15
snackbarkjeder	1	1
snackbarmat	1	1
snackbarn	1	1
snackbarplasser	1	1
snackbarpreget	1	1
snackbars	1	1
snacket	2	2
snackmarkedet	1	1
snackproduksjon	1	1
snacks	148	125
snacks-	1	1
snacks'en	1	1
snacksen	5	4
snackset	1	1
snacksets	2	1
snacksfatene	1	1
snacksgenerasjonen	1	1
snackshåndball	1	1
snackskonsumenter	1	1
snackskulturen	2	1
snackskulturens	1	1
snacksmåltider	1	1
snacksmarkedet	3	2
snacksmoms	1	1
snacksomane	1	1
snackspakninger	1	1
snacksprodukter	3	3
snacksprodusent	1	1
snacksprodusenten	3	3
snacksprosjektet	1	1
snacksrett	1	1
snacksselgende	1	1
snacksspisende	1	1
snackssuksess	1	1
snackstypene	1	1
snacksvane	1	1
snacksy	9	7

Although access is expensive, this is a very efficient way of gathering material, particularly for research on low-frequency lexical words.

Access to machine-readable texts is limited not only by cost but also by copyright restrictions. The copyright issue is a thorny one with machine-readable texts, in spite of proposals like the Xanadu system (Nelson 1989).[7] Corpus workers must abide by the same rules that apply to machine-readable texts in general. This means that texts cannot be copied and shared among researchers unless permission has been obtained from copyright holders. A task for corpus workers is to investigate whether it is feasible to work out special rules for the use of machine-readable texts for non-profit textual research.

20.7 International cooperation

The availability of some major computer corpora has stimulated cooperation among researchers. It is essential to try to carry on, and strengthen, the cooperation which has developed among corpus workers, for example under the auspices of the International Computer Archive of Modern English (ICAME) (see *ICAME Journal*). Promising new possibilities are offered by electronic mail and electronic discussion groups, best exemplified by the *Humanist* discussion group referred to in Section 3 above. Through such contact and cooperation it may be possible to continue sharing material, discuss problems of common interest (such as those connected with copyright and encoding guidelines), and stimulate research in general.

20.8 Corpus work and computational linguistics

There has been an unfortunate gap between corpus workers, who are occupied mainly with language description, and computational linguists, who focus on theoretical matters and are typically concerned with a very restricted range of data. In the last few years we have seen encouraging signs that the gap is narrowing. On the one hand, corpus workers have shown that 'large-scale corpus-based linguistics can be a basis for deriving theoretically interesting insights' (Källgren 1990: 99). On the other, there seems to be an increasing concern with data among computational linguists, as shown by the recent Data Collection Initiative sponsored by the

Association for Computational Linguistics. This project aims at assembling at least 100 million words of text encoded in standard form with SGML tagging, to be made available at cost to researchers.[8] In the future we can perhaps hope for a linguistics which is less divided than it has been in the past.

20.9   Opportunities for research

By making it possible to survey and organize vast quantities of data, the computer has enriched many areas of research. Results of corpus studies have already filtered into some major descriptive works, such as the comprehensive reference grammar by Quirk *et al.* (1985) and the *Collins COBUILD English Language Dictionary* (1987), where a computer corpus played a crucial role in the selection and description of words. In Section 3 I have touched on the significance of corpus work in the study of linguistic variation. After the International Corpus of English is completed and the Helsinki Corpus of Historical and Dialectal English[9] becomes available (and other corpora planned or under way), we will have excellent tools for synchronic and diachronic descriptive work.

Special opportunities are offered for quantitative studies, e.g. of word frequencies, collocations and probabilistic grammar. With a further narrowing of corpus work and computational linguistics, we may be better equipped to develop workable systems of automatic linguistic analysis and practical tools based on such systems (for translation, aids for the handicapped, etc.).

The opportunities for research seem almost endless. The number of corpus-related studies is already very large. A study of the bibliography in Altenberg (1991), which focuses on publications based on or related to the English text corpora distributed through ICAME, reveals the following pattern (the figures have been rounded off to the nearest multiple of ten):

Year	Number of publications
–1965	10
1966–1970	20
1971–1975	30
1976–1980	80
1981–1985	160
1986–	320

We may predict continued growth, as the computer penetrates more and more areas of linguistic study.

20.10   The corpus – *one* of the linguist's tools

In spite of the great changes in the less than three decades since the first computer corpus, there is one way in which the role of the corpus in linguistic research has not changed. The corpus remains *one* of the linguist's tools, to be used together with introspection and elicitation techniques. Wise linguists, like experienced craftsmen, sharpen their tools and recognize their appropriate uses. It is no coincidence that Jan Svartvik has done distinguished work in the areas of both corpora and elicitation.[10] His example is worth bearing in mind, whatever further changes may follow in the future.

Notes

[1] The computerization of the Survey of English Usage Corpus is a much later development. See Svartvik and Quirk (1980), Kaye (1988), and Section 3 below.

[2] See the notice in *ICAME Journal* 13 (1989), p. 89, and Taylor and Leech (1991).

[3] In the course of the last couple of years we have, however, seen a number of encouraging initiatives, perhaps the most important being a project undertaken by researchers at Rutgers and Princeton Universities to plan for a National Center for Machine-Readable Texts in the Humanities. The initial goals will be 'the continuation of an ongoing inventory of machine-readable texts; the cataloging and dissemination of inventory information to the broader scholarly community; the acquisition, preservation and servicing of textual datafiles which would otherwise become generally unavailable; the distribution of such datafiles in an appropriate manner; and the establishment of a resource center/ referral point for information concerning textual data' (*Humanist*, Vol. 3, No. 761, 19 Nov. 1989). Inquiries can be directed to Marianne Gaunt (GAUNT@ZODIAC.RUTGERS.EDU) or Robert Hollander (BOBH@PHOENIX.PRINCETON.EDU).

[4] In research on diachronic variation and change there is, of course, no alternative to corpus study.

[5] See Svartvik (1990).

[6] For access to information about the Text Encoding Initiative, subscribe to the electronic discussion list TEI–L at the University of Chicago by sending the message SUBSCRIBE TEI–L + subscriber's full name to

LISTSERV@UICVM.BITNET. The current proposals from the Text Encoding Initiative are formulated in Sperberg-McQueen and Burnard (1990).

[7] Note also the important contribution by Robert John Kost on 'UseRight' (presented to members of the Library of Congress Network Advisory Committee in 1988 and recently made available through *Humanist*).

[8] For information about the project, contact Mark Y. Liberman (MYL@RESEARCH.ATT.COM) or Donald E. Walker (WALKER-@FLASH. BELLCORE.COM).

[9] For information on the Helsinki Corpus, see contributions by Ossi Ihalainen, Merja Kytö and Matti Rissanen in Meijs (1987) and Kytö *et al.* (1988).

[10] Jan Svartvik's corpus work has already been alluded to. In the area of elicitation techniques we find, for example, Quirk and Svartvik (1966) and Svartvik and Wright (1977).

Appendix: Some computerized English text corpora

The following list gives a brief description of the computerized English text corpora referred to in this volume. Some of the corpora are available in different formats: as running text, tagged text, KWIC concordance, in orthographic or prosodic transcription, on tape, diskette or microfiche. The corpora available through ICAME (International Computer Archive of Modern English) can be obtained from The Norwegian Computing Centre for the Humanities, PO Box 53, University of Bergen, N–5027 Bergen, Norway. More detailed information about these and other corpora can be found in Taylor and Leech (1991), in *ICAME Journal* (editor: Stig Johansson, Department of English, University of Oslo), and on the ICAME fileserver (FAFSRV@NOBERGEN) set up at the EARN/BITNET node in Bergen (coordinator: Knut Hofland).

The Birmingham Collection of English Text
Compiled in collaboration with Collins Publishers by a research team under the direction of J. Sinclair at the Research and Development Unit for English Language Studies, University of Birmingham. The collection includes over 20 million words of contemporary, mostly written British English texts. Available at the Research and Development Unit, Westmere, 50 Edgbaston Park Road, Birmingham B15 2RX. Reference: Renouf (1987).

The Brown Corpus
Compiled by W. N. Francis and H. Kučera, Brown University, Providence, RI. It contains one million words of American English texts printed in 1961. Available through ICAME in various formats.

References: Kučera and Francis (1967), Francis and Kučera (1979), Francis and Kučera (1982).

The Guangzhou Petroleum English Corpus
Compiled by Zhu Qi-bo, Guangzhou Training College of the Chinese Petroleum University. It contains 412,000 words of mainly written British and American English from 1975–86. Available through the compiler. Reference: Qi-bo (1989).

The Helsinki Corpus of English Texts: Diachronic and Dialectal (under development)
Compiled by a research team led by M. Rissanen, O. Ihalainen and M. Kytö at the Department of English, University of Helsinki. The diachronic corpus contains 1.6 million words of British English texts from 850-1720; the dialectal material currently includes 245,000 words of contemporary British dialects. Available through the compilers. References: Kytö (1990) (the diachronic part) and Ihalainen (1990) (the dialectal part).

The International Corpus of English (ICE) (under development)
In preparation by thirteen national groups (including Australia, Canada, East Africa, India, Jamaica, New Zealand, Nigeria, Philippines, UK, USA). Coordinator: S. Greenbaum, University College, London. Reference: Greenbaum (this volume).

The JDEST Corpus of Texts in English for Science and Technology
Compiled at Jiao Tong University, Shanghai. It contains one million words of English scientific and technical texts from 1975–83. Reference: Yang (1985a and b, 1986).

The Kolhapur Corpus of Indian English
Compiled by S. V. Shastri, Shivaji University, Kolhapur. It is modelled on the Brown Corpus and comprises one million words of Indian English texts printed in 1978. Available through ICAME. Reference: Shastri (1988).

The Lancaster/IBM Spoken English Corpus (SEC)
Compiled at the Unit for Computer Research on the English Language (UCREL), University of Lancaster, and IBM UK Scientific Centre, Winchester. It contains 52,000 words of spoken (broadcast) British English. Available through ICAME in several versions. Reference: Taylor and Knowles (1988).

The Lancaster-Oslo/Bergen Corpus (LOB)

Compiled and computerized by research teams at Lancaster (G. Leech), Oslo (S. Johansson) and Bergen (K. Hofland). It is modelled on the Brown Corpus and contains one million words of British English texts printed in 1961. Available through ICAME in several versions. References: Johansson *et al.* (1978), Hofland and Johansson (1982), Garside *et al.* (1987), Johansson and Hofland (1989).

The London-Lund Corpus of Spoken English (LLC)

The spoken part of the Survey of English Usage Corpus, computerized at the Survey of Spoken English, Lund University under the direction of J. Svartvik. It consists of 500,000 words of spoken British English recorded from 1953 to 1987. Available from ICAME in several versions. References: Svartvik and Quirk (1980), Svartvik *et al.* (1982), Greenbaum and Svartvik (1990).

The Longman/Lancaster English Language Corpus

Compiled by the Longman Dictionaries Division, with advice from Professor Sir Randolph Quirk and Professor Geoffrey Leech (among others). 30 million words of British, American and other English, split into two equal halves, one with target percentages, the other collected on a randomized basis, and strongly influenced by the work of Douglas Biber. Available (for academic research only) from Longman.

The Macquarie Corpus (under development)

In preparation by D. Blair, A. Brierley, P. Collins and P. Peters at the School of English, Macquarie University, New South Wales. It is modelled on the Brown Corpus and will contain one million words of Australian English printed in 1986. References: Collins and Peters (1988), Collins (1988b).

The Melbourne–Surrey Corpus

Compiled by G. G. Corbett and K. Ahmad at the University of Surrey, Guildford. It contains 100,000 words of Australian newspaper editorials from 1980–1. Available through ICAME. Reference: Ahmad and Corbett (1987).

The Nijmegen Corpus

Compiled by J. Aarts, University of Nijmegen. It contains 130,000 words of mainly written British English from 1962 to 1968. Available at Nijmegen. Reference: Keulen (1986).

The (Santa Barbara) Corpus of Spoken American English (CSAE) (under development)

In preparation by W. L. Chafe, J. W. Du Bois and S. A. Thompson at the Department of Linguistics, University of California, Santa Barbara. Planned to include c. 200,000 words of face-to-face conversation. Reference: Chafe et al. (this volume).

The Survey of English Usage Corpus (SEU)

Compiled at the Survey of English Usage, University College, London, under the direction of R. Quirk and S. Greenbaum. It contains one million words of British English (50 per cent spoken, 50 per cent written) from 1953 to 1987. Available at the Survey of English Usage only (on the spoken part, see also the London-Lund Corpus). References: Svartvik and Quirk (1980), Greenbaum and Svartvik (1990).

The TOSCA Corpus

Compiled by the TOSCA research group, Department of Language and Speech, University of Nijmegen. It contains 1.5 million words of written British English texts from 1976 to 1986. Available at Nijmegen. References: Oostdijk (1988a, 1988b).

References

Aarts, F. (1971), 'On the distribution of noun-phrase types in English clause structure', *Lingua* **26**, 252–64.

Aarts, J. (1988), 'Corpus linguistics: An appraisal', Paper read at the Fifteenth International Conference on Literary and Linguistic Computing, Jerusalem, June 1988.

Aarts, J. and van den Heuvel, T. (1985), 'Computational tools for the syntactic analysis of corpora', *Linguistics* **23**, 303–35.

Aarts, J. and Meijs, W. (eds) (1984), *Corpus Linguistics. Recent Developments in the Use of Computer Corpora in English Language Research*, Rodopi, Amsterdam.

Aarts, J. and Meijs, W. (eds) (1986), *Corpus Linguistics II. New Studies in the Analysis and Exploitation of Computer Corpora*, Rodopi, Amsterdam.

Aarts, J. and Meijs, W. (eds) (1990), *Theory and Practice in Corpus Linguistics*, Rodopi, Amsterdam.

Aarts, J. and Oostdijk, N. (1988), 'Corpus-related research at Nijmegen University', in Kytö *et al.* (eds) 1988: 1–14.

Ahmad, K. and Corbett, C. (1987), 'The Melbourne-Surrey Corpus', *ICAME Journal* **11**, 39–44.

Aitchison, J. (1987) 'Reproductive furniture and extinguished professors', in Steele and Threadgold (eds) 1987, Vol. 2, 3–14.

Akimoto, M. (1989), *A Study of Verbo-Nominal Structures in English*, Shinozaki Shorin, Tokyo.

Akkerman, E., Meijs, W. and Voogt-van Zutphen, M. (1987), 'Grammatical tagging in ASCOT', in Meijs (ed.) 1987: 181–94.

Alexander, L. G. (1988), *Longman English Grammar*, Longman.

Allwood, J. (1988), 'Om det svenska systemet för språklig återkoppling', in Linell, P., Adelswärd, V., Nilsson, T. and Pettersson, P. A. (eds), *Svenskans beskrivning* 16, Vol. 1.

319

Altenberg, B. (1986) 'ICAME Bibliography', *ICAME News* 10, 67–79.

Altenberg, B. (1990a), 'Spoken English and the dictionary', in Svartvik (ed.) 1990: 177–93.

Altenberg, B. (1990b), 'Speech as linear composition', in Caie, G., Haastrup, K., Lykke Jakobsen, A., Nielsen, J. E., Sevaldsen, J., Specht, H., Zettersten, A. (eds.), *Proceedings from the Fourth Nordic Conference for English Studies*, vol. 1, Department of English, University of Copenhagen.

Altenberg, B. (1991), 'A bibliography of publications relating to English computer corpora', in Johansson and Stenström (eds) 1991.

Altenberg, B. and Eeg-Olofsson, M. (1990), 'Phraseology in spoken English', in Aarts and Meijs (eds) 1990: 1–26.

Atwell, E. and Elliott, S. (1987), 'Dealing with ill-formed English text', in Garside *et al.* (eds) 1987: 120–38.

Bahl, L. R., Jelinek, F. and Mercer, R. L. (1983), 'A maximum likelihood approach to continuous speech recognition', *IEEE Transactions on Pattern Analysis and Machine Intelligence*, Vol. PAMI–5, 2, 179–90.

Bailey, C.-J. (1973), *Variation and Linguistic Theory*, Center for Applied Linguistics, Arlington, VA.

Bald, W.-D. (1980), 'Some functions of *yes* and *no* in conversation', in Greenbaum *et al.* (eds) 1980: 178–91.

Bald, W.-D. and Schwarz, A. (1984), *Active Grammar*, Langenscheidt-Longman, Munich.

Bergenholtz, H. and Schaeder, B. (eds) (1979), *Empirische Textwissenschaft: Aufbau und Auswertung von Text-Corpora*, Scriptor Verlag, Königstein.

Bernard, J. and Delbridge, A. (1980), *Introduction to Linguistics: An Australian Perspective*, Prentice Hall, Melbourne.

Besnier, N. (1988), 'The linguistic relationships of spoken and written Nukulaelae registers', *Language* 64, 707–36.

Biber, D. (1986), 'Investigating macroscopic textual variation through multi-feature/multi-dimensional analyses', *Linguistics* 23, 337–60.

Biber, D. (1987), 'A textual comparison of British and American writing', *American Speech* 62, 99–119.

Biber, D. (1988), *Variation across Speech and Writing*, Cambridge University Press.

Biber, D. (1989), 'A typology of English texts', *Linguistics* 27, 3–43.

Biber, D. (1990), 'Some methodological issues in corpus-based analyses of linguistic variation', ms. University of Southern California, Los Angeles.

Biber, D. and Finegan, E. (1986), 'An initial typology of English text types', in Aarts and Meijs (eds) 1986: 19–46.

Biber, D. and Finegan E. (1988a), 'Adverbial stance types in English', *Discourse Processes* 11, 1–34.

Biber, D. and Finegan, E. (1988b), 'Drift in three English genres from the 18th to the 20th centuries: A multi-dimensional approach', in Kytö *et al.* (eds) 1988: 83–103.

Biber, D. and Finegan, E. (1989a), 'Drift and the evolution of English style: A history of three genres', *Language* 65, 487–517.

Biber, D. and Finegan, E. (1989b), 'Styles of stance in English: Lexical and grammatical marking of evidentiality and affect', *Text* 9, 93–124.

Biber, D. and Hared, M. (1989), 'Form/function associations in English and Somali', paper presented at the 4th International Congress of Somali Studies, Mogadishu, Somalia.

Bloomfield, M. W. (1985), 'The question of correctness', in Greenbaum (ed.) 1985, *The English Language Today*, Pergamon Press, 265–70.

Bolinger, D. (1975), *Aspects of Language*, 2nd edn, Harcourt Brace Jovanovich.

Bonaparte, L. L. (1875–6), 'On the dialects of Monmouthshire, Herefordshire, Worcestershire, Berkshire, Oxfordshire, South Warwickshire, South Northamptonshire, Buckinghamshire, Hertfordshire, Middlesex, and Surrey, with a new classification of the English dialects', *Transactions of the Philological Society*, 1875–6, Trübner.

Boyd, J. and Thorne, J. P. (1969), 'The semantics of modal verbs', *Journal of Linguistics* 5, 57–74.

Briscoe, T. (1990), 'English noun phrases are regular: A reply to Professor Sampson', in Aarts and Meijs (eds) 1990: 45–61.

Brown, P. F., Cocke, J., Della Pietra, S. A., Della Pietra, V. J., Jelinek, F., Lafferty, J. C., Mercer, R. L. and Roosin, P. S. (1988), 'A Statistical Approach to Machine Translation', IBM Research Report, T. J. Watson Research Centre, Yorktown Heights, NY (to appear in *Computational Linguistics*).

Bryan, M. (1988), *SGML: An Author's Guide to the Standard Generalized Markup Language*, Addison-Wesley, Wokingham.

Burton-Roberts, N. (1975), 'Nominal apposition', *Foundations of Language* 13, 391–419.

Carstensen, B. (1972), 'Die Darstellung des englischen Futurs in den Lehrwerken, *Learning English, The Good Companion, English for Today unter anderen*', in Bald, W.-D., Carstensen, B. and Hellinger, M., *Die Behandlung grammatischer Probleme in Lehrwerken für den Englischunterricht*, Diesterweg, Frankfurt am Main.

Carter, R. (1987), *Vocabulary*, Allen & Unwin.

Carter, R. and McCarthy, M. (eds) (1988), *Vocabulary and Language Teaching*, Longman.

Carvell, H. T. and Svartvik, J. (1969), *Computational Experiments in Grammatical Classification*, Mouton, The Hague.

Celce-Murcia, M. and Larsen-Freeman, D. (1983), *The Grammar Book*, Newbury House, Rowley, Mass.

Chafe, W. (1982), 'Integration and involvement in speaking, writing and oral literature', in Tannen, D., *Spoken and Written Language: Exploring Orality and Literacy*, Ablex, Norwood, NJ.

Chomsky, N. (1957), *Syntactic Structures*, Mouton, The Hague.

Chomsky, N. (1962), Paper given at the University of Texas 1958, 3rd Texas Conference on Problems of Linguistic Analysis in English, Austin, University of Texas.

Chomsky, N. (1965), *Aspects of the Theory of Syntax*, MIT Press, Cambridge, Mass.

Chope, R. P. (1891), *The Dialect of Hartland, Devonshire*, English Dialect Society 65, Kegan Paul, Trench, Trübner.

Close, R. A. (1975), *A Reference Grammar for Students of English*, Longman.

Coates, J. (1983), *The Semantics of the Modal Auxiliaries*, Croom Helm.

Coates, J. (1986), *Women, Men and Language*, Longman.

Collins, P. C. (1987), 'Cleft and pseudo-cleft constructions in English spoken and written discourse', *ICAME Journal* **11**, 5–17.

Collins, P. C. (1988a), 'The semantics of some modals in contemporary Australian English', *Australian Journal of Linguistics* **8**, 233–58.

Collins, P. C. (1988b), 'Computer corpora in English language research: A critical survey', *Australian Review of Applied Linguistics* **10**, 1–19.

Collins, P. C. and Peters, P. (1988), 'The Australian corpus project', in Kytö *et al.* (eds) 1988: 103–21.

Collins COBUILD English Language Dictionary, 1987, Collins.

Connor-Linton, J. (1988), 'Author's style and world-view in nuclear discourse: A quantitative analysis', *Multilingua* **7**, 95–132.

Connor-Linton, J. (1989), 'Crosstalk: A multi-feature analysis of Soviet–American spacebrigades', unpublished PhD dissertation, University of Southern California.

Cornish, F. (1986), *Anaphoric Relations in English and French*, Routledge.

Cowie, A. P. and Mackin, R. (eds) (1975), *Oxford Dictionary of Current Idiomatic English*, Vol. 1, Oxford University Press.

Cruse, D. A. (1986), *Lexical Semantics*, Cambridge University Press.

Crystal, D. (1966), 'Specification and English tenses', *Journal of Linguistics* **2**, 1–34.

Crystal, D. (1972), 'Objective and subjective in stylistic analysis', in Kachru, B. and Stahlke, H. F. W. (eds), *Current Trends in Stylistics*, Linguistic Research Inc., Edmonton.

Crystal, D. (1979), 'Neglected grammatical factors in conversational English', in Greenbaum *et al.* (eds) 1979: 153–67.

Crystal, D. (1982), *Profiling Linguistic Disability*, Edward Arnold, Whurr Publishers 1989.

Crystal, D. (1985), *Child Language, Learning and Linguists*, 2nd edn, Edward Arnold.

Crystal, D. and Davy, D. (1969), *Investigating English Style*, Longman.

Crystal, D., Fletcher, P. and Garman, M. (1976), *The Grammatical Analysis of Language Disability*, Edward Arnold, 2nd edn, Whurr Publishers 1989.

Department of Education and Science (1989), *English for Ages 5 to 16*, HMSO.

DeRose, S. J. (1988), 'Grammatical category disambiguation by statistical optimization', *Computational Linguistics* **14**, 31–9.

Dewart, H. and Summers, S. (1988), *The Pragmatics Profile of Early Communicative Skills*, NFER-Nelson.

Dixon, R. M. W. (1991), *A New Approach to English Grammar, on Semantic Principles* Clarendon Press.

Du Bois, J. W., Schuetze-Coburn, S., Paolino, D. and Cumming, S. (forthcoming a), *Discourse Transcription*.

Du Bois, J. W., Schuetze-Coburn, S., Paolino, D. and Cumming, S. (forthcoming b), 'Outline of discourse transcription', in Edwards, J. A. and Lampert, M. D. (eds), *Transcription and Coding Methods for Language Research*, Lawrence Erlbaum, Hillsdale, NJ.

Duncan, S. (1974), 'On the structure of speaker–auditor interaction during speaking turns', *Language in Society* **2**, 161–80.

Eastwood, J. and Mackin, R. (1982), *A Basic English Grammar*, Oxford University Press.

Eastwood, J. (1989), *Grammar You Can Use*, Cornelsen and Oxford University Press, Berlin.

Eeg-Olofsson, M. (1985), 'A probability model for computer-aided word-class determination', *ALLC Journal* **5**, 25–30.

Eeg-Olofsson, M. (1990), 'An automatic word class tagger and a phrase parser', in Svartvik (ed.) 1990: 107–37.

Ehrman, M. (1966), *The Meanings of the Modals in Present-Day American English*, Mouton, The Hague.

Ellinger, J. (1983), 'Substantivsätze mit oder ohne *that* in der neueren englischen Literatur', *Anglia* **57**, 78–109.

Ellis, A. J. (1889), *On Early English Pronunciation: Part V, The Existing Phonology of English Dialects Compared with that of West Saxon*, Early English Text Society, Extra Series 56; reprint, Greenwood Press, New York 1968.

Ellis, M. and Ellis, P. (1985), *Counterpoint*, Nelson.

Elsness, J. (1982), '*That* v. zero connective in English nominal clauses', *ICAME News* **6**, 1–45.

Elsness, J. (1984), '*That* or zero? A look at the choice of object clause connective in a corpus of American English', *English Studies* **65**, 519–33.

Elworthy, T. (1875), *The Dialect of West Somerset* (from *Transactions of the Philological Society* for 1875–6, 197–271, Trübner), Vaduz: Kraus Reprint Limited, 1965.

Elworthy, T. (1886), *The West Somerset Word-Book: A Glossary of Dialectal and Archaic Words and Phrases Used in the West of Somerset and East Devon* (Trübner), Vaduz: Kraus Reprint Limited, 1965.

Erman, B. (1986), 'Some pragmatic expressions in English conversation', in Tottie and Bäcklund (eds) 1986: 131–49.

Finegan, E. and Biber, D. (1986), 'Two dimensions of linguistic complexity in English', in Connor-Linton, J., Hall, C. J. and McGinnis, M. (eds), *Social and Cognitive Perspectives on Language, Southern California Occasional Papers in Linguistics* **11**, 1–23.

Finegan, E. and Biber, D. (1989), 'Parallel patterns in social dialect and register variation: Towards an integrated theory', ms., University of Southern California, Los Angeles.

Fischer, A. (1976), *Dialects in the South-West of England: A Lexical Investigation*, Francke Verlag, Bern.

Fishman, P. M. (1978), 'Interaction: The work women do', *Social Problems* **25**, 397–406.

Francis, W. N. (1979), 'Problems of assembling, describing, and computerizing large corpora', in Bergenholz and Schaeder (eds) 1979: 110–23; also in Johansson (ed.) 1982: 7–24.

Francis, W. N. (1980), 'A tagged corpus – problems and prospects', in Greenbaum *et al.* (eds) 1980: 192–209.

Francis, W. N. and Kučera, H. (1979), *Manual of Information to Accompany a Standard Sample of Present-day Edited American English, for Use with Digital Computers*, Department of Linguistics, Brown University, Providence, RI.

Francis, W. N. and Kučera, H. (1982), *Frequency Analysis of English Usage: Lexicon and Grammar*, Houghton Mifflin, Boston.

Francis, W. N., Svartvik, J. and Rubin, G. M. (1969), 'Computer-produced representation of dialectal variation: Initial fricatives in Southern British English', International Conference on Computational Linguistics, Preprint 52, Stockholm.

Fries, C. (1952), *The Structure of English*, Harcourt, Brace and World, New York.

Garside, R., Leech, G. and Sampson, G. (eds) (1987), *The Computational Analysis of English: A Corpus-based Approach*, Longman.

Grabe, W. (1986), 'Contrastive rhetoric and text-type research', in Connor, U. and Kaplan, R. B. (eds), *Writing Across Languages: Analysis of L2 Text*, Addison-Wesley, Reading, Mass., 115–37.

Greenbaum, S. (1985), Commentator 1, in Quirk and Greenbaum (eds) 1985: 31–32.

Greenbaum, S. (1988a), 'A proposal for an international computerized corpus of English', *World Englishes* **7**, 315.

Greenbaum, S. (1988b), *Good English and the Grammarian*, Longman.

Greenbaum, S. (1990), 'The International Corpus of English', *ICAME Journal* **14**, 106–8.

Greenbaum, S., Leech, G. and Svartvik, J. (eds) (1979), *Studies in English Linguistics for Randolph Quirk*, Longman.

Greenbaum, S. and Svartvik, J. (1990), 'The London-Lund Corpus of Spoken English', in Svartvik (ed.) 1990: 11–63.

Gross, M. (1972), *Mathematical Models in Linguistics*, Prentice-Hall, Englewood Cliffs, NJ.

Grunwell, P. (1985), *Phonological Assessment of Child Speech*, NFER-Nelson.

Haan, P. de (1987), 'Exploring the linguistic database: Noun phrase complexity and language variation', in Meijs (ed.) 1987: 151–65.

Hall, D. (1986), *Working with English Prepositions*, Nelson.

Halliday, M. A. K. (1956), 'Grammatical categories in Modern Chinese', *Transactions of the Philological Society*.

Halliday, M. A. K. (1959), *The Language of the Chinese: 'Secret History of the Mongols'*, Blackwell.

Halliday, M. A. K. (1961), 'Categories of the theory of gammar', *Word* **17**, 241–92.

Halliday, M. A. K. (1970), 'Functional diversity in language as seen from a consideration of modality and mood in English', *Foundations of Language* **4**, 225–42.

Halliday, M. A. K. (1987), 'Spoken and written modes of meaning', in Horowitz, R. and Samuels, S. J. (eds), *Comprehending Oral and Written Language*, Academic Press, New York.

Halliday, M. A. K. (forthcoming), 'Towards probabilistic interpretations', in Ventola, E. (ed.), *Selected Papers from the 16th International Systemic Congress, Hanasaari, Finland, 12–16 June 1989*.

Halteren, H. and Heuvel T., van den (1990), *Linguistic Exploitation of Syntactic Databases* Rodopi, Amsterdam.

Harris Z. (1951), *Methods in Structural Linguistics*, University of Chicago Press, Chicago.

Hasan, R. (1987), 'The grammarian's dream: Lexis as most delicate grammar', in Halliday, M. A. K. and Fawcett, R. P. (eds), *New Developments in Systemic Linguistics. Volume 1: Theory and Description*, Pinter, 184–211.

Hasan, R. (forthcoming), *Offers in the Making*.

Hermerén, L. (1978), *On Modality in English: A Study of the Semantics of the Modals*, Lund University Press, Lund.

Hewett, S. (1892), *The Peasant Speech of Devon*, Elliott Stock.

Hockett, C. F. (1948), 'A note on "structure"', *International Journal of American Linguistics* **14**, 69–71.

Hockey, S. and Martin, J. (1988), *The Oxford Concordance Program: Users' Manual Version 2*, Oxford University Computing Service.

Hofland, K. and Johansson, S. (1982), *Word Frequencies in British and American English*, Norwegian Computing Centre for the Humanities, Bergen.

Huddleston, R. D. (1976), 'Some theoretical issues in the description of the English verb', *Lingua* **40**, 331–83.

Humanist, Humanist discussion group (electronic distribution list): LISTSERV@UTORONTO. BITNET, University of Toronto.

ICAME Journal, Journal of the International Computer Archive of Modern English, Norwegian Computing Centre for the Humanities, Bergen.

Ihalainen, O. (1976), 'Periphrastic *do* in affirmative sentences in the dialect of East Somerset', *Neuphilologische Mitteilungen* **67**, 608–22.

Ihalainen, O. (1987), 'Towards a grammar of the Somerset dialect: A case study of the language of J. M.', *Neophilologica Fennica: Modern Society 100 Years*, Société Néophilologique, Helsinki, 71–86.

Ihalainen, O. (1988a), 'Creating linguistic databases from machine-readable dialect texts', in Thomas, A. R. (ed.), *Methods in Dialectology*, Multilingual Matters, Clevedon, Philadelphia, 569–84.

Ihalainen, O. (1988b), 'Working with dialectal material stored in a dBase file', in Kytö *et al.* (eds) 1988: 137–44.

Ihalainen, O. (1990), 'A source of data for the study of English dialectal syntax: The Helsinki Corpus', in Aarts and Meijs (eds) 1990: 83–103.

Ihalainen, O. (1991), 'The grammatical subject in educated and dialectal English: Comparing the London-Lund Corpus and the Helsinki Corpus of English Dialects', in Johansson and Stenström (eds) 1991.

Itkonen, E. (1980), 'Qualitative vs quantitative analysis in linguistics', in Perry, T. (ed.) (1980), *Evidence and Argumentation in Linguistics*, de Gruyter, Berlin.

Jacobson, B. (1979), 'Modality and the modals of necessity *must* and *have to*', *English Studies* **60**, 195–215.

Jelinek, F. (1985a), '*Self-Organized Language Modeling for Speech Recognition*', IBM Research Report, T. J. Watson Research Center, Yorktown Heights, NY.

Jelinek, F. (1985b), 'The development of an experimental discrete dictation recognizer', *Proceedings of the IEEE* **73**, 1616–24.

Jespersen, O. (1909–49), *A Modern English Grammar on Historical Principles* (7 vols), Munksgaard, Copenhagen.

Jespersen, O. (1967), *Growth and Structure of the English Language*, 9th edn, Blackwell.

Johansson, S. (ed.) (1982), *Computer Corpora in English Language Research*, Norwegian Computing Centre for the Humanities, Bergen.

Johansson, S., Atwell, E., Garside, R. and Leech, G. (1986), *The Tagged LOB Corpus: Users' Manual*, Norwegian Computing Centre for the Humanities, Bergen.

Johansson, S. and Hofland, K. (1989), *Frequency Analysis of English Vocabulary and Grammar* (2 vols), Clarendon Press.

Johansson, S., Leech, G. and Goodluck, H. (1978), *Manual of Information to Accompany the Lancaster-Oslo/Bergen Corpus of British English, for Use with Digital Computers*, Department of English, University of Oslo.

Johansson, S. and Stenström, A. (eds) (1991), *English Computer Corpora*, Mouton de Gruyter, Berlin.

Jones, R. (1987), 'Accessing the Brown Corpus using an IBM PC', *ICAME Journal* 11, 44–7.

Kachru, B. (1985), 'The English language in a global context', in Quirk and Widdowson (eds) 1985: 11–30.

Källgren, G. (1990), 'Review of Garside *et al.* (1987)', *ICAME Journal* 14, 98–103.

Kaye, G. (1988), 'The design of the database for the Survey of English Usage', in Kytö *et al.* (eds) 1988: 145–68.

Kaye, G. (1989), *KAYE the KWIC Analyser: User's Manual*, IBM Scientific Centre, Winchester, UK.

Kaye, G. (1990), 'A concordance browser for tagged texts and bilingual texts', in Aarts and Meijs (eds) 1990: 137–63.

Kendon, A. (1967), 'Some functions of gaze-direction in social interaction', *Acta Psychologica* 26, 22–63.

Kennedy, G. D. (forthcoming), 'Collocations: Where grammar and vocabulary teaching meet', in Aniwan, S. (ed.), *RELC Anthology Series No. 24*, Regional Language Centre, Singapore.

Keulen, F. (1986), 'The Dutch computer corpus pilot project', in Aarts and Meijs (eds) 1986: 127–63.

Kirch, M. (1959), 'Scandinavian influence on English syntax', *PMLA* 74, 503–10.

Kjellmer, G. (1982), 'Some problems relating to the study of collocations in the Brown Corpus', in Johansson (ed.) 1982: 25–33.

Kjellmer, G. (1987), 'Aspects of English collocations', in Meijs (ed.) 1987: 133–40.

Kjellmer, G. (1990), 'Patterns of collocability', in Aarts and Meis (eds) 1990: 163–78.

Knowles, G. and Alderson, P. (eds) (forthcoming), *Working with Speech*, Longman.

Knowles, G. and Lawrence, L. (1987), 'Automatic intonation assignment', in Garside *et al.* (eds) 1987: 139–48.

Kost, R. J. (1988), 'UseRight', *Intellectual Property Issues in the Library Network Context: Proceedings of the Library of Congress Network Advisory Committee Meeting, March 23–25 1988*, Network Planning Papers of the Network Development and Marc Standards Office, No. 17 (also available through *Humanist*).

Kučera, H. and Francis, W. N. (1967), *Computational Analysis of Present-Day American English*, Brown University Press, Providence, RI.

Kytö, M. (1990), *Manual to the Diachronic Part of the Helsinki Corpus of English Texts 1: Coding conventions and lists of source texts*, Department of English, University of Helsinki.

Kytö, M., Ihalainen, O. and Rissanen, M. (eds) (1988), *Corpus Linguistics Hard and Soft*, Rodopi, Amsterdam.

Kytö, M. and Rissanen, M. (1988), 'The Helsinki Corpus of English Texts: Classifying and coding the diachronic part', in Kytö *et al.* (eds) 1988: 169–76.

Labov, W. (1966), *Social Stratification of English in New York City*, Center for Applied Linguistics, Washington, DC.

Labov, W. (1972), *Sociolinguistic Patterns*, University of Pennsylvania Press, Philadelphia.

Leech, G. (1971), *Meaning and the English Verb*, Longman.

Leech, G. (1981), *Semantics*, 2nd edn, Penguin.

Leech, G. and Coates, J. (1980), 'Semantic indeterminacy and the modals', in Greenbaum *et al.* (eds) 1980: 79–91.

Leech, G. and Garside, R. (1991), 'Running a grammar factory: The production of syntactically analysed corpora or "treebanks"', in Johansson and Stenström (eds) 1991.

Liberman, M. (1989), 'Text on tap: The ACL/DCI', in *Proceedings of the DARPA Speech and Natural Language Workshop, October 1989*, Morgan Kaufman, San Mateo, CA.

Live, A. H. (1973), 'The *take–have* phrasal in English', *Linguistics* **95**, 31–56.

Ljung, M. (1980), 'Two American blasphemes', in Allwood, J. and Ljung, M. (eds), *ALVAR. A Linguistically Varied Assortment of Readings*, Department of English, University of Stockholm, 116–29.

Ljung, M. (1986), *Om svordomar*, Akademilitteratur, Stockholm.

Lodge, D. (1975), *Changing Places*, Penguin.

Longman Dictionary of Contemporary English, 1987, 2nd edn, Longman.

Longman Webster English College Dictionary, 1984, Longman.

Lyons, J. (1977), *Semantics* (2 vols), Cambridge University Press.

MacWhinney, B. and Snow, C. (1990), 'The Child Language Data Exchange System', *ICAME Journal* **14**, 3–25.

Marino, M. (1973), 'A feature analysis of the English modals', *Lingua* **32**, 309–23.

Marshall, I. (1987), 'Tag selection using probabilistic methods', in Garside *et al.* (eds) 1987: 42–56.

Matthews, P. (1981), *Syntax*, Cambridge University Press.

McDavid, V. (1964), 'The alternation of *that* and zero in noun clauses', *American Speech* **39**, 102–13.

Meijs, W. (ed.) (1987), *Corpus Linguistics and Beyond*, Rodopi, Amsterdam.

Meyer, C. (1986), 'Computer corpora: Their availability, capabilities, and limitations', *SECOL Review* **10**, 38–51.

Meyer, C. (1987), 'Apposition in English', *Journal of English Linguistics* **20**, 101–21.

Meyer, C. (1989), 'Restrictive apposition: An indeterminate category', *English Studies* **70**, 147–66.

Meyer, C. (forthcoming), *Apposition in Contemporary English*, Cambridge University Press.

Mindt, D. (1987), *Sprache – Grammatik – Unterrichtsgrammatik: Futurischer Zeitbezug im Englischen I. Darstellungen*, Diesterweg, Frankfurt am Main.

Mitchell, B. (1985), *Old English Syntax* (2 vols), Oxford University Press.

Moore, R. K. (1989), 'Speech technology corpora', unpublished background paper for the SALT Workshop on Corpus Resources, Wadham College, Oxford, January 1990.

Müller, E. A. (1978), *Funktionsverbgefüge vom Typ 'Give a Smile' und ähnliche Konstruktionen*, Peter Lang, Frankfurt am Main.

Nation, P. and Carter, N. (eds) (1989), 'Vocabulary acquisition', *AILA Review 6*, Free University Press, Amsterdam.

Nattinger, J. R. (1980), 'A lexical phrase grammar for ESL', *TESOL Quarterly* **14**, 337–44.

Nattinger, J. R. and DeCarrico, J. (1989), 'Lexical phrases, speech acts and teaching conversation', in Nation and Carter (eds) 1989: 118–39.

Nelson, T. H. (1989), *Literary Machines*, Mindful Press, Sausalito, CA.

Nesbitt, C. and Plum, G. (1988), 'Probabilities in a systemic grammar: The clause complex in English', in Fawcett, R. P. and Young, D. J. (eds), *New Developments in Systemic Linguistics. Volume 2: Theory and Applications*, Pinter, 6–33.

Nevalainen, T. and Ramoulin-Brunberg, H. (1989), 'A corpus of early Modern Standard English in a socio-historical perspective', *Neuphilologische Mitteilungen* **90**, 67–110.

Nickel, G. (1968), 'Complex verbal structures in English', *IRAL* **6**, 1–21.

Nordenstam, K. (1987), 'Kvinnlig och manlig samtalsstil', research report, Department of Scandinavian Languages, University of Gothenburg. [In Swedish]

Ogura, M. (1978), '*Verba dicendi* in Old English poetry', *Bunken Ronshu* **3**, 1–26.

Ogura, M. (1979), '*Cweðan* and *secgan* in Old English prose', *Bunken Ronshu* **4**, 1–30.

Olsson, Y. (1961), *On the Syntax of the English Verb with Special Reference to* HAVE A LOOK *and Similar Complex Structures*, Almqvist & Wiksell, Stockholm.

Oostdijk, N. (1988a), 'A corpus for studying linguistic variation', *ICAME Journal* **12**, 3–14.

Oostdijk, N. (1988b), 'A corpus linguistic approach to linguistic variation', *Literary and Linguistic Computing* **3**, 12–25.

Oostdijk, N. (forthcoming), *Issues in the Automatic Processing of English. A Corpus Linguistic Study*, PhD dissertation, University of Nijmegen.

Oreström, B. (1983), *Turn-taking in English Conversation*, Lund University Press, Lund.

The Oxford Dictionary of English Etymology, 1966, Clarendon Press.

The Oxford English Dictionary, 1933, Clarendon Press.

Oxford University Computing Service, 1983, *Text Archive* Document available from OUCS, Banbury Road, Oxford OX2 6NN.

Painter, C. (1984), *Into the Mother Tongue: A Case Study in Early Language Development*, Pinter.

Palmer, F. R. (1974), *The English Verb*, Longman.

Palmer, F. R. (1979), *Modality and the English Modals*, Longman.

Partridge, E. A. (1974), *A Dictionary of Slang and Unconventional Language*, Routledge & Kegan Paul.

Pawley, A. and Syder, F. H. (1983), 'Two puzzles for linguistic theory: Nativelike selection and nativelike fluency', in Richards, J. C. and Schmidt, R. W. (eds), *Language and Communication*, Longman, 191–226.

Perkins, M. (1983), *Modal Expressions in English*, Pinter.

Peters, A. M. (1983), *The Units of Language Acquisition*, Cambridge University Press.

Prince, E. (1972), 'A note on aspect in English: the take-a-walk construction', in Plötz, S. (ed.), *Transformationelle Analyse*, Athenäum, Berlin, 409–20.

Qi-bo, Z. (1989), 'A quantitative look at the Guangzhou Petroleum English Corpus', *ICAME Journal* **13**, 28–38.

Quirk, R. (1960), 'Towards a description of English usage', *Transactions of the Philological Society*, 40–61. (Revised and reprinted in Quirk, R. (1968), *Essays on the English Language: Medieval and Modern*, Longman, 70–87.)

Quirk, R. (1965), 'Descriptive statement and serial relationship', *Language* **41**, 205–17.

Quirk, R., Greenbaum, S., Leech, G. and Svartvik, J. (1972), *A Grammar of Contemporary English*, Longman.

Quirk, R., Greenbaum, S., Leech, G. and Svartvik, J. (1985), *A Comprehensive Grammar of the English Language*, Longman.

Quirk, R. and Svartvik, J. (1966), *Investigating Linguistic Acceptability*, Mouton, The Hague.

Quirk, R. and Widdowson, H. G. (eds) (1985), *English in the World: Teaching and Learning the Language and Literatures*, Cambridge University Press.

Renouf, A. (1984), 'Corpus development at Birmingham University', in Aarts and Meijs (eds) 1984: 3–39.

Renouf, A. (1987), 'Corpus development', in Sinclair (ed.) 1987: 1–40.

Renouf, A. (forthcoming), 'General patterns of phraseology in English' (provisional title).

Renský, M. (1964), 'English verbo-nominal phrases. Some structural and stylistic aspects', *Travaux Linguistiques de Prague* 1, 289–99.

Rieger, B. (1979), 'Repräsentivität: Von der Unangemessenheit eines Begriffs zur Kennzeichnung eines Problems linguistischer Korpusbildung', in Bergenholz and Schaeder (eds) 1979: 52–70.

Rissanen, M. (1989), 'Three problems connected with the use of diachronic corpora', *ICAME Journal* 13, 16–19.

Rissanen, M. (forthcoming), 'Computers are useful – for *auht* I know', *Edinburgh Studies in English Language* 2, Edinburgh.

Rogers, N. (1979), *Wessex Dialect*, Moonraker Press.

Romaine, S. (1982), *Socio-historical Linguistics, its Status and Methodology*, Cambridge University Press.

Rydén, M. (1987), 'Syntactic variation and paradigmatic typology', *Studia Linguistica* 41, 48–57.

Sampson, G. (1987a), 'Evidence against the "grammatical"/"ungrammatical" distinction', in Meijs (ed.) 1987: 219–26.

Sampson, G. (1987b), 'Probabilistic models of analysis', in Garside *et al.* (eds) 1987: 16–29.

Schegloff, E. (1982), 'Discourse as an interactional achievement. Some uses of *uh huh* and other things that come between sentences', in Tannen, D. (ed.), *Analyzing Discourse: Text and Talk*, Georgetown University Press, Washington, DC, 71–93.

Schmidt, A. (1902), *Shakespeare–Lexicon*, Reimer, Berlin.

Schmied, J. (1989), 'Text categorization according to use and user and the International Corpus of English', *Computer Corpora des Englischen in Forschung, Lehre und Anwendungen (CCE Newsletter)* 3, 1–11.

Sebba, M. (1989), *The Adequacy of Corpora*, unpublished MSc dissertation, Centre for Computational Linguistics, UMIST, University of Manchester.

Shannon, C. and Weaver, W. (1949), *The Mathematical Theory of Communication*, University of Illinois Press, Urbana, Ill, 8–16.

Sharman, R. (1989a), *An Introduction to the Theory of Language Models:*

Lecture Notes, IBM Research Report 204, IBM UK Scientific Centre, Winchester.

Sharman, R. (1989b), *Observational Evidence for a Statistical Model of Language*, IBM Research Report 205, IBM UK Scientific Centre, Winchester.

Shastri, S. V. (1988), 'The Kolhapur Corpus of Indian English and work done on its basis so far', *ICAME Journal* **12**, 15–26.

Sinclair, J. (1982), 'Reflections on computer corpora in English language research', in Johansson (ed.) 1982: 1–6.

Sinclair, J. (1985), 'Lexicographic evidence', in Ilson, R. (ed.), *Dictionaries, Lexicography and Language Learning*, Pergamon and The British Council.

Sinclair, J. (1987a), 'Collocation: A progress report', in Steele and Threadgold (eds) 1987: 319–331.

Sinclair, J. (ed.) (1987b), *Looking Up: An Account of the COBUILD Project*, Collins.

Sinclair, J. (1989), 'Uncommonly common words', in Tickoo, M. L. (ed.), *Learners' Dictionaries: State of the Art*, RELC Anthology Series No. 23, Regional Language Centre, Singapore.

Sinclair, J. and Coulthard, M. R. (1975), *Towards an Analysis of Discourse*, Oxford University Press.

Sinclair, J., Daley, R. and Jones, S. (1970), *English Lexical Studies*, Report No. 5060, Office of Scientific and Technical Information, London.

Sinclair, J. and Renouf, A. (1988), 'A lexical syllabus for language learning', in Carter, R. and McCarthy, M. (eds), *Vocabulary and Language Teaching*, Longman, 140–60.

Sopher, H. (1971), 'Apposition', *English Studies* **52**, 401–12.

Sperberg-McQueen, C. M. and Burnard L. (eds) (1990), *Guidelines for the Encoding and Interchange of Machine-Readable Texts*, Draft Version 1.0. Association for Computational Linguistics/Association for Computers and the Humanities/ Association for Literary and Linguistic Computing. Chicago and Oxford.

Stankiewicz, E. (1963), 'Problems of emotive language', in Sebeok, T., *Approaches to Semiotics*, Mouton, The Hague, 239–63.

Steele, R. and Threadgold, T. (eds) (1987), *Language Topics. Essays in Honour of Michael Halliday* (2 vols), John Benjamins.

Stein, G. (1991), 'The phrasal verb type *to have a look* in modern English', *IRAL*.

Stenström, A.-B. (1982), 'Feedback', in Enkvist, N. E. (ed.), *Impromptu Speech: A Symposium*, Åbo Akademi, Åbo, 319–40.

Stenström, A.-B. (1984a), *Questions and Responses in English Conversation*, Lund University Press, Lund.

Stenström, A.-B. (1984b), 'Discourage tags', in Aarts and Meijs (eds) 1984: 65–81.

Stenström, A.-B. (1986), 'What does *really* really do?' in Tottie and Bäcklund (eds) 1986: 149–63.

Stenström, A.-B. (1990), 'Lexical items peculiar to spoken discourse', in Svartvik (ed.) 1990: 137–77.

Storms, G. (1966), '*That*-clauses in modern English', *English Studies* 47, 249–70.

Svartvik, J. (1966), *On Voice in the English Verb*, Mouton, The Hague.

Svartvik, J. (1968), *The Evans Statements: A Case for Forensic Linguistics*, Almqvist & Wiksell, Stockholm.

Svartvik, J. (1980), '*Well* in conversation', in Greenbaum *et al.* (eds) 1980: 167–77.

Svartvik, J. (ed.) (1990), *The London-Lund Corpus of Spoken English: Description and Research*, Lund University Press, Lund.

Svartvik, J., Eeg-Olofsson, M., Forsheden, O., Oreström, B. and Thavenius, C. (1982), *Survey of Spoken English. Report on Research 1975–81*, Lund University Press, Lund.

Svartvik, J. and Quirk, R. (eds) (1980), *A Corpus of English Conversation*, Lund University Press, Lund.

Svartvik, J. and Wright, D. (1977), 'The use of *ought* in teenage English', in Greenbaum, S. (ed.), *Acceptability in Language*, Mouton, The Hague, 179–201.

Swan, M. and Walter, C. (1984), *The Cambridge English Course, Book 1*, Cambridge University Press.

Tannen, D. (1984), *Conversational Style, Analyzing Talk among Friends*, Ablex, Norwood, NJ.

Taylor, L., Grover, C. and Briscoe, T. (1989), 'The syntactic regularity of English noun phrases', *Proceedings of the European Chapter of the Association of Computational Linguistics*, UMIST, Manchester.

Taylor, L. and Knowles, G. (1988), *Manual of Information to Accompany the SEC Corpus*, UCREL, University of Lancaster.

Taylor, L. and Leech, G. (1991), 'Survey of English machine-readable texts', in Johansson and Stenström (eds) 1991.

Tesch, F. (1990), *Die Indefinitpronomina 'some' und 'any' im authentischen englischen Sprachgebrauch und in Lehrwerken: Eine empirische Untersuchung*, PhD dissertation (microfiche), Freie Universität, Berlin.

Thompson, H. S. (ed.) (1989), *Speech and Language Technology – Strategy for Research and Development Support*, London, Department of Trade and Industry.

Tottie, G. (1985), 'The negation of epistemic necessity in present-day British and American English', *English World-Wide* 6, 87–116.

Tottie, G. (1988), 'A new English–Swedish dictionary: Towards a balanced British–American norm', in Hyldgaard-Jensen, K. and Zettersten, A. (eds), *Symposium on Lexicography III*, Max Niemeyer, Tübingen.

Tottie, G. (1989), 'What does *uh-(h)uh* mean?', in Odenstedt, B. and

Persson, G. (eds), *Instead of Flowers. Papers in Honour of Mats Rydén on the Occasion of his Sixtieth Birthday August 27, 1989*, Almqvist & Wiksell, Stockholm, 269–81.

Tottie, G. (1990), 'Backchannels in dyadic and multi-party conversations', paper read at the 8th Sociolinguistics Symposium at the Roehampton Institute, March 28–30.

Tottie, G. and Bäcklund, I. (eds) (1986), *English in Speech and Writing*, Almqvist & Wiksell, Stockholm.

Traugott, E. and Romaine, S. (1985), 'Some questions for the definition of "style" in socio-historical linguistics', *Folia Linguistica Historica* 6, 7–39.

Trudgill, P. and Hannah, J. (1982), *International English*, Edward Arnold.

Ullman, S. (1964), *Language and Style*, Blackwell.

Ungerer, F., Meier, E. H., Schäfer, K. and Lechler, S. B. (1984), *A Grammar of Present-Day English*, Klett, Stuttgart.

van den Heuvel, T. (1987), 'Interaction in syntactic corpus analysis', in Meijs (ed.) 1987: 235–52.

van Ek, J. A. and Alexander, L. G. (1975), *Threshold Level English*, Pergamon.

Viereck, W. (1980), 'The dialectal structure of British English: Lowman's evidence', *English World-Wide* 1, 25–44.

Viereck, W. (1985), 'Linguistic atlases and dialectometry: The Survey of English dialects', in Kirk, J. M., Sanderson, S. and Widdowson, J. D. A. (eds), *Studies in Linguistic Geography*, Croom Helm, 94–112.

Wakelin, M. (1975), *Language and History in Cornwall*, Leicester University Press.

Wakelin, M. (1977), *English Dialects: An Introduction*, 2nd edn, Athlone Press.

Wakelin, M. (1984), 'Rural dialects in England', in Trudgill, P. (ed.), *Language in the British Isles*, Cambridge University Press, 70–93.

Wakelin, M. (1986), *The Southwest of England*, Varieties of English around the world, Text Series, Vol. 5.

Warner, A. (1982), *Complementation in Middle English and the Methodology of Historical Syntax*, Croom Helm.

Webster's New Dictionary of Synonyms, 1978, Merriam, Springfield, Mass.

Webster's Third New International Dictionary, 1961, Merriam, Springfield, Mass.

Wells, J. C. (1982), *Accents of English 2: The British Isles*, Cambridge University Press.

Weltens, B. (1983), 'Non-standard periphrastic *do* in the dialects of south west Britain', *Lore and Language* 3, 56–64.

West, M. (1953), *A General Service List of English Words*, Longman.

White, S. (1989), 'Backchannels across cultures: A study of Americans and Japanese', *Language in Society* 18, 59–76.

Wiegert, H. (1921) *'Jim and Nell' von W. F. Rock. Eine Studie zum Dialekt von Devonshire*, Mayer and Müller, Berlin.

Wierzbicka, A. (1982), 'Why can you *have a drink* when you can't **have an eat?*', *Language* **58**, 753–99.

Wolfson, N. (1976), 'Speech events and natural speech: Some implications for sociolinguistic methodology', *Language in Society* **5**, 189–209.

Yang, H. (1985a), 'The JDEST computer corpus of texts in English for science and technology', *ICAME News* **9**, 24–5.

Yang, H. (1985b), 'The use of computers in English teaching and research in China', in Quirk and Widdowson (eds) 1985: 86–101.

Yang, H. (1986), 'A new technique for identifying scientific/technical terms and describing science texts', *Literary and Linguistic Computing* **1**, 93–103.

Yngve, V. (1970), 'On getting a word in edgewise', *Papers from the Sixth Regional Meeting of the Chicago Linguistic Society*, University of Chicago, 567–77.

Ziff, P. (1974), 'The number of English sentences', *Foundations of Language* **11**, 519–32.

Zipf, G. K. (1935), *The Psychobiology of Language*, Houghton Mifflin, Boston.

Index